D0098103

Q SCHOOL CONFIDENTIAL

Q SCHOOL CONFIDENTIAL

INSIDE GOLF'S CRUELEST TOURNAMENT

DAVID GOULD

ST. MARTIN'S PRESS
NEW YORK

THOMAS DUNNE BOOKS.
An imprint of St. Martin's Press.

ISBN 0-312-20355-1

Designed by Michelle McMillian

First Edition: December 1999

10 9 8 7 6 5 4 3 2 1

For Rachel

CONTENTS

Acknowledgments   *ix*

A Note on the Text   *xiii*

1. Play Scratch, Feel the Itch   1

2. The Journey and the Men   18

3. How They Built the Gate   46

4. Pulling Rabbits from the Q School Hat   76

5. Chaos on Bentgrass   101

6. Good Enough to Dream   122

7. One Trip Through, or 17   150

8. First Day of School   165

9. Groundhog Day   191

10. On the Number   207

11. The Reshuffle   227

Appendix: Facts and Records   *237*

Afterword   *309*

ACKNOWLEDGMENTS

Unlike professional golf's regular schedule of tournaments, the qualifying events have been sparsely documented. The records that do exist are not so easily accessible, even to experienced staff people at the PGA of America and the PGA Tour. I am grateful to many who took the time to track down Q School archived data on my behalf, including Bob Hyde, Karen Rose, Dave Lancer, and Denise Taylor. Ken Anderson of the PGA of America was extremely considerate in locating very early records and providing background material from his own memories and experiences.

As they do for all reporters and writers who cover their pro tournaments, PGA and Nike Tour media officials were generous in responding to my continuing requests during the Nike Tour and PGA Tour events I attended during the three-year research effort. Thanks in particular go to Joe Chemycz and Joan van Thron.

PGA Tour rules officials, I discovered, are among the best sources of anecdotal information on Q School. The encouragement and cooperation of Arvin Ginn, George Boutell, Vaughn Moise, Mark Russell, and Glen Tait was of much help in piecing together this narrative, and are greatly appreciated.

Among those who cooperated in lengthy interviews, only to endure repeated follow-up calls with patience, were Joe Black, Max Elbin, David Eger, Jim McLean, Jack Tuthill, Jack Burke, Jr., and Jackson Bradley. My thanks go to each of them.

Player representatives were also of great help in the information-gathering process, in particular Mike Biggs of Cornerstone Sports; Rich Katz of Pinnacle Enterprises; Mac Barnhardt of Pros, Incorporated; and David Parker of Links MMG.

Several magazine assignments helped defray expenses along the research trail. I am particularly grateful to Ken Van Kampen, Geoff Russell, and Terry Galvin during those times. Special thanks are owed to Mike D'Antonio, Jim Dodson, Rick Lipsey, and Tom Hanson—just a few of my fellow writers who offered guidance and help along the way. The same goes to the photographers, Mitch Haddad and Paul Lester, who helped assemble the photos that go along with this text. A debt of gratitude is also owed to Rand Jerris of the USGA library for help with late-stage archival research, to Maury Kelley, who provided videotapes of golf events that would otherwise have been missed; and to Mark Lex, for his assistance with digital backup of my manuscript-in-progress. I must also express a general thank-you to Ross and Randy Henry for their friendship and insights for over more than a decade. I would be far less knowledgeable about the golf swing, golf equipment, and the tour player's inner thoughts without their contributions.

Randy Voorhees, my literary agent, deserves recognition for originating this book's concept and helping shepherd the project through all its many stages. Pete Wolverton of Thomas Dunne/ St. Martin's Press is owed special thanks for believing in the idea from the start as well as shaping and sharpening the manuscript along the way. Rachel Basch, my wife and fellow author, is the inspiration behind anything I write to the best of my abilities. My gratitude to her is deep and eternal. To our children, Nathaniel and Hannah, I offer thanks for their many well-timed appearances at the writing table while this work was in progress. Every visit they made brightened the moment and leveled out the steep path I was climbing.

A NOTE ON THE TEXT

The terms "Q School" and "tour school" are colloquial, throwback phrases that exempt regular people from having to use the phrases "PGA Tour Qualifying Tournament" or (its official precursor) "PGA Tournament Training and Qualifying Program."

"Q School" and "tour school" are used more or less interchangeably in this book. The former is capitalized because the solitary *q* makes it typographically preferable to capitalize it—it is likewise preferable visually to match the *q* with an uppercase *s* for "School." The alternative term, "tour school," is spelled lowercase because it lacks the solitary letter that demands capitalization. There is also some sense on the part of the author that players, officials, and others use "Q School" to refer more particularly to the final stage of the PGA Tour Qualifying Tournament and "tour school" in a somewhat more generic way to describe the entire three-stage process.

La Quinta is a town in the California desert near Palm Springs, and home to the internationally recognized La Quinta Resort.

PGA Tour Qualifying's final stage has been held in the town of La Quinta five times since 1986, using one golf course on the La Quinta Resort grounds and another course across town at the sprawling PGA West golf community. At times in this book, a phrase like "the 1988 finals at La Quinta" is used in place of more cumbersome language restating the PGA West–La Quinta split-siting.

Likewise, the reader will see references to "Smith's final round at Matanzas Woods in 1987," which seems to suggest that all 183 players in the 1987 Q School final played all six of their rounds at Matanzas Woods. In fact, the field shuttled between Matanzas Woods and Pine Lakes Country Club, as other fields have shuttled between Grenelefe (pronounced *greenleaf*) West and Grenelefe South or between TPC at the Woodlands and the Woodlands Inn and Country Club (both located in a Houston suburb called The Woodlands, Texas).

In cases of geographical confusion, the reader may wish to consult the summary listing of all tour school finals as contained in archival form in chapter 12. In that summary, certain players are listed with their full names in some cases and a shorter version in other cases ("Patrick Burke" one year, "Pat Burke" another year). This is to preserve as closely as possible the original tour records.

1

PLAY SCRATCH, FEEL THE ITCH

I could not have known it at the time, but the dramatic heart of this book began beating on the first tee of the Woodland Golf Club during opening-round play of the 1973 Massachusetts Open. Banners hung from the old club's iron gates and two-tone Coupe de Villes idled on the entrance road as our 12:48 P.M. group commenced play. Two balls rested far down the fairway, waiting for a third contestant, the blond, blocky club pro who was my boss and my sometime hero, to hit his drive.

Beside me in the shade stood his green-and-white staff bag, which carried a set of MacGregor MTs and the name "Mike Smith" in a hopeful flourish of black script. Having already gone 18 holes in the third pairing of the morning (I caddied for an amateur who had shot 73), my legs and feet tingled with fatigue. The starter, who had announced my amateur's name six hours earlier and was still manning his post, sounded a bit weary himself.

But Mike was brimming with energy. Fidgeting, you might

even say. I watched him crunch his shoulder blades together and sweep a few ribbons of hair across his forehead, where pebbles of perspiration had recently emerged. Jitterbugging between the tee markers, he squinted at the fairway and the treelines pinching it. His small but ape-strong hands traveled along the club handle, trying to agree on a grip. He tugged at his glove and hitched up his sans-a-belt waistband, reestablishing that wavy border between a bulge of belly and his narrow, quick-turning hips. Many times had I witnessed this routine, including Mike's familiar pre-round benedictions: "Tee it high and fly," "Stick it in the ground and go," and so on, which today came out more in a croak than in his singsong rendition of a Rhode Island working-class accent.

My elders on the tee didn't know Mike Smith, but they knew about tournament golf. I had the case covered a different way—didn't know the game too well but I did know Mike. Which is how all of us simultaneously realized the guy was choking. Gagging uncontrollably. Constricted in the throat and in every other bodily orifice. Once I grasped what was happening, anxiety skipped from him to me like a flamelick in dry woods.

Examining my shoelaces, I steeled myself for an out-and-out whiff. Rejecting that possibility, I pictured the coldest of cold tops, a "hey boss look at me" company-outing special.

There were a few final spasms of Mike's false nonchalance, then he coiled back. His downswing was slashy and quick, and then came impact. About six dimples' worth, I estimated, occurring along that bony ridge where a persimmon driver's neck and soleplate meet.

The ball sizzled audibly. I pictured its cover carved open like a heavyweight's eyebrow. The shot tracked low and left, exploring the woods like a finch. Once it passed the first small grove—a copse of trees that could have pinballed it for a few loud *thwocks* then burped it back onto the forward tee—the torn ball found a sliver of daylight. As golf shots go, I remember thinking, this one was more exciting to watch than any high, booming drive would have been. It battled the evil forces of sidespin and topspin for 80 or 90 yards then finally succumbed. Though it had taken a fairly deep angle into the trees, this patch of woods must have been recently thinned, allowing the ball to skip crazily forward after it touched down. The terrain of the woods sloped upland from the fairway's edge, creating a valley effect that sent the ball trickling back toward safety. It came to rest 130 yards away, in a little clearing from which a reasonable recovery shot could be played.

Grim disaster had somehow been avoided. All parties to the incident, with the exception of the starter, legged it off the first tee like johns fleeing a raided brothel. By the time Mike retrieved his driver's headcover he had by some miracle gotten his wits about him, as well. Soon he was conversing with himself in full tenor, and I let myself believe that a scrambling 74 might be possible.

Twenty-five years later, I don't remember exactly what Mike shot. Closer to 80 than 70, certainly. What mattered is that I had finally seen him up close in a real tournament, and thus understood that his game was nothing special, to say the least. Mike was 34 years old at the time and I was 16. We had met the prior October when he was hired as head pro at Needham Golf Club, a nine-holer where my younger brother, Peter, and I were caddies. That fall, Mike chose me from among the "A" caddies to be his bag-room attendant and caddie master for the upcoming summer, a favor for which I was then and still am eternally grateful. Our previous pro was Mr. Burke, a tall, tanned, smooth-featured gentleman who had given up golf for full-time whiskey drinking. In three years of caddying at the club, I had seen the man play perhaps one round. Our new pro, as the officers on the search committee promised, was destined to be a great improvement, due to his youth and modern training and his downright respectable behavior. "Respectable" meaning he did most of his drinking after the golf shop was closed.

Given what we had heard of his professional skills, it was hard to imagine that Mike had worked at four or five clubs without ever being offered a head-pro position. The members at his most recent place of employment claimed he could reshaft, regrip, and rejigger the swingweight of a persimmon driver on an hour's notice. They said he could teach all day in the hot sun with skill and patience. Given his keen eye for merchandise, they predicted the Needham shop would soon be a colorful showcase of the latest gear. His tournaments would run like clockwork, they said, right down to the scoresheets he hand-lettered so swiftly and artfully. Mike knew the rules of our royal and ancient game, inside and out. He was a storyteller, he was an early riser and a hard worker, and he was more than happy to fill out a Saturday foursome of members, even the high-handicappers.

The Needham membership buzzed with anticipation. Their pro shop, which had become a wax museum, was about to be transformed. Extolling the virtues of this incoming firebrand became the only form of conversation allowed. "And he's a heckuva player, too," was how the members' speeches generally concluded. "Got a super swing." If a question then arose as to Mike's lack of tournament victories, a postscript would be added: "Guess he's been struggling with the putter the last couple of years," the members would note. "Yeah, putter is what's killin' him."

When you're 15 and living in a golf backwater like Needham, Massachusetts, you think anybody who can break par on an average course is mere steps away from stardom. I signed on not only as Mike's bag-room attendant but as his personal rooting section for the golfing comeback this great new job would allow him to mount. First off, he would need me and the rest of the staff to help get the golf program organized. Once things were running smoothly, he could buckle down to work on his game. Of course "comeback" may not have been the appropriate term, since Mike's raw talent had never been harnessed to produce those telltale high finishes in the New England PGA section's important tournaments. Or even in recent Monday pro-ams, for that matter.

But the man had played great golf in his time. Lately, however, it had all come at those odd hours when an overworked assistant pro might seize the chance. Mike would wait for the long evenings of summer, he explained to me, after club parking lots emptied and the shop doors were locked, to race through his unwitnessed rounds of 66, 67, 68. That had been his only serious playing time for the past several years, he explained, but now things would be different.

Somehow, the great comeback never did materialize. The drinking was mostly confined to after hours, but it hampered his progress all the same. And the shop staff responsible for getting things organized turned out to include one longtime crony of Mike's who did all his heavy lifting from the till. Some kind of cyst or spur cropped up at the base of Mike's thumb, an ailment the doctors couldn't seem to repair or even conclusively diagnose. In keeping with his reputation, Mike taught all day on our makeshift range and had no energy left to practice. I caddied for him the following summer when he and our greenkeeper teamed up to win a New England PGA Pro-Superintendent title, but that was all the fame and glory we could muster.

During that first summer, when my naïve rooting and his powers of self-deception produced their symbiotic revelries, I would ask him about his early career, his flashes of raw potential, his moments when it seemed destiny was beckoning him toward the big time. He would oblige me with a tournament golfer's standard narrative—the tips he had received from area pros whose names I recognized, the little grip changes and swing changes that had fine-tuned his ball flight and added distance or control. Putting, that prissy detail of the game that had proved such a nuisance even to greats like Hogan and Palmer, would come in for its few words of scorn, along with fresh words of resolve. There was a seriousness in all these explanations that convinced me Mike's playing goals—which in hindsight were wildly modest compared to the prospects I harbored for him—would one day be reached.

He would head off on Mondays to play in section tournaments and Tuesday's paper would list the top scores, none of which happened to be his. Then came the week of the Mass Open, and after that we spoke less and less about the comeback. When we did talk about his playing career, I noticed a bitter realism starting to creep into the conversation. Finally he related an incident that relieved me of my ignorance.

One of Mike's prior bosses had been Paul Harney, perhaps the finest tournament golfer New England has produced since the days of the great amateur (and 1913 U.S. Open champion) Francis Ouimet. Harney, who won seven PGA Tour events in his career, won three of those while engaged as the working head professional at Pleasant Valley Country Club in Sutton, Massachusetts, during the 1960s and early 1970s. Mike Smith, like the typical Harney assistant, was inspired to the point of awe by a man who could succeed wildly in both pro-golf arenas at once. Mike dedicated himself to seeing how good he could possibly be at the game Harney made look easy. The golf course, Pleasant Valley, was a PGA Tour stop, and thus a fitting test of any pro's potential. Mike would hit balls in the morning or at lunch, close the shop at dinnertime, and roar out onto the golf course. He had always been a hard swinger, but now he was adding finesse to his power game. The more he played it, the more this championship layout yielded low scores to him. He strode in one night after covering Pleasant Valley in another tidy 67. Unexpectedly, Harney was still on the premises. Mike knocked the grass clippings from his spikes and swaggered into the shop.

"I've made a decision I need to tell you about," Mike said to the boss. Then he drew in his breath. "Mr. Harney, I'm goin' on the tour."

Noticing the effect his long-abandoned declaration was having upon me, Mike paused for emphasis.

"Harney just looked at me," Mike recounted, "then he said, 'Son . . . you're not goin' anywhere.' "

And Paul Harney didn't mean, "Gosh, Mike, you're too valuable an employee—I need you around here." He meant, "You can't beat anybody, kid, so don't waste your time dreaming."

For all of Mike's tendencies toward self-delusion, his tone as he replayed Harney's words that day was one of door-slamming authority. An hour later, walking the mile of railroad track between the golf club and my house, I imagined that the great pro's reply must have stung Mike at first, and then eventually liberated him. That's when I realized that in Mike's mind, the competitive comeback his new job was going to spark would never ticket him for a return to Pleasant Valley and a stab at "Monday qualifying" for the Classic. His playing ambitions had to have been confined to respectable finishes in the Mass Opens and Rhode Island Opens and maybe the fall Cape Cod Pro-Am Series. Never would they approach the great, gaudy PGA Tour, as I had let myself imagine.

I remember feeling relieved that I hadn't made a big deal about my belief in Mike's playing ability to anyone, not even to my brother, Pete. At the same time, I felt disgusted with the game of golf, with its absurd randomness. So many players with classy swings and a passion to compete, and try as you might to discern superiority, you could go to your grave not knowing why one succeeded and the next one stood no chance.

Less than a decade later, I found myself legging it around professional tournaments with a set of pairing sheets and a notepad in my hand. The game's eternal riddle—why certain players were destined for stardom and certain others bound for obscurity— had worked its way into a vocation. By no means did I solve any mysteries right away, nor have I developed an eagle eye for budding greatness in the dozen years since. Unpredictability is still the essence of top-level tournament golf, and all the swing doctors, stat-masters, and sports psychologists in the world can only shed a certain amount of light on it. At the 1997 PGA Tour "Q School" finals in central Florida, I met a philosophical tour caddie (I suppose that's a redundancy) named Bob Ming, aka "Cowboy." Bob made an obtuse observation about the challenge of tour qualifying that I still find oddly helpful.

"Tour school is the final exam, it's there waiting for you. And every year, the questions on the test are the same," said Cowboy. "Problem is, every year the answers are different."

Those ever-changing answers to the big, simple question: "How good do you need to be?" are what make a Nike Tour event on the Golf Channel so disorienting. Watching these "developmental tour" events, an average fan asks, Haven't we seen a lot of these Nike Tour players competing on the PGA Tour? Aren't these Nike Tour players driving it as far as PGA Tour players do? Aren't they holing the six-footers and missing the 12-footers, same as on the PGA Tour?

The lack of visible differences among the various levels is one reason so many of us confine our rooting to the very elite players. We don't know exactly why they're better, we just know we can stick with them and never seem ignorant. Football fans can follow the NFL draft safe in the belief that most of the players in the first couple of rounds will have successful careers, even if some quit due to injury and a few others simply don't pan out. Basketball fans who turn themselves into "NBA draftniks" during the annual selection pageant have the luxury of adopting just about any first-rounder as their personal hero and knowing their guy will romp through the league for several seasons, anyway. The enormous no-cut contracts of these incoming players virtually assures it, whether the player excels or not.

In golf, being named rookie of the year (Mark Carnevale, Woody Austin, and Robert Gamez have all won the award in the '90s; all three have returned to Q School since) is a dubious honor—on the pro tour early success is usually fleeting. As fans and reporters, we wait for excellence to repeat itself over many campaigns before we adopt a player as one of our favorites. The media—newspapers along with television—try to skirt risk by fixating on the top 10 or 15 players, the superstars who dominate the major tournaments and get invited to all those easy-money side events. Most of the audience, most of the time, will be content to hear about the front-runners and turn a blind eye to the players who scuffle along. Whenever one of the scufflers goes on a tear in a big tournament, you can hear the media guidebooks crack open to the page containing his capsule bio.

I used to see the world from that angle myself, complaining inwardly about the unknowns and little-knowns who cluttered the landscape while I was busy trying to watch Jack Nicklaus, Tom Watson, and Greg Norman. Now, after three years researching this book, I find myself paying more attention to marginal players than stars. Perhaps it's out of vestigial loyalty to my old boss, Mike, who lived hard and wound up dying young. The main reason, I suppose, is that I've come to appreciate that special inner architecture to the sport and society of golf, the web of joists and rafters that connects all the participants to each other in a six-degrees-of-separation manner. There is a spontaneous kinship within golf, a summoning instinct. It works from the ground up and causes people like Eddie Lowery, Ouimet's schoolboy caddie, to grow up, move to California, and nurture the careers of Harvie Ward and Ken Venturi, who thrived under Lowery's patronage and have, in turn, adopted their own protégés. This kinship is powerful, and yet when it reaches the top of the professional pyramid, where the corporate dollars and megadeals become exponential, it gives way to some other force.

Up at the pinnacle of success, a Nicklaus, Watson, or Norman—these days a Tiger Woods or a David Duval—can unlink from tribal golf society and turn into an orbiting golf planet unto himself. "It's not that Greg Norman isn't a nice guy by nature," tour veteran Peter Jacobsen once told me. "It's just this commercial machine that's been built around him, like some kind of wall. I saw Greg at a tournament a couple of weeks ago and he must have had eight business guys walking stride for stride with him. I waved, and he waved back, but I remember thinking to myself, 'Was that Greg Norman who just walked by or was that a multinational corporation?'"

Arnold Palmer is the biggest star this game ever produced, but Palmer never orbited out of reach of his galleries or the average golfer. In the first place, it wasn't in his nature. Secondly, at the time of Palmer's rise to stardom, the economics of the game were not as complex and turbocharged as they are now. And since Palmer is both the ultimate golf superstar and perhaps the last icon to keep that earthy, personal connection to the proletariat, it's worth noting that golf's universal denominator—which is humility, the stark public experience of being humbled—played an important role. Arnold Palmer won early and often, he won major championships, he was coronated golf's king, but he lost his championship form while still in his prime years and became completely eclipsed as a player by Nicklaus. Palmer's putting yips in general and his nightmarish fumbling of the 1966 U.S. Open, after that title was well in hand, cast him as human, fallible, and ever approachable.

Nicklaus, by contrast, never suffered a cathartic, humiliating defeat between the gallery ropes. Dry spells and missed opportunities, yes, but no naked failure. Meanwhile, he followed his ambition and pride into course design and club manufacturing, treating these sidelines as serious competitive arenas. Palmer was involved in similar enterprises, but always the opportunities came to him. Any venture that bore the Palmer name would be high quality—Arnold insisted on that. But there was nothing dog-eat-dog about the Arnold Palmer golf-equipment company or his course-design and course-management outfits. If you really wanted to see Palmer's competitive fires burn, you had to watch him play golf tournaments.

As for Greg Norman, the supposedly humbling effect of defeat—even catastrophic collapse, such as Norman endured at the 1996 Masters—never seems to fully take hold. Norman's horse gets shot out from under him and he falls, but he doesn't hit the turf. Defeat is nominally accepted, but not its harsh implications. Instead, Norman dusts himself off, counts his blessings (after being overtaken by Faldo in 1996 at Augusta, he even publicly counted his money), and moves on. To the next business deal, the next tournament, the next appointment with his rightful destiny. Tiger Woods, who came to us prepackaged, is similar to Greg Norman—separate from you and me. The current star system in golf makes it impossible for Woods to be an extension of the lineage that connects 20-handicappers to 10-handicappers, 10s to 5s, 5s to scratch players, scratch players to minitour pros, and so on up through Q School and the Nike Tour to the PGA Tour. That being the case, we look elsewhere for people to identify with. At least I do. When the giants battle it out in major championships, the show is still spectacular and it's still history-in-the-making. But if you're used to feeling a subtle, personal identification with the people inside the ropes—a distant, genealogical link—then Palmer was surely the last super-star to whom that feeling extended.

Pro golf's overall unpredictability, that seemingly random se-lection process I once walked along the railroad tracks cursing, is actually a great unifier of everyone who plays the game, or even just follows it. As long as it's basically impossible, early on, to distinguish the can't-miss player from the prohibitive long shot, then we're all entitled to spot future PGA Tour mainstays in our own backyards. Take any junior-golf champion from any club in any town who shoots 69–68 to win by eight shots—automatically this boy is Tour Material, at least to the folks around him. When tournament-goers sit in the driving-range grandstand watching PGA Tour pros practice, there are always a few who are picturing Billy Elwood or Jason Appleton or some other local phenom who could hit it longer and straighter than half the contestants on the tee. ("Jason ought to be out there," you almost hear them sigh.) It's both their burden and their natural right.

Then the next big tournament starts and one of the big names outduels a few other big names and, yes, a few lesser-knowns along the way. The big-name player's familiar face gets splashed on the magazine covers and he moves a few notches up the World Ranking. With the start-up of the World Golf Championship tour-naments, and other changes in the PGA Tour's structure, elite players are being separated from the rest of the population even more dramatically than before. The gap opening up between top-tier pros and the rank and file naturally brings these professionals one peg closer to the real world, where the rest of us live. It connects us to the walk-ons who bloomed a bit late and were coached by the local pro instead of David Leadbetter. When one of these scufflers can escape his purgatory and establish himself at the top professional level, it's a victory that feels straight out of the hometown newspaper. To paraphrase Bobby Jones's famous comment about Nicklaus, these mid-level pros play a game with which we *are* familiar.

Meanwhile, they are scarcely any better at gauging or predicting their success than we are. As their careers progress and then stall, they struggle with the question of how good they'll need to be to achieve their next goal. They look ever inward to try and learn exactly how much ability they possess. And Q School, the annual PGA Tour feeder tournament, is their official spawning grounds. In recent years, the scuffling life in general has become a bit easier and Q School in particular has begun to seem less of a tour stepchild. The purse money it offers is actually worth battling for, and if you come up short of PGA Tour eligibility, the Nike Tour offers consolation and semigainful employment. But despite the safety net, veteran pros in their late 20s and 30s often find tour qualifying to be a more harrowing, humbling ordeal than ever before. Players who have spent even one season on the big tour are shocked at how easily they accustomed themselves to its comforts and prestige. When they lose eligibility, it's the equivalent of having sinned and been kicked out of paradise.

"I missed getting a card at my first tour school in '87," explained Nolan Henke, winner of three tour events in the 1990s, "then I came back in '88 and requalified. Unfortunately, that year I finished out of the top 125 [Henke ranked 159th in earnings], so I had to go through it all again. Coming back to the school after a year on tour, I remember thinking how much easier earning a card had been that first time. The second time, you know what you're missing if you don't make it."

The PGA Tour Qualifying Tournament, and this chronicle of

it, is a view of pro golf from the bottom looking up. These stories celebrate the journeyman. They shed light on the working-class heroism found in the lower end of the results sheet, where every Monday morning from January to October there is a 70–72–74–71—$4,672 that matters a great deal to an individual player, his wife, his inner circle of two dozen family and friends and sponsors. After so many conversations with the obscure names listed beside those numbers, you begin to see the condo payments, the insurance bills, and the coach class airfares that have to be extracted from their modest winnings. Anyone who has breathed easier when a struggling coworker returns to the cubicle next to theirs holding a performance review that's one or two notches above the termination line can appreciate what a PGA Tour event's bottom few inches of final results represent. Elevating the importance of the scufflers does not imply a lack of respect for the athletes who dominate pro golf. Like Duval or Tom Lehman, some of them are repeat qualifiers who once spent long years grinding away at their games with minimal success.

But in a time when pro athletes play for sums of money that will keep their grandchildren from ever having to work, it's clear that pro golf's qualifying ritual is not the equivalent of draft day for the NBA or NFL. There are 900 athletes who make the NFL rosters each year. Big-league baseball's combined player count is 700. In pro hockey there are 550 roster slots, and in the NBA about 360. On the PGA Tour (where the bottom one-fourth of eligible players don't earn enough money to cover expenses), there are only 150 to 180 eligible players. And still, any golfer's grand entrance into the big time stands a good chance of being followed by a departure. Then a reentry. Then two or three more repetitions of the cycle. Not to say that basketball players don't get cut from one team and either head for Europe or look for tryouts with other American clubs, but can you imagine how glamorous the NBA draft would be if players continually reentered it?

Inside these pages are the triumphs, turnarounds, failures, and confessions of the obscure and unwashed athletes who populate the cruel and unusual tournament known as Q School. Every serious golfer is a dreamer, and most professional golfers down through the years have kept secret, unwritten diaries full of fond dreams for what they might accomplish in competition. The mystery of who makes it and who misses has turned them inside out looking for some blessed edge or advantage that could put them over the top.

One of those hopefuls was Rick Vershure, now a club professional in suburban New York, who made it to the Q School finals eight times but never got his tour card.

"The last time I tried, the finals were at Palm Coast, Florida," recalled Vershure recently. "Every other time I showed up at a final, I felt unnerved," he said. "That last time, I honestly felt equal to the other players." Vershure's ball-striking that week was reliable to the point of monotony, but he found he was tapping in for par instead of holing his birdie putts. "I came to the 107th hole [out of 108 total] needing to finish par-par," he recounted. "I was still hitting the ball well, but I wasn't making many birdies. That wore on me. I felt like I was out there just playing and playing and playing." The monotony was broken when Vershure three-putted to bogey hole number 107.

"The first putt was a level 20-footer that hit the hole and slid two feet by," he explained, for perhaps the 100th time. Two feet, the ultimate panic-attack distance for any make-or-break putt.

"I hit the hole again, coming back, but the ball wouldn't drop," Vershure confessed. As he later recalled it, that afternoon on the Matanzas Woods course "was as mentally exhausting as anything

I've been through. To come that close and miss . . . it can cost you so much, and for such a long time, if you let it."

In the years since, Vershure has served as head professional at the prestigious Quaker Ridge Golf Club and competed successfully in sectional and national club-pro competition. His colleagues in the Metropolitan section of the PGA sometimes speak like men who have seen a ghost when they talk about the period after Vershure returned from his '87 Q School crack-up. "A couple of us had lunch with him about a month after it happened," recalled Mike Diffley, head professional at Pelham Country Club in New York. "He told the story, and it still shook him to tell it. We all knew what it was like to give away a tournament. But this was, you know, a career. Watching him talk about it, you could see he was in the act of resigning himself to being a club pro."

Vershure, with the benefit of a decade's hindsight, sensed where our conversation about his tour-qualifying quest was going. He anticipated the question about a different life, a life that had slipped away, and offered his answer.

"If I had only made it onto the tour, all the tournaments and money I would have won . . . Are you about to ask me if I think about that all the time?" Vershure inquired. "No, not me. I may have that fantasy moment every once in a while, but I can honestly say I never wasted any time wondering what might have happened."

That "fantasy moment" defines PGA Tour Qualifying School. The Q School's field contains players who have fantasy moments and draw inspiration from them, players who live almost permanently inside those fantasy moments and are enslaved by them, and a few players who have forgotten what the fantasy moment really feels like and are trying to capture it all over again.

And I suppose there are also a few who aren't chasing a fantasy but are running from a curse somebody once laid on them—a curse that went something like, "Son, you aren't goin' anywhere." Players burdened in that way seem to stay on the move, competing in places most of us have barely heard of, dropping out of sight for long stretches at a time. They are hard guys to keep track of, and your best bet is to try and find them at Q School. They tend to show up for that annual test of golf where the questions are always the same, hoping that this time—finally—they know all the right answers.

2

THE JOURNEY AND THE MEN

The parking-lot sentry wore the work clothes of a California carrot grower, not the fashionable knitwear normally seen on PGA Tour volunteers.

"You fellas players?" he asked.

Slouched on the passenger side, I imagined how the contestants had been answering this question.

"Media," answered my colleague, tapping the wheel.

Small talk ensued, until it was obvious the volunteer was there directing traffic, not checking credentials. We prowled ahead without flashing any. They still don't require a media badge at the PGA Tour Qualifying Tournament, nor do they charge admission. They don't send out marshals, they don't erect grandstands, they don't rope the fairways, and they don't print up a program. The few reporters who attend the weeklong competition check in at the makeshift media center upon arrival, then drift onto the grounds and set to work—skulking, lurking, scoping out disaster as it unfolds. All is glum and gray through the early going, until the 108-hole ordeal spirals down to its anguished conclusion. Since 1996, the last few rounds have been telecast by the Golf Channel, whose arty logo and energetic reporters manage to cheer the proceedings up a bit.

If the PGA Tour is a magnificent ocean liner, this tournament is its bilge room. From the Masters to the Skins Game, pro golf is a bentgrass battlefield where college-bred warriors take turns winning the big prize money. Beyond the pageant of saddle shoes and high fives, we assume no madness lurks. Indeed, if there were a tragic side to professional tournament golf, could we even glimpse it? The fact is we could wallow in it, simply by attending the annual PGA Tour Qualifying Tournament.

Better known as "Q School" or "tour school" or even the "Fall Classic," this is the one tournament Samuel Beckett might have competed in. At six full rounds—with no cut—it is longer than most heavyweight fights, and it unfolds like a black-and-white gangster movie in which most characters come to a bad end. The tournament is a specter of failure on which all the success of the pro-golf tour is built. You can't understand the U.S. Open or the PGA Championship or even the importance of 18th place at the John Deere Quad City Classic if you don't understand Q School. Survivors often walk away feeling numb relief rather than triumph.

The Qualifying Tournament screen-tests golf's newcomers but it also acts as a reform school for older delinquents. To appreciate how festive and fun a PGA Tour stop is, you have to watch the tour's cast-off veterans and aspiring rookies trudge through the annual 108-hole qualifier in December. Tour school is young families killing time in motel rooms waiting for Dad to shoot two strokes better than a pack of guys who have equal ability, in which case the family might live semicomfortably for the next 12 months. It's a steady drip-drip-drip of athletic pressure, dreams dissolving here, dreams coming true over there. When a player makes it to his first "final stage" (two earlier stages, local and regional, reduce the original 1,000-plus entries down to about 170) and misses by a few shots, he either wallows in heartbreak or he seeks out a series of experts and pseudoexperts who offer him the missing ingredient.

Q School provides proof that watching highly skilled pros shoot low scores on a difficult golf course is not, in itself, entertainment. When athletes are playing for the right to compete in their chosen sport for an entire year—and most will fail to earn that right—the atmosphere is grim and unpleasant. What you see before you is a golf competition with the air sucked out of it. There are no corporate tents at Q School, no courtesy cars, no junior clinics, no pro-ams, no Gillette Shootouts, no trophy ceremonies, no beer-slaked fans bellowing "Ish shin na hole!" Players experience the strange irony of being intensely examined—and at the same time hardly noticed.

"You don't have to play great golf to get your card at tour school." That comment, which is Q School's most persistent truism, proves how strongly professional golfers feel about the achievement of victory in tournament play. Because finishing 35th in the annual qualifier is basically equal to finishing first, the stronger players in the field have traditionally played it cozy, pacing themselves in the early going while others faltered, or starting strong then loping home in 72–70–71 when they could easily have attacked the course and gunned for scores in the 60s every day. Likewise, many a lesser player has stumbled, scrambled, and rallied his way to a cliff-hanger finish that earned him a card but chipped away at his personal dignity. It's not that ragged golf down the stretch never wins a PGA Tour event—or a U.S. Open, for that matter—it's just that tour school's card-earners always include

a few players who hacked their way home but ran out of holes to screw up before they totally blew it.

The scoreboard at Q School is the same colorful wall of calligraphy and clever symbols you see on display at other big-league golf events, but the people staring at it seem more like visitors to the Vietnam Memorial than tournament-goers. In comes a threesome, up go three scores. Every afternoon, the scorer recalibrates the line separating the cut-makers from the cut-missers. Players whose names are listed above that line can indulge the thought: "If the tournament were over today I'd be in." After only the first or second round, that fact carries little import. But with each passing day there is more and more temptation to feel "safe" because you are "inside the number."

Mike Swartz is a longtime tour hopeful with a lanky build and a sober, serious demeanor. Swartz has been on the pro scene for years but is just one for nine in his attempts at qualifying school. "In a regular tournament you don't see the extremes of emotion you see at Q School," he commented. "You stand on the first tee and say, 'It's just a round of golf,' but you can't convince yourself of it. I shot 65 in the second round one year, then I came out the next day and told myself that my 65 had never happened—the job was to just keep playing as hard as I could."

Kelly Gibson made it through Q School on his sixth try. "It's the toughest experience in golf," says Gibson. "You see players crying, wives crying. The pressure is almost physically painful. You have to think all week about what you eat and whether you can keep it down." The most recent twist in Gibson's career brought him back to the tour-school final of 1998, where he shot 77–67 the last two days to miss requalifying by one bitter stroke. Somehow, Gibson had lost focus during the penultimate round.

Harry Taylor, a journeyman who has earned and lost a walletful of tour cards, has an interesting method of trying to avoid the one-day letdowns that have become less and less survivable in recent years, due to intensified competition. "People talk about taking tour school one day at a time, one round at a time," said Taylor. "I don't do it that way. It doesn't help me focus. I play a tour-school final as if it was one long round, first hole to the 108th hole."

Reporters and other observers wander final-stage qualifying tournaments like refugees trying to spot their fellow villagers in a teeming Red Cross camp. You can spend the whole week at one of these tournaments, shuttling among the multiple golf courses, and never once cross paths with a player or caddie you may have known for years. The daily pairing sheets indicate where and when each of the 170 golfers is due to tee off, but with so many stories to follow and so little information to go on, the spectator never feels he or she is in the right place at the right time. Even a conventional leaderboard wouldn't be much help, since knowing who will finish first, second, or third is of such little importance compared to the crucial information about who ties for 35th.

Day two and day three clunk by, and the contestants you're tracking either "play well and pass guys" or "play lousy and get passed." But no matter how glacial the pace or how repetitive the early and middle rounds of Q School may be, the endings are always tumultuous. In every final round, the field inevitably "backs up," so that a standing of, say, 10-under, which at the end of day five had been a stroke or two outside the top 35, emerges as a cherished number—a bona fide card-earning score—when day six finally ends.

The last 90 minutes of the final stage goes by in a flash, especially for friends and family of the 15 or 20 players still tightroping along the in-or-out line. Around one-thirty or two o'clock, the triumphs and tragedies begin to crash on the shore, three at a time every nine minutes. Contestants who started the day with little or no chance for a PGA Tour card are in the locker room having a quiet beer by then. And the few players who are so far "inside the number" they could shoot 80 without blowing their chance for a card are just making the turn and are no longer the lead actors on the stage.

At that point, the tightropers, the golfers who started the sixth round with a chance to play their way inside the number— or shoot themselves out of it—are coming down the stretch. Spectators with rooting interests in one of these pros will have hustled out to the 15th or 16th hole an hour earlier to root them home, begging for the one birdie their player apparently needs or else praying against the one bogey that, based on the semi-official projections being passed about, would ruin the whole week and the whole upcoming season—maybe even the player's whole career. These galleryites, like the officials and players, have been known to make a mistake in either direction. They have rejoiced at three straight pars out of a belief that their player was already low enough, or cursed a bogey when conventional wisdom (incorrectly) had their man right on the number, lacking so much as a one-shot cushion. It all adds up to a thrilling Monday afternoon.

It's worth mentioning that Tour Qualifying School ends each year on a Monday. There is surely a logical and practical reason for this, but it goes against the karma of tour qualifying to ask what it is. Possibly, the schedule is a bureaucratic expression of Christian piety—to dispense this much misery and anguish on the Sabbath would subvert the divine plan. Monday tournament golf is what local club pros do on their day off—it doesn't suit the pro tour. Even a jamboree like the AT&T Pebble Beach Pro-

Am seems allergic to Mondays, ending its annual battle against wind and rain by declaring a 54-hole winner on Sunday evening. Complaints of inconvenience and anticlimax fill the air even when something as high profile as the U.S. Open settles ties with its Monday 18-hole playoff. But the Q School makes a conscious choice, year in and year out, to finish on a Monday. Perhaps the goal is to prevent all involved from mistakenly thinking of golf as something other than work.

Preliminary tour qualifying takes place at a dozen or more regional sites and narrows the original field of 1,000-plus to about 170 men. Final stage is six rounds, 108 holes. The rounds are mentally grueling as well as physically tiring (even more so since 1997, when cart-riding, a Q School tradition, was prohibited). Then there are the six merciless motel nights prior to each round. Asked recently about his four appearances in tour school finals, Bob Tway, who finally made it through in 1984 after some twitchy near misses, said he only kept one thought in mind throughout: "Be consistent." Asked how nervous the qualifier made him, Tway answered with a straight face: "Let's just say I couldn't eat."

Until 1997, a cut was made at final stage following the fourth round, down to the low 90 and ties. Since that year, the cut has been eliminated and every member of the field has been allowed to play the full six rounds. When the sixth round finally ends, PGA Tour eligibility cards are printed up for the low 35 players, including ties. "Q School is the only tournament I've ever played where you look behind you instead of ahead," says David Sutherland, who was making his sixth attempt at Q School in 1997.

"Instead of thinking how low a score I need in order to win, or place in the top ten, I think about how high a score I could shoot and still qualify."

And despite the drama, despite the intensity of the competition, scarce few spectators come out to watch the players practice their craft at Q School. Fine golf is played on terrific golf courses, yet the only ones on hand are caddies, wives, girlfriends, parents, and of course the players themselves. Along with hopeful new-comers, Q School also attracts those hard-luck tour vets who have veered off the trail, playing too poorly the previous year to keep their cards (or too poorly the past five years to regain one), and hoping to make it back.

In 1999, this oddly named, sparsely chronicled, unusually run tournament finds itself approaching 35 years of unique his-tory. The tour school spins a deep, dense tale of heartbreak, black humor, back-room politics, and sometimes magnificent golf under dire circumstances. In the Q School's near and dis-tant past, many of the vintage moments involve pressure. The classic, often whispered stories of final-stage qualifying are all about breakdowns of the body and soul. The happier stories tell of emotional sinews that twist and fray but somehow keep the mind and golf swing together. Breakdown stories can haunt a pro for years: Eric Epperson's six bogeys on the back nine of the last day of the '95 tournament to ruin his previous five days of solid play, or Jim Carter's complete choke act on the last day of the 1996 event. Even success is wrenching: Mike Weir and Esteban Toledo, crying in front of TV cameras after earning their PGA Tour cards in 1997, were only doing what others had done privately in Q Schools past.

Play a solid week of golf, snag the world's greatest job for one year. That's the devil's bargain of tour school, and its effects are manifold: Players slipping into men's room stalls to purge their digestive systems before final-round play. Seasoned pros so pre-occupied they arrive at the course without clubs, wallets, golf shoes, contact lenses. Veteran reporters snapped at and glared at until they no longer dare approach a player with questions. At the 1990 finals in Palm Springs, Patrick Burke came to his final hole convinced that he needed a birdie to regain his tour eligibility for the 1991 season. Burke hit a decent drive on the long par-4 but was still 185 yards from the hole, which was cut near the back edge of a narrow, deep green.

"Under any other conditions I would have hit 5-iron," groaned the pugnacious Burke. "But I hit the 4-iron, thinking I had to carry the ball to the back of the green and try to stop it near the pin." Burke's 4-iron turned out to be too much club. And the birdie he was gunning for turned out to be too much score. Par on the last hole of that '90 qualifier would have given him 428, good enough for full PGA Tour exemption. Burke recovered from the back rough to 10 feet but couldn't sink his putt. He signed for his bogey and his 429, got in his Pontiac Trans Am and slammed the door viciously.

"The ride from Palm Springs to my house in Asuza takes an hour and forty-five minutes on an average day," said Burke, looking back with a trace of disbelief. "I made it home from Q School that day in one hour. I was in the left lane the entire way, with the accelerator floored. The radio was up at full volume, but you couldn't even tell it was on."

Eight years later, with the finals again held in Palm Springs, another player who felt the sting of missing by a single shot set off for home in disgust. The player was Tim Loustalot, who had been to the Q School finals every year since 1989 and had missed by just one stroke before. Loustalot (the 33-year-old nephew of 1970 tour-school graduate Victor Loustalot) drove away from the sprawling PGA West golf complex and headed east to his home in Phoenix. He stopped halfway at a fast-food taco shop in Blythe, California, to call his wife and commiserate. When she picked up the phone, Loustalot blurted out a curse of regret while his wife,

Jamie, sang out congratulations. Their conversation momentarily halted.

"I missed by one," he moaned. "You made it," she said. "I was 10-under," he countered, "Ten-under made it," she insisted. "Some guy chipped in for birdie but everybody watching thought it was an eagle. They thought he dropped to 11-under and filled out the top 35." Jamie herself had shut off the Golf Channel telecast thinking Tim had missed, only to receive a congratulatory phone call from a caddie who had formerly worked for Loustalot. Initially, Mrs. Loustalot had maligned the caddie for what seemed to be a sadistic prank, but he held his ground and told her to double-check, which she did. "I looked on the Tour's Web site," she said to her husband. "It's official, Tim, you're in." Back in Palm Springs, Loustalot's father was being interviewed by the Golf Channel, saying his son had left the course unhappily but would "be in for a nice surprise when he got home."

We parked the rental car beside a mud-spattered green Ford with Wisconsin license plates and 180,000 miles on it—some 24-year-old who had shocked himself and his buddies by making it through two prior stages of qualifying. "Long ride home in that thing," we each muttered to ourselves. On the dashboard of our rental car there was now a scrap of lined paper, torn from the back of my notepad, on which "Media" had been scrawled by the volunteer. "Keep this where we can see it for the rest of the week," he said, with a faint twang of authority. And thus we had our answer to the question of when Q School first reveals its perverse, unholy, undernourished essence: right as you enter the parking lot.

For opening day of the 1996 final-stage qualifier at La Purisma Golf Course in Lompoc, the sky was as gray as wet cement and bruised purple in a few spots. Half the field was here, half was 40 miles away at Sandpiper Golf Course in Goleta, near Santa Barbara. In a small house that stood about 40 yards from the first tee and seemed to predate construction of the course, members of the PGA Tour communications team, dressed in jackets and sweaters, knelt beside a woodstove and rolled the previous day's newspapers into tight cylinders as fuel for a fire. The compact, two-story house, which apparently lacked central heating, had been converted into a media headquarters for the week. After half an hour of stoking, the balky fire in the stove had fouled the main room with unwanted smoke, and it still seemed colder inside the house than outside.

Up a walkway toward the clubhouse and the 18th tee, La Purisma's unpretentious grill room proved considerably warmer and more comfortable. At one end of the building a long service counter offered cheeseburgers, french fries, beer, and other 19th-hole essentials. At the other end, a group of players' wives had rearranged several tables to create a walled-off nursery and play area for the babies and toddlers. The mothers had laid out a "splat mat" to handle the food rejected by tykes in their Li'l Golfer cloth bibs and had designated a far corner of the small play area as the diaper-changing station. Anyone who came in out of the raw wind for more than 30 minutes was likely to witness the endearing sight of at least two tiny bottoms undergoing a cleanup. The whole scene called to mind descriptions of barbarian Europe provided by the Roman historian Tacitus, who reported that during battles among Saxon tribes, women would bare their breasts along the sidelines to remind clansmen of the dark fate their wives and daughters were sure to suffer at the hands of a victorious opposition army.

The young La Purisma course, stretched across the green breadloaf foothills a few miles from the Pacific, will surely go down as the last risky site choice in PGA Tour Qualifying Tournament history. Not surprisingly, finding a home for the Q has seldom been easy. People who manage golf courses don't like to shut them down for a full week just to host this obscure, melancholy event. The Tour antes up reasonable rent money and lets you display its logo on your billboards and scorecards, but meanwhile you've turned away your regular customers without gaining any real glamour.

Notwithstanding this odd exception of 1996, Q School's final stage requires at least two usable 18-hole courses adjacent to one another, in a Sunbelt location with on-site room accommodations. The Tour angles for resort golf complexes like the TPC at the Woodlands, in Houston, or La Quinta, in the desert golfopolis of Palm Springs, or the colorfully misspelled resort Grenelefe, outside Orlando. According to Tour rules official George Boutell, there may not be 20 golf facilities in the entire U.S. where the event could properly be staged. La Purisma and Sandpiper are two wonderful layouts, but there is no course on earth fine enough to offset the chill rains of the week to come and the delays and confusion they will cause.

This would be the infamous Q School in which 20 players went off the first tee in a downpour for the scheduled sixth day, only to be called back in and told that scoring had been closed out after five rounds. This would be the last Q School with an insulting, afterthought purse ($150,000) that equated to 10 percent of what normal tour events pay. It would also be the last time a player could arrive without a caddie, request a golf cart, load his bag, and ride off into competition unaccompanied. Come 1997, a policy change would go into effect requiring players to walk the full distance. However, in keeping with the perversity that surrounds this event, a legal injunction granted to handicapped Stanford graduate Casey Martin would strike down the no-carts rule before it was ever enforced, allowing players at the 1997 school to ride if they so chose—albeit in stripped-down carts (no roofs or windshields) that could ferry the player only—his clubs would have to be lugged by a caddie.

In the 1996 edition of Q School, 49 players were handed eligibility cards, and out to the big tour they ventured for the 1997 season—where only two of them finished in the top 50 on the money list and a full two thirds of them failed to finish in the top 125—thus buying themselves a return trip through the qualifying grinder. The bottom fourth of the tour money list is ridiculed by many as pro golf's Easy Street, a picnic area populated by semi-motivated underachievers who get vertigo when they see their names on a leaderboard. But to the thousands of golf jocks trying to squeeze into that bottom bracket, it may as well be Fort Knox or Buckingham Palace. The basement floor of the annual money list is where golf's bell curve takes a sharp bend, allowing a cluster of the just-about-good-enough to enter, then opening a trap door beneath them once the season starts. Q School, for many of them, is a revolving door, reminiscent of the contraption in the Dr. Seuss story that tattoos a star on the plain-bellied Sneetches and then removes the stars from the star-bellied Sneetches as they pass through a second time.

Law-school graduates can flunk the bar exam on their first attempt and try again as often as necessary until they pass. But lawyers don't survive the exam and join the bar only to slip so far down in their profession over the ensuing year that they have to retake the test. By passing once, an attorney successfully joins a privileged guild and is welcome to make a living in it as long as he or she works hard and keeps out of trouble. But professional golfers, even more than team-sport athletes, come and go. Q School contestants sometimes compare the six long rounds of tour school to the Harold Ramis film *Groundhog Day*, in which Bill

Murray is compelled by some unseen force to relive the same moribund day over and over again, until he acknowledges his self-centered ways and vows to change.

This *Groundhog Day* comparison is accurate—but more so than players realize. Certainly those 108 holes of grim combat take on a morbid repetitiveness, but it isn't the six days that repeat themselves agonizingly, it's the six years, or the eight or 10 or 12 years. These decades of wandering, in which so many men in their 20s and 30s cling to their goal of becoming successful PGA Tour players, can become a disheartening internal exile within one's chosen profession. In many cases, the journeyman player will taste just enough success to keep him spinning the wire drum inside his hamster cage, but never enough to secure a good living for his family and a fulfilling identity for himself. There's something bleakly pitiful about it, if you ask a deadpan golf philosopher like Jack Burke, Jr.

"Guys will go through the qualifying five or six years in a row," mused Burke, a flinty Texan who won two major championships and 13 other tour events a generation ago. "Half the time they won't get their card, then when they do, they can't keep it for the next year. Now wouldn't that tell you it's time to get a job changing tires or something?" There has always been a scuffling life for borderline tour pros, and there always will be. But these days it's a different kind of journey and a different breed of men. Burke recognizes that the financial rewards of a semi-successful golf career loom large, but to him the irresistible attraction of PGA Tour life comes more from the "athletic idolatry" America has created for itself. When Burke was growing up between the wars, every kid without rickets or polio either worked or played ball all day until dark, then hustled home for supper.

"The whole culture changed when sports at school became organized," said Burke. "The coach would come along in grade school and pick the best athletes, and you and I, if we weren't the best, would end up in the stands, watching. Same thing would happen in junior high, and in high school, too. It's like one big system for turning a few people into athletes and most people into permanent fans.

"Eventually," he said, "you end up with guys standing half-naked in the freezing cold with their faces painted the team colors, making fools of themselves. They never got to play as kids, so they're desperate to be a part of something, and they channel all that energy into worshiping the top athletes."

The club-pro job, the real estate license, the father-in-law's insurance business—all the classic bailout options for unsuccessful tour pros are still there, but many more players seem to forgo them, especially as the purse money on the "big tour" spirals upward. "No matter how many times the door shuts in his face, the young pro of today acts like it's mandated by God that he play the PGA Tour," marveled Burke.

A player who returns year after year to this ritual can end up feeling part of his manhood carved away. For other athletes, the paradigm of Sisyphus rolling his boulder up the mountain doesn't apply. Most sports require a young man to submit to a rite of passage that takes him from boyhood stardom into the pro ranks or out the back exit. When the sports dream fails to come true, he takes his final bush-league bus ride and selects a new path in adult life, tinged with the knowledge of having "almost made the bigs." This held true for golfers in the early years of Q School, when purse money was so-so and getting a tour card did not exempt a new player from the grind of Monday qualifying. These days, however, a golfer turns pro, makes the big leagues, then very likely finds that he has slipped off the roster unnoticed. He qualifies again, performs below the set standard, and has to requalify. Over and over again. Because the physical demands of the game can be met by players in their 30s and early 40s, it's possible to stay locked in the would-be, could-be cycle for a decade, maybe two.

There is indeed more work available these days for golfers who fit the category of journeyman. And there also seem to be more pathways to improvement. The cycle of semisuccess in pro golf causes most of its inhabitants to seek help from performance experts like the sports psychologist Bob Rotella, who wrote *Golf is Not a Game of Perfect* and other mind-building books for golfers. Rotella's long client list includes champions and would-be champions alike. Some of the players from the latter category stumble badly along the way, perhaps badly enough to take Jack Burke's advice and try something else. But it's not as simple as it sounds, the psychologist maintains.

"You don't see pro golfers holding press conferences to announce their retirements, that's just not the way it works," Rotella pointed out. "But every year a certain number of players do give it up," he said. "It's a very hard decision, because tour-caliber golf skills don't develop overnight, and if a player has talent, he owes it to himself to try and bring it out. Then maybe it goes away and he has to find it again. I don't care who you are or how long you've been around this game, you can never predict when the whole package is going to fall into place for a player."

All tour hopefuls have support groups, according to Rotella, whose job it is to help their man persevere through dry spells. Beyond that inner circle—or even inside it—there are always doubters. "When are you going to quit dreaming and face reality?" says Rotella, paraphrasing the questions some of his most successful clients have heard during down periods. "Everybody in golf hears that from somebody. As a sports psychologist, my job is to help a client work toward improvement. When the player's most loyal supporters start talking negatively, it can sometimes lead him toward giving up. But that's for the player alone to decide."

For obvious reasons, many players have chosen Q School as the place to lay down their guns and surrender. Ken Lindsay is former president of the PGA of America and a golf-rules expert with long experience officiating tour qualifiers. Lindsay has found himself the recipient of more than one 28-year-old's impromptu retirement announcement after the Q School ax has fallen. Later, he has been heartened to learn that not all the resignations were final. "One year at tour school," recalled Lindsay, "I saw a guy standing next to a trash barrel and I swear he was just about to stick his bag of clubs into it. 'There's one that's bit the dust,' I thought to myself, figuring the player had hung it up for good. But a year later I was working a regional qualifier and over on the putting green I saw that same player." Lindsay was fairly certain he recognized the golf bag, too.

Rich Katz, a sports agent and course-management executive with Virginia-based Pinnacle Enterprises, hears hard-luck stories about aspiring tour pros all year round, but autumn is always his busy season for journeyman gossip. When the final day of final-stage qualifying rolls around, Katz prefers to be back at the office, not down at ground zero. But he sits by the telephone, which at times in the past has been transformed into a crisis hot line.

"One player I represented called me up from Q School and cried for 20 minutes straight," reported Katz, who actually specializes in Senior PGA Tour clients for the very reason that their emotional demands are much less. "He was hysterical. He kept saying, 'Now I have to go on the Nike Tour, how the hell am I going to support my family?' The guy had just spent his last few thousand bucks to enter the Q school and come up empty. 'Man, I failed, I'm afraid I won't get another chance,' he kept saying. I told myself to give him some positive reinforcement, but what do you say?" lamented Katz, who looks back on that phone call as his "worst experience ever as a sports agent."

A tour victory is a thing from *The Iliad*. The journeyman's life is different—a page from *The Odyssey*. The repeated test, the repeated question. And pro golf does seem at times to be developing a permanent underclass, with Q School and the Nike Tour the headquarters for golf's in-between players. That being the case, some of them will one day break through and become stars. One of the tour bureaucracy's current fears is that players will become career Nike Tour golfers, clogging up the "developmental tour" by their permanent residence. But there is only so much stage-management professional golf is capable of. There will always be nonstars in this game, working-class heroes who develop slowly, postponing pleasure and leaning on their wives for moral support and creative financing at home. Most Q School repeaters who speak at any length about their travails will bring up names like Loren Roberts and Tom Lehman, players who attained dominance on the PGA Tour following long years in the wilderness.

Thirty-five years after its invention, the PGA Tour Qualifying Tournament is still the primary apparatus for measuring and passing judgment on the borderline pro golfer's abilities. What has never changed is the numbing truth that the Q School gate cannot be locked behind you once you pass through it. In fact, a player can finish as medalist in the annual pressure cooker and still meet all manner of hazards once he puts his token on the game board. Of the 54 players who have been medalist or comedalist at a tour qualifier, only five (Ben Crenshaw, Fuzzy Zoeller, Jerry Pate, Paul Azinger, and Steve Jones) have won major championships. At least one-third of all medalists have never even won *a* tournament. From 1990 through 1997, only 109 Q School graduates out of 251 total (or 30 percent) played well enough the following year to retain their PGA Tour eligibility.

The PGA Tour is a business that supplies a field of stellar or at least competitive players to three dozen tournament cosponsors each year. Thousands of professionals aspire to play these tournaments, and there are spots for only 120 to 160. Add up all the exempt and semi-exempt and slightly exempt "members" of the PGA Tour and you reach a total far in excess of what any particular tournament needs. The system for filling fields works somewhat like a university's course offerings, in which all registered students gain entry into at least some of the courses they wish to take—though seldom all. Players on the PGA Tour quickly learn to become their own clubhouse lawyers as they struggle for entry into early and big-money tournaments.

Eligibility for any weekly tournament starts with the top 125 from the previous year's money list, then works its way down an alternating list of tour-school qualifiers and top-15 finishers on the previous year's Nike Tour money list. Once a Q School grad receives the brass PGA Tour money clip engraved with his name—the physical evidence of membership—he is likely to start writing letters to the sponsors of the first half-dozen tournaments on the schedule. These letters say, in essence, "I am now a tour member, but my eligibility status is too low to get me in just by the numbers—would you consider offering me a sponsor's exemption?" The consensus among tour members, both veteran and rookie, is that "they give you enough chances to keep your card." By the end of the season, a solid 20 to 25 entries have been extended to every card holder. But the early events—especially the smaller-field tournaments at Palm Springs, Phoenix, Hawaii, and Orlando—are well attended by veteran tour members and thus difficult to crack. Which sometimes puts a chance for early momentum—the ideal tension-reliever for any Q School grad—beyond reach.

During the last eight or 10 weeks of the PGA Tour schedule, school avoidance becomes the dominant concern for dozens of members. At Milwaukee and San Antonio and Endicott, New York, the school issue is ever present—it seeps in through the ventilation system. Scott McCarron once detoured off the tour to spend several late-summer days in north Idaho with Randy Henry, who had coached McCarron and also designed a set of golf clubs for him that were built at the Henry-Griffitts custom-club factory in Coeur d'Alene. Henry had coached and club-fit dozens of players on all three major U.S. tours, but he remembers clearly the seriousness of McCarron's visit and the added urgency of meeting the struggling young pro's expectant wife.

"You realize what one little swing change or a slightly different shaft in the driver are all about," said Henry. "It's the difference between a guy supporting his family or falling off the map." McCarron, much to his own and Henry's relief, left the Henry-Griffitts research center and battled to a third-place finish in the Las Vegas Invitational, which vaulted him to the relative safety of 128th place on the money list, up from the dirt-cellar depths of 212th. Over the long week of tour-school competition, even the input of the caddie into the club-selection process takes on a make-or-break quality. "One bad club a week—that's about average for a top caddie who knows his player," estimates caddie Bob Ming. "And one bad club is sometimes all it takes at tour school."

Q School is part and parcel of a system that includes the controversial "all-exempt" PGA Tour. In case you forgot, that's the punching bag so many golf pundits have taken pleasure in battering. What's strange is, all golf writers dote on Q School as the hell-week event that makes grown men cry and makes very good copy in the process. However, these same writers throw no end of tomatoes at the all-exempt system—without which there would be no Q School as we know it.

Once a year, at least, some columnist reprimands the PGA Tour for giving 150 professionals the right to show up for a season's worth of tournaments on the basis of qualifying school success, high finish on the Nike Tour, or top-125 status on the prior year's money list. The editorial writer works himself into a state of righteous indignation while dusting off terms like "charity case," "journeyman," "bottom-feeder," "free pass," and "cushy living." He refers with scorn to courtesy cars, free golf equipment, complimentary meals, and all the other perks of PGA Tour life—with the distinction that while these benefits are more or less acceptable dividends for the stars, they ought to be forbidden fruit for the low-echelon players who come and go each year.

And usually there will be one pro singled out as the poster child for undeserved exemption. That player will have competed in 30-plus events the prior year, with an average finish of about 30th (and seldom more than two or three top-15 finishes), all of it yielding per-event earnings of around $7,500. Only when multiplied by his gaudy number of tournaments entered will that per-week average squeeze the player into the top 125 for the year, allowing him to pluck from the low branches for yet another season. In a strongly worded 1998 *Golf World* column about exemptions and journeymen, the player singled out for scolding was Scott Gump, who was derided for making "an extremely nice living" as a "plodder" who turns in one "season of mediocrity" after another.

And as the 1998 season drew to a close, Gump was up to his old tricks, making cuts and retaining his tour eligibility. Only this time around his per-event dollars were about double the previous year's. And his rank on the money list was 73rd—a far cry from 125th. In one of the tour's nine statistical performance categories, Driving Accuracy, Gump had finished tied for eighth. Apparently, at age 33, after six full seasons on tour, Scott Gump was noticeably improving—a pro named Ben Hogan followed a similar cycle, if memory serves. When the 1999 season rolled around, Gump broke form and went on a roll of his own. After 11 tournaments, his winnings had totaled $724,279 and his rank on the money list was a lofty 16th. "Gump needs to understand his own limits" is how the photo that accompanied the anti-Gump editorial had been captioned. Instead of shredding that issue of *Golf World*, Gump must have clipped out the article and tucked it into his golf bag for inspiration.

The recurrence of these editorials proves that a pundit can never go wrong by attacking privilege. And since American athletes in general are coddled and insulated, fans of any sport will tend to nod their heads when a writer suggests ways of making things tougher on them. Watching sports of any kind, we are never far removed from the Romans who filled the Colosseum whenever the Christians and the lions squared off. Ballplayers used to ride trains, wear wool uniforms, and deliver coal in the winter. Prizefights used to drone on all day in the hot sun, not a skimpy 15 rounds. And do football players really need oxygen tanks and those machines that blow cool mist on the sidelines?

Defending athletes against the charge that they are indulged and pampered is a lost cause before you begin. By all means, the PGA Tour's second-tier and third-tier players could be stripped of their season-long exemption and forced to jump through weekly hoops for the chance to play. Fields could be made up of 60 or 70 players instead of the standard 156. Purse distributions could be made more top-heavy, squeezing out guys who have a knack for making the cut but who seldom move up during the weekend. When and if they turn the competitive screws that tightly, it will certainly send some of the marginal tour pros down the road. And should that happen, the tribal connections that loosely link every member of the Golf Nation will suffer a bit more. The pro tour is no different from any other traveling entertainment—it's always had its bit players and character actors as well as its leading men.

Sammy Rachels got his tour card in 1975, emerging from the swamps and stubblefields of DeFuniak Springs, a farm town in the Florida Panhandle. Rachels hated tour life, and he knew plenty of other players who didn't like it much more than he did. "Fear of real work was and is a huge motivator for some people," says Rachels. "But that motivation to reach the top, get rich and famous, that's overrated," he says. "People assume it's universal, but there's less of it going around than you think."

There are different breeds of cat in any Q School field. In the 1990s, many submit their applications with the idea of making it onto the Nike Tour. When they survive second stage, they can be nearly sure that a Nike card is sewn up, in which case they can look forward to starting their apprenticeship. Then there are players who intend to either get their PGA Tour card or head back to the European or Australasian tours, where they may have separate exemptions. There are players in the Q School final stage who have finished in the 126–150 zone of the PGA Tour money list and are using tour school as a way to improve their status from conditionally eligible to fully eligible. There are players in their 40s who want to get back into the competitive fire as preparation for a run at the Senior PGA Tour. There are young players who have plans for law, business, or medical school if the tour thing doesn't work out. Then there are follow-the-sun diehards, players who are professional tournament golfers for life and will find some place or other to tee it up, come what may.

As for those who are out on tour, many of them see the agony of Q School drifting toward them as early as July. That's when the rush to climb the money list is on in full force. You can't shrug off your low money total and say you're still looking for the groove. You have to turn it on right then and there, or face the fact that you'll be stuck playing in the Fall Classic. One of golf's great stories is of a dead-broke Ben Hogan having the wheels stolen off his car on the eve of the 1938 Oakland Open. That tournament was to be his last if he failed to finish among the top five. Q School often feels like our only relic of that on-the-brink legacy from the early days of professional tournament golf.

Constantly broke, living out of a suitcase, enduring the whispered ridicule of friends and family—the conditions a journeyman pro endures are often characterized as ennobling. But the postwar generation may be correct in wondering whether the same lifestyle that made them tough and realistic is making the next generation permanently juvenile and dependant. One bit of moral high ground tour pros of the '50s and '60s can claim is that their sweat and toil was helping build something that didn't exist when they returned from France and Africa and the South Pacific. By contrast, today's struggling tour pro finds the gravy train already built and running. And even when we hear about Woody Austin's long, dull days as a bank teller and Scott McCarron's three-year stint helping run his family's apparel company, it's not the same level of adversity that comes through when Jack Burke gets to growling about the wartime generation's blue-collar grit.

"We didn't grow up thinking golf was something that would make you a living," remarked Burke. "Tommy Bolt was a carpenter. Ernie Vossler was a plumber. The rest of us worked at clubs or did some other kind of job," mused Burke, implying that the toughness a man needs to succeed on tour is more likely to emerge if his hands are callused from something other than hitting golf balls. Contributing to the widening gap between hardscrabble reality and the young touring pro's footloose existence was the emergence in the late 1950s of individual sponsors and syndicates. Again, this was simply early evidence of the connections within the golfing tribes: Throw some money in a pot and underwrite the golfer among us who happens to be good enough to go on a journey we'd all love to take ourselves. Burke chooses to marvel at the foolishness of the original backers, even when they had their wagons hitched to a Billy Casper or a Gene Littler. "Hands down, it was the worst investment in the world, sponsoring a tour pro," he said. "When you compared the expenses to the purse money, it was obvious that even if your guy won every week he couldn't earn a profit for you."

Down deep, Burke understood that the checks these men wrote were symbols of the kinship golf creates. Sponsorship money had unintended effects, however. It allowed the journeyman population to rise well beyond what it otherwise would have been in the late '50s and '60s. Jack Tuthill, a PGA tournament coordinator who started in 1960 and went on to supervise the first three Q Schools, was part of an ongoing internal PGA debate about purse distribution during that period. He was aware that the new players—and their sponsors back home—favored a payout system that spread tournament purses among an increasingly large number of entrants. They may not have expected to get rich, but they wanted at least a nominal return on investment—enough to just reinforce their relationship with what was an increasingly glamorous golf tour.

The older pros saw things differently. They were accustomed to putting aside money from their club jobs, paying their own travel expenses, and restricting purse dollars to the group that truly contended on any given week. The pre-Palmer-and-Nicklaus players knew the talent pool was small ("Trust me," said Vossler by way of explanation, "when I was on tour, there were 40 pros, at the most, who could play.") and they knew that even 30th-place money was hardly worth arguing about. But as the country prospered and television money began to appear, the graybeard ethic of paying just a few spots was overruled.

"When I first started," said Tuthill, "we paid about 30 spots. But it gradually grew and grew. The cut number got bigger, up to 50, then 60, then 70 and ties. A fellow could play and make cuts and not make any money. That was the bad part about paying so many spots. There were guys who hung on and never got anywhere. The ones with sponsors would stick it out the longest. I remember one kid—from New Jersey, I think—he could hardly break 80. But he had a contract with a sponsor who was writing off the sponsorship money against business income. The kid told me once, 'I'm not stupid, I know I don't belong out here, but my sponsor won't let me quit.' It was a sad situation. Finally he must have worked it out, because we didn't see him anymore."

A generation or two later, the sponsored touring life of Michael Clark II and his wife, Ryndee, appears to be a half-and-half mixture of comfort and tribulation. Clark, who received a bachelor's degree in management from Georgia Tech in 1992 while playing on the same varsity golf team as David Duval, turned pro and assembled a syndicate of five backers who continue to provide him with a very reasonable monthly check. "That money covers expenses, pays the rent, pays medical insurance, and we usually put a little away in savings every month, too," explained Clark, who, unthinkable as this sounds, has missed getting his PGA Tour card by one shot in three straight years: 1996, 1997, and 1998.

"We're not living a dream, by any means, but I'd say I'm doing as well or better financially than 90 percent of my friends from college."

Say this for Paul Harney: He was bluntly honest with a young assistant pro when it might have been easier to offer the mild encouragement that starts a journeyman on the path to potential disappointment. Jim Albus, a Senior PGA Tour pro who took one run at Q School some 30 years ago before settling into club life on Long Island, would often be asked to evaluate a young player who had thoughts about trying the tour. Bill Britton and Bruce Zabriski were the best-known tour aspirants in greater New York during Albus's club-pro years, and both made it to the tour, as Albus and other sages expected. But, in general, being asked the "should I or shouldn't I" question was never something Albus looked forward to.

"You've got to have some tact, and you've got to be honest at the same time," said Albus. "Going off the scores will tell you a lot, but we've all seen can't-miss guys fall flat and we've all seen players who seem no good at all make it. I learned over the years not to tell someone they have no chance.

"There are definitely a lot of Walter Mittys out there," he asserted. "Otherwise you wouldn't see first-stage qualifying scores up around 100. I have older guys who are 10-handicaps telling me they're thinking seriously about trying for the Senior Tour. But that's not the worst thing in the world, really. I don't think it hurts a guy to dream—as long as he can afford it."

The pros of the early 1950s never considered tournament golf a livelihood and they laughed at men who sponsored aspiring tour pros and expected a financial return on the investment. The only solid money in the golf profession were the wages paid to working club professionals, some of whom did well, most of whom squeaked by. But money was on its way into tournament

golf, and a debate would soon be brewing within the golf profession over how to regulate this money and who had a right to
play for it. The pro tour had never been a job, but it had been an
adventure. And it was on its rocky way toward becoming a business.

3

HOW THEY BUILT THE GATE

Eldrick "Tiger" Woods hunches over a shop counter, double-checking scores for the Ladies One-Day Member-Guest. A salesman spreads out his line of Gore-Tex rainsuits while Randolph Grainger IV, club president, addresses the dire need for new range balls. "Let's order them without stripes, eh, Tiger?" suggests Grainger. "I've always said the practice balls at a private club should be plain white."

In the back room, two assistants scramble through file drawers in search of a purchase order for six dozen Junior Club Championship hats Tiger was supposed to have ordered. Recalculating *Mrs.* Grainger's score, the young pro quietly gasps. Her net 107 was actually a net 117—meaning the crystal prizeware Tiger just presented to the club president's wife will have to be taken back. "Something amiss with Mrs. G's card?" Grainger whines, peering over the young pro's shoulder. "Tiger, don't tell me you've bungled another tournament. We vote on renewing your contract next month. What sort of operation are you running here?"

Cut to: Tiger Woods sitting bolt upright in a swirl of designer sheets, panting for breath and realizing it was all a bad dream.

That scenario would be rich in irony if it weren't completely implausible. Superstardom doesn't exempt you from having nightmares, but visions of screwing up as a club pro could scarcely haunt the slumbers of Tiger, Justin Leonard, or any other young titan of the pro tour. These players (neither Woods nor Leonard, by the way, has been to a Q School) belong to a generation of pro golfers who have never labored as club pros and never will. As far as they know, the PGA Tour has been accommodating full-time professional golfers with a richly funded, well-oiled tournament machine since the days of the gutta-percha golf ball. But by no means is that the case.

"Cary Middlecoff and Billy Casper were the first ones to play the tour without having worked at clubs," said Jack Burke, Jr., who was a longtime touring/club pro hybrid when he won the Masters and the PGA Championship in 1956. "Those two came on tour in the '50s with the idea of making a living just by playing, which was a foreign concept to us. We had never seen a person like that."

In the '50s, even the names of Hogan and Snead could be found on shingles hanging outside pro shops. Granted, Sam Snead and Ben Hogan had risen high enough in stature to shed all shop duties, so their "employment" at the Greenbrier resort in White Sulphur Springs, West Virginia, and Century Country Club in Purchase, New York, (respectively) was symbolic. But Hogan and Snead were rare exceptions to the norm, which demanded a dual existence of any PGA pro who wanted to play the tour and still pay his bills. According to Frank Beard, who joined the tour just prior to the Q School era, Burke was once asked by a reporter if he planned to continue his successful winter-tour campaign by playing competitive golf full-time through the spring and summer.

"No, thanks," the Texan reportedly barked. "I got me a $33,000-a-year job up in Erie, Pennsylvania. That beats tournament money hands down."

The origins of what we call Q School belong to a tumultuous era in the mid-1960s when the pro tour was finally beginning to prosper and the Professional Golfers Association, after 50 years of unified leadership, was about to crack apart. As it turns out, Q School, the split-up of the PGA, and a suddenly flourishing pro tour were causes and effects of one another. Today, we view the Q School as a monolithic presence that seemingly dates back to the hickory-shaft era, but annual qualifying is a fairly young institution and, until recently, one that was subject to frequent experimentation. The tale of Q School's origin is part of a larger story, one that ends in bitterness with the original Professional Golfers Association losing control of its pro tour and PGA leaders grudgingly recognizing a new era—one in which tournament-playing pros would be divorced from the lesson-giving, shop-managing life that had been the basis of their profession for so long.

Half a century ago, the PGA's officers and the vast majority of its members were full-time club professionals who taught lessons, sold merchandise, and organized the annual club championship. The tournaments they and most other pros played in were local and relatively low-key. Among the professionals in the top echelon of playing talent, a few were national heroes and the rest lived double lives—club pros by trade and pro golfers when time and money allowed. But by 1965, when the PGA of America announced its inaugural Tournament Training and Qualifying Program, the pro tour it operated had moved beyond its postwar relaunch. The age of Palmer, Nicklaus, and TV was at hand, pushing prize money to the point where a core of top players could actually make a living without holding down a club job. As the tour's visibility increased, it seemed inevitable there would be more Caspers, Middlecoffs, Palmers, and Gene Littlers—young men who would apply for a slimmed-down version of PGA membership known as Approved Tournament Player status. These pros would arrive on the scene with no intention of working in clubs or ever taking the coursework and exams required for full PGA membership.

Over the years, the courses, tests, and other apprenticeship requirements for Class A PGA membership had been stiffened, all in the name of better employment relations and improved working conditions. The organization had been founded in 1916 as a means of combating the serfdom endured by anyone who tried to make his livelihood off the game. Golf history books delight in telling how Walter Hagen, with his surpassing talent and Roaring Twenties flamboyance, had swept in and conferred a new dignity on the golf profession. But Hagen's efforts only started that process. The bluebloods who controlled club golf in America were accustomed to employing Scottish-born professionals who deferred to their social superiors like indentured servants. Hagen was practically in retirement by the time the first American-born pro to be elected PGA president, George Jacobus, took the gavel in 1933. With the country mired in economic depression, attempts to elevate the status of any working-class occupation must have seemed curious, indeed. And yet, along with their competitive urges as players, PGA guild members in that transitional era had a survival instinct that compelled them toward higher standards of professional service. Their business-education programs and other standard-raising efforts were well in force three decades later, with even stricter requirements and longer training periods planned for the future.

That made sense for the club-pro path, where schooling and experience would always be needed to ensure adequate performance (and where the population of certified pros had to be controlled to prevent oversupply). But for golfers who turned professional simply in order to play, pure ball-striking talent merited swift entry into the ranks. As purses rose, the number of unindoctrinated men competing in PGA-sanctioned golf tournaments was rising, too. This loophole in the pro-golf establishment troubled its protectors. They could only hope that once on tour, the so-called Approved Tournament Player who performed well enough to hang around would gradually absorb the values and beliefs of the PGA members around him.

Of course, the loophole was hardly a barn door. ATP applicants could not simply flash a few news clippings and expect an invitation to the next Monday qualifier on the PGA tournament schedule. They had to receive written recommendations from two Class A PGA members in their part of the country, at least one of whom would have recently played two rounds of golf with the applicant. ATP applicants were also required to show written proof of financial wherewithal and an in-force liability insurance policy. Still, if you had talent, it all amounted to a low barrier to entry, compared to the expanding requirements for full Class A PGA membership. From the officers' perspective, that signaled a likely loss of control over players' attitudes and behavior, and image problems for the association.

Meanwhile, organizing and promoting the pro-golf road show was already a "mammoth undertaking," in the words of then–tournament director Joe Black. To the 30 or 40 players who took turns winning all the purse money, it was clear that the club pros in charge of the PGA were too busy running their trade union to give tour business more than a halfhearted effort. The tour's big money winners tended to be free-spirited and adventurous. The PGA's ranking officers tended to be classic "home pro" types, cautious and fond of order. In two previous eras, impresarios Bob

Harlow and Fred Corcoran had been hired to ride herd on the "winter tour," as it was called. Harlow and Corcoran, both news-papermen by trade, would whistle-stop their way from tourna-ment site to tournament site, cobbling deals together on the spot and drumming up publicity however they could. But by the late 1950s, the exploits of Hogan, Snead, Demaret, Tommy Bolt, Ken Venturi, and others had bolstered professional golf's leverage. Perennial beggars, the tour players began to see themselves as choosers. The more marketable they noticed their tour becoming, the more they longed for a latter-day Harlow—a deal-maker out front, properly armed by the PGA with a generous budget and aggressive negotiating tactics.

"We went through terrible arguments with the PGA officers," said Jackson Bradley, whose career bridges two eras and whose loyalty was split between true-blue, traditional PGA and the in-creasingly maverick attitude of a touring pro. Bradley had played a few events in his native southern California before joining the Pacific fleet in World War II. His club affiliations would include Austin Country Club, River Oaks Country Club in Houston, and several others around Chicago. Bradley was a gutty competitor who often found himself elected or simply elbowed into a lead-ership role by his fellow tour pros. "Right after the war, we were happy to be home and playing anywhere," he recalled. But while pro golf was still far from marquee entertainment, Bradley and his fellow troupers perceived that sponsors were starting to come out ahead.

"The people putting on the tournaments were keeping way more than their share," he asserted, "and we were big enough suckers to show up and play, no matter what the deal was.

"I entered 11 tournaments on the '53 winter tour, made a check in eight of them, and still couldn't cover expenses," said Bradley. "The PGA could have helped, but the officers were very weak in standing up for our rights. I can remember guys finishing in the top 10 and still not being able to fill their gas tanks on Sunday night."

It particularly rankled the players that their entry fees were handed over to sponsors or funneled into the tournament operations budget, not used to bolster prize purses. Tour pros of the 1930s and early 1940s had operated with no more supervision than contestants in a flagpole-sitting contest. Chandler Harper, winner of the 1950 PGA Championship, told a story about the 1933 St. Petersburg Open that typified the autonomous status of early touring pros. As related in Al Barkow's oral-history compendium *Gettin' to the Dance Floor*, Harper's play-off with Johnny Revolta in that tournament was for a sum of prize money not even determined until the morning of the match—and eventually redistributed by the players, acting unilaterally. Harper recalls:

"They were putting up a $3,000 purse and the club said they were having a hard time—this was during the Depression—and how about us [the club and the two players] splitting the gate receipts for the play-off three ways? Normally then the players got the play-off gate money. I said fine and so did Revolta, then he said to me, 'Boy, you want to split the prize?' Of course, he was older than me, and was the leading money winner right then on the winter tour. I thought, Hell, I'd like to play this guy. But we did split."[1]

Arrangements like the one Harper and Revolta made with the operators of the 1933 St. Petersburg Open were the essence of pro golf before World War II and would not have been meddled with by PGA officials any more than an after-hours game of five-card stud would have. After the war, however, new attempts were

---

[1]Al Barkow, *Gettin' to the Dance Floor* (New York: Atheneum, 1986), pp. 107–108.

made to both support and regulate the pro tour. In the 1950s and into the 1960s, tournament administrators like Howard Capps, Harvey Raynor, and Joe Black had the respect of the players but often their pity, as well. Running the tour in those days meant driving ahead to upcoming tournament sites looking for local amateurs willing to fill out the fields and local volunteers willing to serve—by and large ineptly—as rules officials. Of course, the issue that would throw off the hottest sparks was television revenue. Until 1962, the PGA's standard contract ceded broadcast rights to the local tournament sponsor. Initially, those rights weren't worth bickering over. But as time passed the PGA's mistaken generosity would further frustrate players and officials alike. When the PGA finally appropriated television rights to its pro tour events, the stage was set for profound and lasting changes.

The rift between PGA officers and the players who competed on tour would eventually lead, in late 1968 and early 1969, to a complete and final split, with the staging of a player-run Q School as the most dramatic and flagrant gesture in the entire feud. Like any other, this feud was two-sided. Tour players of the '50s and early '60s were justified in feeling neglected, but the PGA's leaders had legitimate concerns of their own. Going back to the PGA's founding, elected officers had carefully upgraded the club professional's image from that of an unwashed laborer hunched in an outbuilding, tapping his flask and deciding which members to hustle. The new pro was steady, dependable, and bound by the PGA Code of Ethics. Any backsliding in regard to the professional's image sent up red flags back at PGA headquarters. The pro tour, which bore the PGA logo, was assuming a renegade atmosphere, the officers believed, flouting rules and regulations even as it grew in prominence.

Second in command of the PGA at the time was the dedicated, dignified Max Elbin, whose spit-and-polish operation at Burning

Tree Country Club outside Washington, D.C., had earned him the respect and friendship of members like President Dwight D. Eisenhower. Elbin, along with the PGA's then-president, Warren Cantrell, considered his cherished association to be only as strong as its weakest link. From where Elbin sat, the need for a Q School–type feeder system for the tour was all about maintaining image and high standards. It irritated him, for example, that fields for PGA tournaments would include a non-PGA contestant like Don Cherry.

"This fellow sang in nightclubs for a living," Elbin said of Cherry, as he recalled the rancor of the era. "He was a fine player, and he may have trained briefly for the golf profession when he was younger, but what was a cabaret singer doing playing professional tournaments? The answer is, they had an old-buddy system out there, and if you were pals with the influential players, you got to play."

While the golfing crooner in question was surely an oddity, he was actually envied by many of his fellow travelers on the tour. One of them, Billy Maxwell, had grown up with Cherry in Texas, playing golf by day and rattling around the honky-tonks by night. Often, upon their arrival at a new tour stop, the pair would play a swift practice round, then mosey over to the club where Cherry was booked to perform. Maxwell is quick to point out that Cherry had played on victorious U.S. Walker Cup teams with such gentlemen of the sport as Bill Campbell (later to serve as USGA president), Ken Venturi, and the noted amateur Billy Joe Patton. According to Jackson Bradley, Cherry was not only a skilled vocalist and golfer, he had a head for business, as well. "The fact that Don kept up his career as a nightclub entertainer while he played in tournaments just proves he had enough smarts and talent to make a good living," explained Bradley. "That was more than most of us could say."

More to the point, Cherry was not a crony who had to be back-doored into tournaments through sponsor invitations that came at the request of the tour's top dogs. He had applied through a sectional PGA office for his Approved Tournament Player status, received his letters of recommendation, and been approved by national headquarters. What the PGA's system needed, perhaps, was a stricter set of ATP requirements, or at least stricter enforcement of the ones that existed. And from time to time, the ATP rules were indeed reviewed and sometimes stiffened. For example, after a policy memo of 1956, a large group of week-in-week-out tour players who were PGA members without ATP status, Joe Black included, found themselves compelled to undergo the ATP application process.

Unaffected by this policy change was the PGA's oddest strand of red tape concerning tour players, the so-called six-month rule. Under this rule, an amateur who turned professional and submitted his ATP application had to wait six months before becoming eligible to win prize money in a PGA event. The rule effectively prevented opportunism on the part of top amateurs, who otherwise may have been able to pounce on a weak field, win a top prize, then apply for quick reinstatement of their amateur status. It also gave the tour a space of time in which to vet the applications and sniff out any miscreants. But like most protective guild rules, this one eventually did more harm than good.

The vast majority of new professionals simply waited out the six months before ponying up entry money to compete in a tournament, but Black remembers with admiration a few, including Palmer and Venturi, who refused to wait, actually paying entry fees to compete in pro tournaments with no chance of claiming prize money, even if they were to win. Expeditions to such outposts as Cuba and Panama, where at least one big pro event would be played every year, helped keep Palmer flush with travel money while he served his "apprenticeship," as some players actually called it. But Palmer's disdain for the rule dramatized its anticompetitive nature and helped speed its demise. Billy Maxwell clearly remembers Palmer coming out of the service, turning pro, and going straight into PGA competition, money or no money. "Arnold was such a competitor," said Maxwell, "you couldn't hold him back. And when that six months was finally up, he could taste it. He showed up at Hartford [for the 1956 Insurance City Open] right after he became eligible for prize money, and don't you know he wins the tournament."

To Elbin, the presence on tour of irregulars like Don Cherry was a minor irritation compared to other controversies. In 1963, one of the 43 events on the PGA schedule was a tournament called the Frank Sinatra Classic, staged in September at Palm Springs. It was won by Frank Beard, then in his second year as a pro. According to Elbin, the idea for the tournament came directly out of Sinatra's acquaintance with the established, influential members of the tour, Toney Penna in particular. Sinatra had endured wide swings in popularity since entering show business, along with more than his share of legal scrapes. It was only natural for him to envy the cachet and legitimacy soaked up by contemporaries like Bing Crosby and Bob Hope through their association with pro golf events.

When Sinatra floated his offer, the tour's inner circle, including Gardner Dickinson, Doug Ford, and Dan Sikes, was only too glad to back it. They had grown accustomed to hearing news or even direct statements from organizations and individuals wishing to establish tournaments, only to have these proposals disappear with no information as to why. Such perceived blundering helped send Dickinson into what would be a lifelong harangue against the PGA (and later its offshoot, the PGA Tour). Ford was equally free with his opinions, when it suited him, and Sikes, nicknamed

"Lawyer Dan," had been a member of the bar before joining the tour and was able to summon his advocacy skills in times of conflict. The PGA had won its showdown with sponsors over television rights the year before, but the improvements this new revenue stream would provide were too slow in coming to appease core activists. They were leading an ad hoc self-help program for the tour, and politics be damned.

"Sinatra wanted to have his tournament in Palm Springs, the same place we played the Bob Hope. To make matters worse, he wanted dates just a couple of weeks in front of Hope's tournament," Elbin recalled. "And the players thought that was fine. They encouraged the idea." Officially, the Palm Springs Golf Classic would not take on Hope's name until two years later, but the comedian was already a visible presence in the tournament. Hope, who personally employed as many as five press agents at a time, was able to put his publicity machine to work promoting the Classic throughout the desert community. However you looked at it, Elbin argued, letting Sinatra's new event upstage Hope's was bad business.

According to Ernie Vossler, now a respected course-management executive and a successful 50's-era tour pro, players warmed to the Sinatra proposal in part due to its format, which did not require four days of golf alongside amateurs, as the Hope and Crosby events did. For this and other reasons, Elbin and his fellow officers came to believe the players were prepared to bypass the Palm Springs Golf Classic in favor of the Frank Sinatra.

"Hope was a good friend of the PGA," Elbin noted. "It was still the PGA's tour, and we were not willing to kick a sponsor in the face." What galled Elbin most was the fact that Hope's tournament benefited a local hospital that went by the name of the Eisenhower Medical Center. Somehow, Elbin's gallivanting brethren had forgotten that Dwight Eisenhower—who held his namesake hospital dear to his heart—was not only a war hero and a former president of the United States, he was also a member of the club where Elbin worked. "The Sinatra tournament," said Elbin, "was when I cracked down."

Bill Clarke, who was a PGA officer at the time and would eventually become its president, to this day cannot click past a Sinatra movie on television without thinking back to the controversy. "Plenty of the players on tour were against that original plan for the Sinatra tournament," said Clarke. "The PGA agreed with that group of players. But the other group pushed for it hard. Even some of the businesspeople they had advising them said it was a bad idea."

Beard, Vossler, Bradley, and other pros of the time play down the significance of the Sinatra controversy. The two tournaments were months apart, not weeks or days, they contend, an assertion that also fits with Black's recall. "The Frank Sinatra was played in the off-season," insisted Vossler. "It was never a major threat in the Palm Springs area." Perhaps, but we won't ever know, since the event was put to rest after just one playing. And even if Elbin had overreacted on this issue, the players, Burke included, do not deny that Elbin and his fellow officers had reason for concern. Bradley proved particularly sympathetic.

"Max was the consummate golf pro," Bradley said. "He was pointing out that there was a code of conduct you had to honor to be a member of the PGA, and we weren't abiding by it. There was definite chaos out on the tour. I got into a lot of brouhahas with the guys. You could pick up $5,000 in appearance money to run off and play in Mexico, and guys would skip their own PGA tournament to do it. I was violently against anything that would detract from our contract to play a tournament, but some of the guys had no concerns about that—if they saw some cash to be made."

. . .

PGA Tour competition has become a kingdom in the sky, whose knights, the players, gallop in all directions seeking wealth and fame. It is a lifestyle so desirable that the tour's guardians have been forced to erect a secure gate at the kingdom's entrance, limiting the number of aspirants who might enter at any one time. What is ironic is how little time has passed between the days when tournament fields went begging and today's scenario, in which college programs bulge with pro prospects and an entire developmental tour, sponsored by Nike, operates parallel to the main tour. Jack Burke, Jr., described the talent pool for the tour of the early '50s in simple and practical terms. "We only had 40 or 50 guys driving," commented Burke. He didn't mean driving themselves to perform at a peak level, he meant driving from stop to stop in their automobiles.

Since the 1983 rule change that created the "all-exempt" PGA Tour, we've been taught to associate exemption from Monday qualifying (what few Monday-qualifying spots remain) with marginal players who haunt the Q School and the Nike Tour. The big stars of the PGA Tour are simply fixtures to us—Fred Couples, Phil Mickelson, Justin Leonard, and Davis Love III, for example, have exemptions that run five or more years into the next century. The fact that many other big names enjoy only one-year or two-year exemptions seems irrelevant. We don't imagine them failing to keep their eligibility.

Thus, when the issue of exemption is raised, fans think automatically of the borderline players. They are used to a process in which every year one of these players finishes 125th on the PGA Tour money list, edging the 126th player by a few hundred dollars and sending poor Mr. 126th back to Q School. Fans are generally aware that on the Nike Tour money list, the number 15 player at season's end will get a PGA Tour card while number 16 will tumble back into the qualifying pool. News and commentary about this game of musical chairs for exemption filters through in late season, nearly always in reference to unproven young players or scuffling veterans.

But the original purpose of exemption is diametrically different from our current bottom-rung emphasis. Exempt status began in the days when purses were too small to support the players and the depth of talent was barely enough to guarantee a good show. With only "40 or 50 players driving," to use Burke's words, there could be no 126th place worth fighting for, and no Mr. 126th struggling to hang on. Players like Hogan, Snead, and Byron Nelson were made exempt from qualifying as a signal to sponsors that golf's biggest names would be available throughout the season. Forcing the players who had proven their worth and their marquee value to compete in weekly qualifying would have been folly. From a scheduling standpoint alone, it was not feasible.

As the postwar period wore on, exemption from Monday qualifying was extended beyond the previous year's top 25 money winners to include the top 30—then the top 40, top 50, et cetera. Players would receive exempt status for a given tournament by winning it the previous year or, in a later modification of the rules, by making the cut in the previous week's event. You were granted a full-year tour exemption for winning the U.S. Amateur prior to turning pro, or for winning the U.S. Open, the Masters, or the PGA. Making a Ryder Cup team also exempted a player from having to qualify on Mondays the following season. Billy Maxwell, who earned exemption from the Monday scramble by winning the 1951 U.S. Amateur title, felt the exemption rules did a decent job of building a solid core of worthy players and at the same time cutting down on cronyism. "It seemed like we had ourselves 10 or 12 different ways to qualify," said Maxwell. "They tried anything they could to eliminate the buddy-buddy system and make sure the best players got into each field."

But exemptions rarely seemed to outpace the number of players capable of winning a tournament. And once spring returned to the large northern cities, only a skeleton crew of pros—PGA members, ATP-status qualifiers, or the exempt—was likely to show up for tour events. As a result of the often thin talent pool, Joe Black would have to approach exempt players with hat in hand, imploring them to help beef up the field for a future event. "It was dicey at times," recalled Black, "but I knew which players had the right attitude about helping the tour." Black's request would often require a player to shake off an injury or postpone a vacation or even forgo a paying gig like an outing or golf exhibition. "Our contracts assured the sponsor a 'representative field' of players," said Black. "Of course, nobody ever defined what a 'representative field' was. About the only way to do that would have been through some kind of lawsuit, which we were determined to avoid."

The one exception was the tour's winter swing through California and Arizona, whose cornerstones were the Los Angeles Open, first played in 1926; the Phoenix Open, inaugurated 10 years later; and the Bing Crosby Pro-Am "clambake" tournament, first played in San Diego in 1937. These events had recovered smartly from their wartime shutdowns and were soon receiving heavy demand for playing spots. The most extreme case was Los Angeles. "In my day, if somebody said 'Monday qualifying,' the stop that came to mind was L.A.," explained Maxwell. "The clubs back East were shut down for the winter and all the pros who worked at them would come out to California and give the tour a try. There would be hundreds of pros trying for a couple dozen spots. A few of the new guys who qualified would manage to make the cut, which exempted them for the following week. And if they could play well enough to make the second week's cut, before you knew it they were tour players."

Seen in retrospect, the L.A. Opens of the 1950s assume a unique role in the history of American pro golf. That string of tournaments, with its hordes of would-be entrants, represents a vital burst of nearly democratic conditions throughout the golf profession. For earlier generations, there had scarcely been a tour worth playing. For those who came later, the disparity in talent between themselves and a bona fide tour player would have been proven early and often, through junior golf, college, and the mini-tours. In the '50s, not only was there a playing field finally worth competing on, that field had an open and reasonably level appearance. Ten years before the PGA created its Q School, at a time when tournaments that followed the Masters might hold Monday qualifying for 45 spots and award one each to the 35 local pros who entered, the Los Angeles Open found itself besieged with club professionals from the East and Midwest, all wondering if they had the talent to leave club life behind and compete every week against the game's top performers.

With a staff of just four or five full-timers, Black and his predecessors would stage sprawling Monday qualifiers for the L.A. stop, stretching the prelims over four packed golf courses and calling in volunteers the way Hollywood rounded up extras for the Cinemascope epics it had then begun to produce. The tour was protected by a castle wall, but it was low enough to let aspiring players see across to the other side. This was tour qualifying quick and dramatic, no drudgery required. The process of weeding out the mediocre players from the truly gifted ones was taking place at or near the top level of competition. If you were a PGA member with a sweet swing, an eight-cylinder coupe, and a rack of alpaca sweaters, who could say you weren't ready for the big time?

"Every year at L.A. it was a cast of thousands," said Burke. "But there was something simple about it, too. It gave a club pro or a top amateur the chance to see if they wanted any part of this tour thing. Now you can't do that without turning pro and spending years getting ready." Until 1964, when he quit his PGA tournament directorship to take a corporate golf job in Dallas, Black reserved his deepest dread for the Monday before the L.A. Open.

"I would set up my scoring in an office at the Junior Chamber of Commerce downtown," Black recalled. "The scores would come in all afternoon from the various courses—400 or 500 entries. Some names I had seen before, most I had never heard of." Central scorers would take the scores down by hand and start by knocking out the especially high ones. "There would usually be some 90s and high 80s—the real dreamers," noted Black. To try and reduce the size of the L.A. Open qualifier, the PGA doubled its entry fee, but Black never felt the extra $50 charge dissuaded any hopefuls. Phones would ring off the hook as he and his helpers pounded their manual typewriters, piecing together pairing sheets and starting times for Wednesday's pro-am and Thursday's first round. For every call they received from a scoring tent, the Junior Chamber office received a passel from players hungry to learn their fate.

On a per-worker basis, this was probably as hard as any tournament committee ever labored in preparation for a single event. After hammering wooden stakes to mark the hazards at each qualifying course and using hand-operated lime tanks to put down lines denoting out-of-bounds and ground under repair, the advance team would struggle through the scoring process with whatever energy they had left. The office photocopier was yet to be invented, which meant the tournament team had to lug heavy mimeograph machines with them from stop to stop. Each time they found a way to survive their Los Angeles ordeal, the tournament staff would beseech their bosses back in Florida to overhaul the process. Decent players were coming out of the woodwork, they pointed out, and the need to leave qualifying so wide open was disappearing.

The inaugural Q School of 1965 marked the beginning of a much more closed and controlled system of selecting fields for pro-tour events. As it prepared for the new qualifying process, the PGA headquarters and its sectional offices shut down the existing ATP apparatus, apparently for a full year. One of the pros who participated in both the 1965 and 1966 Q Schools, John Molenda, remembers being discharged from the Army in late 1963 with plans to file an ATP application the following spring. He was put off. "To get themselves ready for the new qualifying school, the PGA froze everything, the whole application process," said Molenda, who would miss his card at the first Q School but make it through successfully the following year.

Along with its start-up of the Q School, the PGA sped up the pace at which it was revoking the ATP cards of unsuccessful tour players who had earned that status under the old system. As the decade came to a close, players who had not gone through the Q School began to feel less and less entitled to their shot at Monday qualifying, which once had been a birthright of the PGA member. L.A.'s Monday mob scenes had in a way foreshadowed the Q Schools that would follow, and now they were on their way to extinction. A more controlled, less haphazard system was going into place. By then, however, Joe Black, weary from the travel and the grind of Monday-qualifying marathons, had left the pro tour for good. Years later, when war drums began to beat between the PGA and the tour, he would be summoned back to his old position, only to stand down when a bitter peace was made.

As much as a player who endures PGA Tour Qualifying might learn about his talent, his heart, and his nerves, the terms

"Q School" or "tour school" are still ludicrous designations for the dog-eat-dog atmosphere of the annual pro qualifier. They are a vestige of the three-year period when the presplit PGA of America still ran the tour and therefore took responsibility for its new screening program. The original "PGA Tournament Training and Qualifying Program," as it was christened in 1965, was not intended as a spawning ground for additional gunslingers in the Doug Ford/Gardner Dickinson mold. Instead it seemed bent on turning out restrained, rules-abiding competitors. Toward that apparent end, the organizers established a calm, nurturing atmosphere for the first Q School, something akin to an Eagle Scout meeting or the tryouts for a debating society.

The home pros who designed tour qualifying would send their recruits to the battlefield for eight grueling rounds, but along the way they consoled and mentored them like brothers in a low-key fraternity. On the Sunday midway through 1965 the school's qualifying 49 participants were invited by the PGA National's owner, John D. MacArthur, for a cocktail reception in the clubhouse. At the tour schools of today, players pay $4,000 to enter (instead of the few hundred originally charged), and they may or may not get free breakfast as part of the package.

Photographs from the original 1965 Q School reveal an obvious fellowship between the applicants and the PGA personnel on hand to guide them. The panelists and speakers tended to be warm, reassuring personalities like Dave Marr, Tommy Jacobs, and Chick Harbert. The paneled walls of the PGA National clubhouse (it was renamed JDM Country Club when a new PGA National was built up the street), the rep ties and blue jackets, the clean-shaven faces, all enfuse the proceedings with a sense of unity and mission. In advance articles that appeared in the PGA's house-organ magazine, *Professional Golfer*, the first Q School was billed as a fraternal, cracker-barrel-style convocation.

While there would be 144 holes of grueling golf to play, descriptions of the inaugural Training and Qualifying Program were light on the golf competition, heavy on the indoctrination aspect. One *Professional Golfer* article praised the new program for its capacity to provide "greater depth of analysis in regard to a player's conduct, temperament, and suitability for rigid Tour competition." The program's agenda was modeled on the training programs—courses like Basic Accounting, Club Repair, Displays and Merchandising—required of golf pros who aspired only to the club life. The new screening process "might be compared," the article preeningly added, "to the now famous PGA Business Schools, which have become so important to the PGA Club Professionals."

Even for a game as steeped in etiquette and protocol as golf, this new, 11-day qualifying regime launched by the image-conscious PGA seemed comically high-minded. The program, being new and not heavily publicized, attracted a grand total of 49 applicants, all of whom were approved for registration at the old PGA National Golf Club resort in late October. The 49 (or possibly 48—written records disagree) who arrived at Palm Beach Gardens, Florida, for the qualifier were not shortchanged on book-learning. Over three half-day sessions during the mornings of October 25, 26, and 27, they sat through no fewer than 15 separate lectures. Topics included: The Player's Obligation to the Game; Player Conduct On and Off the Golf Course; Public and Press Relations; Relationship of Tournament Sponsors and the PGA; and a vaguely named seminar, The Tournament Player in Action.

There were no portraits of Eisenhower or Bob Hope on the classroom walls, and no reports of a player with slouching posture being forced to walk with a stack of books balanced on his head, but the emphasis on polish and poise comes through nonetheless. The PGA officers' reasoning seems clear: The conservative Cold War politics of the 1950s was rapidly disappearing, and the PGA's freewheeling golf tour—not unlike the nation's increasingly radical college campuses—was more and more prone to rebellion, even to talk of secession. But at least the new inductees, fresh from their benign boot-camp experience at Q School, would be familiar with the PGA's side of the story.

In fairness, the PGA also seemed honestly motivated by sympathy for mediocre players who might waste their money and youth chasing rainbows. But even that motivation seems naïvely paternalistic compared with our present-day sense of the tour as an appropriately harsh, unyielding ordeal that abandons its victims like road kill.

"Under the formerly used procedures," the PGA acknowledged, "Approved Tournament Player status was awarded on the basis of recommendations of Sectional officials. These men had no current measure of a player's ability under national professional tournament conditions, nor was there any opportunity to provide the newcomers with any schooling before sending them onto the Tour trail." Equipped with its new qualifying apparatus, the PGA felt that it could "eliminate or at least reduce the 'hit-or-miss' decisions on the chances of a man's success on the Tour." Ken Anderson, a tournament administrator who began his long PGA career in 1965, says the seminar material taught the new tour players about proper conduct and public image, but it also tried to help them conduct their individual affairs profitably. "The classes were aimed at helping them find sponsors," said Anderson, "and learning how to negotiate a reasonable agreement not only with sponsors but with the golf companies, too, on things like club endorsements."

But along with this altruism, the PGA's sense that it could use the Q School to enfuse its tour with a dose of proper manners is obvious. The good-conduct seminars at its inaugural school were not only held in advance of the 144-hole tournament, they were actually set up to weed out applicants whose test scores showed spotty command of the dos-and-don'ts material being presented. According to official reports, the decorum lessons were not lost on the applicants. "A lengthy written test," wrote *Professional Golfer*, "disclosed that none of the well-behaved first class was wanting in understanding and comprehension of the lectures."

What was truly amazing about the written test was its scheduling. Players at the school had to be well behaved, indeed, given that they were scheduled to endure 90 of the 144 tournament holes before even sitting down to take the written examination. As decreed by the original agenda, players would find themselves one solid week and 90 holes of golf into the program before learning whether their written-test scores were high enough to keep them from washing out of the school. For similar reasons, they would also be unaware of how many cards were to be granted, since the final number was projected to be based on how many applicants made it through the written part of the test. Preliminary documents called for the qualifier's first two 18-hole rounds to be played on Thursday, October 28, and Friday the 29th, followed by 36 holes on Saturday the 30th. "Sunday," a *Professional Golfer* article proclaimed, in tones appropriate to a Bible-camp brochure, "will be reserved for rest, relaxation, and study."

The article further notes that "the second 72-hole tournament will begin on November 1 with 18 holes," and that "testing will be conducted on Monday evening, November 1." To any pro who has competed in a modern tour qualifier, it would seem preposterous that the tournament could be half over before the number of cards being granted was disclosed. Players who competed in the 1965 Q School were not totally in the dark, however. Many recall hearing, at or near the outset of the program, an approximate number of tour cards to be issued. The eventual total of 17, by the players' recall, was even a bit higher than the earliest estimates. As for when the actual written test was administered, players also seem to recollect that it took place prior to the fifth round of the on-course competition. So perhaps a less contrived, more straightforward agenda was settled on. Be that as it may, the contrast between our modern, no-nonsense tour schools and the original finishing-school version of the event is striking.

The PGA's new training program was buttressed by its continuation of many existing ATP policies, including the need for would-be tour players to show written proof of "financial wherewithal." This rule, like so many other paternalistic policies, would disappear in the more Darwinian age that followed the PGA–PGA Tour split, although letters of reference from Class A PGA professionals "verifying personal character and golf ability" are still required of first-time Q School applicants.

With their original rules still in place and the qualifying school fully established, the officers may have imagined that wildcat tour players prone to anti-PGA sentiment would become less and less of a worry. A sense of relief does come through in the official PGA statements following completion of the first Qualifying Program and the "graduation" of the class of 1965.

"Through this new program," the association's magazine wrote, "the PGA feels it will be sending onto the Tour players more likely to succeed in tournament golf and better prepared to comport themselves properly and intelligently on the circuit." But as for the potential of the new screening process to prevent future insurrections, that cause was already lost, as the next chapter of this book will describe.

Furthermore, as things turned out, the first Q School was not a harbinger of success for most of its graduates. Of the original

17 qualifiers, only Jim Colbert enjoyed what could be called a long and productive tour career. Colbert, who made it through "on the number," won seven tournaments and just over $1.5 million during his 17-year PGA Tour career. Then, after starting up a company that owned and managed public courses, Colbert went on to a Senior PGA Tour career that far outstripped what he had accomplished on the regular tour. In the 1995 senior season alone, Colbert basically equaled his entire PGA Tour money winnings.

The medalist of the class of 1965 was John Schlee, a Memphis State University grad who had already served two years as an Army paratrooper before heading out on tour in 1964. Through his solid early play, Schlee helped confer some early legitimacy on the new Training and Qualifying Program. The rawboned Arizonan enjoyed a productive 1966 season, finishing with over $21,000 in official money, which was good enough for 47th place on the money list. That performance earned Rookie of the Year honors for Schlee, not to mention a year-long exemption from Monday qualifying. His next four seasons were vaguely disappointing, but 1971 through 1974 would turn out to be prime years. During that period, Schlee averaged about $70,000 in winnings. His one great year was 1973, which began with his only tour win, a victory in the Hawaiian Open. In the 1973 United States Open at Oakmont, Schlee's second-place finish earned him the cold comfort of reflected fame, as his 280 total was bettered only by Johnny Miller—on the strength of Miller's electrifying and record-setting final round of 63.

The 17 card-earners from 1965 also included David Marad, a Massachusetts native who had left the University of Houston after his freshman year to play the tour, with minimal success, in 1964. Marad, then 20 years old, had tuned up for 1965 tour qualifying by "playing the Indian Summer Pro-Am series on Cape Cod and winning everything," he recalled. Like many other men who entered the first several tour schools, Marad was eligible for something else—the military draft. The likely call to service was an ongoing consideration, but Marad pressed ahead. He lined up a sponsor, learned the ins and outs of tour life from veterans like Julius Boros, George Bayer, and Paul Harney, and gave it his best shot for most of a decade, never emerging from the phantom zone of enforced Monday qualifying. The closest Marad came to victory in his tour career was a play-off loss to Grier Jones in a 1972 event called the Robinson's Fall Classic. As for his service obligations, Marad opted to fulfill them by pulling a six-year hitch in a fighter wing of the Air National Guard, juggling tournament golf with weekend drills and summer duty.

The first Q School graduating group included Frank Whibley, as well, a 31 year-old Ontario club pro with five children; second-place finisher John Josephson, who stood six feet four inches tall and was the only player able to keep within hailing distance of Schlee; and Jim Langley, a Cal-Berkeley graduate who had never taken a golf lesson before age 28 and was working for the International Paper Company when the father of a boyhood friend suggested he tune up his game and try for the pro tour. Langley, who ended up tying Colbert for the final spot, holds a special place in Q School history. He is the first player to earn a card at Q School, lose his eligibility through insufficient earnings, and then go back through the qualifying process and successfully earn another card.

"That's true," said Langley, now head golf professional at the hallowed Cypress Point Club in Pebble Beach, California. "I was the first guy to repeat at Q School. I'm not sure that's any great distinction."

Langley and his wife had one child and a second on the way when he accepted the sponsorship offer and took a leave of absence from his sales job. In one six-month period, he found a teacher, Bob Moore; sharpened his mechanics notably; entered several amateur tournaments; and went through the application process for the trip to Palm Beach Gardens in October of 1965. Out on tour in 1966, Langley found that playing against only 49 other players—with a full 17 spots up for grabs—was not exactly the acid test of his golf game, even if the examination did go a full eight rounds. "The experience of playing the PGA Tour was great," he said, "unfortunately my own play wasn't." When the 1966 season wound down, Langley returned home having made just three cuts and with a measly $301 in official winnings.

That $301 didn't help him much. Prior to the establishment of the "all-exempt" tour in 1983, players who gained ATP status via Q School were spared a return trip to the school if they could muster a certain minimum in prize money over the length of the season—even in the mid-1970s that figure was a mere $5,000. But Langley had washed out. He found work selling insurance, teamed up with a new coach, and prepared for his second attempt at tour qualifying. At the 1967 tour school, playing on the same golf course, scores in general were about 10 shots lower than they had been in 1965. Langley's 144-hole was 592, three shots lower than the 595 necessary. He once again had a tour card, and this time he took his wife (who was once again expecting) and his three sons on tour in a specially outfitted van.

"We made a journey of it," said Langley. "I finished second a couple of times, made the top 20 a bunch of times. That's just enough success to let you fool yourself. Sooner or later, reality sets in. You realize you aren't good enough to really succeed out there." Ironically, Langley believes his finest hour on tour came in a Monday qualifier. He found himself at the tour stop in Westchester, just outside New York City, competing on a demanding, tree-lined golf course against "about a hundred other players for about four or five spots." He made it in that day, but

Langley's run would be a short one. In the late '60s, he found himself a retired tour player and full-time lettuce loader back in Salinas. Dave Stockton, a fellow Californian whom Langley had known on tour, encouraged him to become a teaching professional. Langley took Stockton's advice and in 1971 he had the splendid good fortune to parlay his skills and personality—and a résumé burnished by the aura of a few years playing the tour—into one of the most prestigious head-pro positions in all of golf.

Along with those who made it through the first school, there were recognizable names among the also-rans, including Jerry McGee, who would win four PGA Tour events; Harry Toscano, better known for his exploits several decades later on the Senior PGA Tour; and J. C. Snead, who switched from professional baseball to golf and would end up playing on three Ryder Cup teams. The first Q Schoolers ever to soldier through an entire week on their way to stunningly *high* scores were Lloyd Harris of Elko, Nevada, and Don Desio of Port Chester, New York, who missed getting their cards by 41 and 48 strokes, respectively. Desio's low 18-hole round was 77, not a good sign, and his collection of rounds in the mid-80s ballooned him far above the average entrant.

Another near-miss player in the first school was Marty Bohen, a tall, powerful Southern Californian who shared a hotel room with Colbert that first year and missed joining him in the first graduating class by eight strokes—one stroke per round. That was a frustration, but Bohen's most disappointing tour school would be the 1966 edition, when 30 cards were up for grabs and Bohen began the final, 36-hole day in 20th place. "Early in the second nine of that first round I was hitting out of fairway bunker and I broke a 7-iron," recalled Bohen, now a club professional north of New York City. "The head buried in the sand and the ball went about 10 feet. It kind of shook me, and I ended up shooting about a 42 for that nine." Bohen pulled himself together, even birdied the day's final hole, only to miss his card again, this time by one solitary shot. "I was destroyed," he admitted, vaguely aware of his role as the original Q School poster boy for narrow defeat.

Another footnote to the story of 1965 involves a 57-year-old Illinois golf course owner and PGA club pro named Larry Suhre. After four rounds of play in the first-ever tour qualifier, Suhre became the first golfer in the event's 35-year history to withdraw. His cumulative score was only six shots higher than the four-round score of an eventual qualifier, Frank Whibley, but Suhre didn't like his chances at the midpoint one bit. He was a short hitter, and his running tally of 74–82–77–76 foretold a nearly guaranteed elimination.

"We played the first, third, and fourth rounds on the West Course, which was the shorter of the two," Suhre recalled "My 82 was on the East Course, after about 10 inches of rain had fallen the day before. On three par-4s I had to hit driver-driver. It was so wet our tee shots were landing and hopping back a couple of feet. That 82 got me depressed." Wet weather had pushed back the start of play by one day and altered the originally scheduled course rotation. Players were informed that the East Course, due to its superior drainage, would be the site of the concluding four rounds. Suhre took stock of things and went looking for Jack Tuthill, the tournament supervisor. When he found Tuthill, Suhre announced that he was dropping out.

"I probably should have stayed and stuck it out, but I just knew I couldn't come up with the scores I would have needed playing on that East Course," he said. Suhre went back home to southern Illinois and together with his father built a nine-hole golf course on farmland the family had owned. After winning a prestigious amateur tournament in 1968, Suhre went back through tour school for one last shot the following year, missing by seven or eight strokes. He returned to the family course, Oak Brook Golf Club in Edwardsville, which later expanded to 18 holes and has acreage currently designated for further expansion. For years, Suhre studied the tour money lists and calculated his success as a golf businessman against what he might have done as a tournament player. Most of the time, he came out well ahead of the average tour player. Reality is a concept Larry Suhre, unlike some other aspiring pro golfers, can put his arms around. But he got a little more of it than he wanted on day two of the 1965 Q School.

"When I came off that wet, mucky golf course with my 82," he recalled, "and I heard somebody say John Schlee had shot a 69, that was the most depressing moment of my life. I told myself, 'I'm in the wrong league. I don't belong here.' "

Suhre and most of his fellow cut-missers at the first couple of Q Schools gave up their dreams of life on tour and found some other way to make a living in the golf business, most of them as "home pros." And the home pros who governed the tour felt satisfied after 1965 that a sense of order had been established regarding entry into the touring life. They had built a proper gate.

Very soon, however, the keys to that gate would taken out of their hands. Q School would be taken by force and become the bailiwick of the frontier types who played for money instead of working for it. Once that change occurred—and as the money in the purses kept growing—tour qualifying could go on to become the wide-open, stripped-down survival test it was always meant to be.

4

PULLING RABBITS FROM
THE Q SCHOOL HAT

At the PGA Tournament Training and Qualifying Program of 1968, a Seattle native named Mike Reasor shot a rain-soaked 83 in the final round and missed getting his card by eight strokes. Rather than return home, Reasor talked his way into a part-time job at PGA National and spent the entire winter trying to undo his costly mistakes. Come spring, he would have a chance at redemption, thanks to a policy change that, beginning in the spring of 1968, had made Q School a twice-yearly event. What Reasor couldn't know for sure was whether the next PGA qualifier would be an official one—or whether it would take place at all.

Unwittingly, in setting up their original once-a-year Q School, the good shepherds of the PGA had created a 12-month no-man's-land for aspiring tour players.

"If you were an amateur who turned pro in order to compete in the tour school," the PGA's Ken Anderson pointed out, "you either got your card or you ended up in limbo. Your amateur status was gone, but you weren't a PGA member. That meant you were stuck with no place to play and no experience that might help you catch on somewhere as an assistant pro. The PGA hadn't intended it, but trying for an ATP card at the first few schools was costing a lot of guys a whole year of their life."

The tendency of Q School washouts to return for another try established itself early. Of the 31 players who missed getting cards in 1965, 16 returned the following year to take another shot. Of those 16, six were successful in gaining eligibility, including Harry Toscano, the 1966 medalist, and Jerry McGee, who had missed qualifying by a shot in 1965 and, card in hand following the 1966 school, would go on to win four PGA Tour titles in the late '70s. J. C. Snead returned for more Q School pressure in 1966, missing by only five strokes the second time. As for Don Desio, the Port Chester, New York, player who had stumbled to a regrettable 654 in 1965 (average round: 81.8), he was okayed for a retest in 1966, which he underwent with somewhat improved results. Desio brought his average round down to 77.1 and tallied a 144-hole 617—still 14 strokes off the number that was needed.

To PGA officials, the change in spring of 1968 that reduced a failed qualifier's wait from 12 months to six was an important act of compassion. In its dealings with young tour aspirants, the PGA had proved itself once again solicitous. But when it came to the gripes and grievances of disgruntled tour veterans, PGA officers never could find that conciliatory touch. Halving the yearlong limbo status for those who failed at Q School cut no ice with the hard-boiled regulars, whose complaints were many and whose talk of mutiny grew in volume. Toward the end of the 1968 tour season, a breakaway movement took clear shape, and a third Q School was scheduled and announced for that fall. It was to be conducted simultaneously with the fall 1968 PGA qualifier under the name Association of Professional Golfers, or APG. This sly transposition stirred immediate talk of a PGA trademark lawsuit, but before any injunctions could be granted or peace talks commenced, Doral Country Club in Miami was rented out and the APG version of Q School was under way.

"People didn't know whether to play at our school or theirs," said the PGA's Anderson, recalling the 1968 confusion. "Everything was up in the air, you didn't know whether the old order or the new order would win out. When a player chose one school over the other, he was taking a gamble."

Ross Randall, who hailed from Alameda, California, had played varsity golf at San Jose State with Craig Harmon, a New York native whose father was Claude Harmon, winner of the 1948 Masters and head professional (prior to Tom Nieporte) at Winged Foot Golf Club. Randall came East to work under Harmon and hone his game for a try at the tour. When he announced himself ready to do so in 1968, another of Harmon's sons, Butch, was also primed for a run at tour qualifying. Needing advice on which school to attend, the two decided to heed the suggestion of another former Harmon assistant, Dave Marr, 1965 PGA Champion and, despite his teaching stint at the original 1965 qualifier, a political pragmatist.

"Dave told us, 'Go with the players,'" said Randall. "He felt that when all was said and done, the players would be the ones deciding what happens."

Without actually making a final decision, Randall and Harmon packed their golf clubs and flew down to Florida from New York. "When we got there, we weren't sure which direction to go," Randall recalled. "We could have driven south to Miami or north to Palm Beach Gardens." They drove south, played in the APG qualifier, and earned their cards. Randall, who is now the golf coach at the University of Kansas, acknowledged that "with the field diluted, we had an easier time getting through." Randall played eight years on the pro tour, finishing low on the money list and never becoming a fully exempt member. Harmon, who shot 615 that week to get his APG eligibility "on the number" (i.e., with no strokes to spare), has earned fame in the golf profession as a teacher to such high-profile students as Tiger Woods.

Martin Roesink, the brawny, Dutch-born medalist at the breakaway APG school, remembers feeling complete confidence in the APG tournament's validity. "It was an official qualifier, that's how the players felt. As long you finished in the low 20 or whatever it was, you got a tour card," claimed Roesink, who shot 585 for 144 holes and found himself out on the rabbit trail with every other 1968 qualifier, including those who had received cards at the spring and fall PGA-sanctioned schools.

Like the original 1965 PGA Q School, the alternative APG school of 1968 was not well advertised. One of the stars of the Senior PGA Tour in the mid-1990s, Jim Albus, competed unsuccessfully in the fall 1968 Q School run by the PGA, never knowing he had a choice. Albus withdrew with one round to play and too big a gap between his own score and the projected score necessary to earn a PGA card. Albus was well aware of the rift between the pros on tour and the pros running the PGA, but when he showed up to play in the "official" fall 1968 tour school, he was completely unaware that a rival qualifier would soon be staged. "I remember a lot of talk about the tour getting out from under the umbrella of the PGA," said Albus, "but I don't remember having a choice between one qualifying school or another."

Alabama native Steve Lyles ended up with Roesink and 38 others in the breakaway APG school at Doral. He recalls the Doral APG school "as kind of a thrown-together deal," that took place sometime near Thanksgiving, with the resort virtually empty except for this brand-X qualifier. "Whoever ran it did a good enough job as far as the rules and organization," said Lyles, who shot an eight-round score of 620 to miss out by five strokes. "The only problem was the lack of information about what would happen next. They had this school, and nobody knew exactly why. There was a lot of apprehension among the players about whether the cards they were giving out would mean anything."

Ken Ellsworth, a young pro who played out of Harbor City, California, was well connected to a West Coast grapevine known for spreading reliable rumors about the tour players' plan of secession. "We had to weigh the possibilities between those two qualifiying schools," said Ellsworth, familiar to some golf fans from his guest spots on Golf Channel instruction segments. "I was good friends with Jerry Heard [who was a fellow Californian and would go on to become a five-time PGA Tour winner before being injured in a lightning storm in 1975], and Jerry and I decided to stay with the PGA's school. Looking at it realistically, I knew the PGA would survive—it had been around since 1916 and it wasn't going out of business. Depending how the dust settled, the PGA might still be running the tour. With the APG group, you weren't sure what was going to happen."

Ellsworth mentions Gene Littler, John and Tommy Jacobs, Billy Casper, and several other Southern Californians among the more active pro-split players on tour. "Those guys had a certain influence on players from the area like Lee Davis and Curtis Sifford [cousin of tour veteran Charlie Sifford], which is probably why Lee and Curtis played in the APG school," he surmised. According to Ellsworth, the political significance of the renegade tour school was openly discussed. "We could see that if the APG was able to attract the most promising players to their Q School," he said, "it would have given them more leverage" in their struggle against the PGA.

But the APG's tour school would be able to lay no such claim. The spring and fall qualifiers run by the original PGA in 1968 produced the likes of Hale Irwin, Grier Jones, Jerry Heard, Ed

Sneed, and Mike Hill. Meanwhile, the insurgent AGP's qualifier at Doral had produced a graduating class of 21 players who were destined for near-total obscurity. From Roesink at 585 (plus-9) down to Robert Cox at 615, this wave of players stands absolutely unrecognizable to the attentive fan—with the exception of Harmon, whose reputation is owed to his skills as a teacher. Dramatizing what took place at the 1968 APG tour school is the line score of the 33rd finisher, who goes into the record books as the player with perhaps the most outrageously high Q School score ever:

> Herman C. Matthes, Jr. Wilmington, Del.
> 99–89–94–86–93–91–102–91—748

Averaging over 93 strokes per round, Matthes finished 135 strokes out of contention and 78 strokes behind the next-worst score, a 670 total shot by Clyde Williams of Brunswick, Georgia. That Matthes was allowed to complete play seems strange, but the talent pool in general was nothing too impressive. Of the twenty-one APG players who qualified, over half of them recorded at least one round of 80 or higher.

One other high-scoring APG entrant gives rise to an interesting footnote. The player in question is:

> Salvatore "Joe" DiPietro, Canton, Ohio
> 83–77–86–78–77–82—WD

DiPietro had withdrawn from the 1966 qualifier two years prior, after rounds of 93–82–78–90 plunged him to the absolute bottom of a 99-player field. But his week at Doral in 1968 enabled DiPietro to make connections with that school's medalist, Martin Roesink. Three decades later, Roesink could be found still in

DiPietro's employ as head pro at Tam O'Shanter Golf Course in Canton, where DiPietro owns not only Tam O'Shanter but the Skyland Pines Golf Course and a Papa Bear's Pizza Oven restaurant, as well. Which proves that Q School is a place where careers of many types can get their start.

There was bungling to be found at the PGA's 1968 fall tour school, as well, but most of it came in the wind, rain, and muck of the eighth and final round. Heard's final-round 80 and Ellsworth's 84 were part of the last-day debacle in which 21 of the 30 players who would qualify shot 77 or higher. "Between the fatigue, the pressure, and the awful conditions," said Ellsworth, "I had all I could do just to finish. I was coming off a 69, so I went into the last day knowing I couldn't miss unless I shot some huge number, then I went out and I nearly did it. I was gassing on that last hole. I either bogeyed or double-bogeyed it, for the 84. When I came off the course I really thought I had blown it."

High scores notwithstanding, that obscure Q School at Doral served as physical evidence that the Association of Professional Golfers actually existed (other written records refer to the group as the American Professional Golfers—most likely a hastily contrived alternative that kept the same APG initials while providing a less likely target for trademark infringement suits). From the day the school ended to the night several months later when tour players and the PGA reached a nominal truce, the issue of what the 1969 pro-golf season would be called, who would run it, and who would compete on it remained unsettled. The PGA put out a call to Joe Black and persuaded the former tour director to go on sabbatical from his position at Brookhaven Country Club in Dallas and operate what would apparently be one of two rival golf tours.

"We were working on a schedule, planning to go out on our own," said Bill Clarke, who was president of the PGA in the mid-

'70s and later on a member of the tour's policy board. "There was a date sitting on the calendar when this whole wasteful fight would have gotten started. Week after week, our tournament up against their tournament, that's what was going to happen. And which one would people go to? No one knew. But then," noted Clarke, "it all got put to rest with the eight-to-seven vote."

The so-called eight-to-seven vote took place not in an Appomattox courthouse but in a Scottsdale, Arizona, hotel called the Safari. The vote came at the end of an exhausting 15-hour meeting in which the PGA of America's leaders, Clarke among them, narrowly decided to cut their losses and allow "the three letters," PGA, to continue being associated with the professional golf tour in America. As a result of the vote, which proved a heartbreaker for Max Elbin and other PGA leaders who stood against accommodating tour insurgents, the APG name was put to rest and the U.S. pro tour went forward under the banner of the TPD, for Tournament Players Division. The TPD would be a more-or-less autonomous division of the PGA, under the direction of Joseph C. Dey, a former executive director and eminence grise of the USGA, and a man considered the world's highest authority on the Rules of Golf.

Given the acrimony that caused the split, it's interesting to note how much the PGA of America kept its hand in the tour-qualifying system, even after the TPD attained sovereignty over all tour matters. For one thing, the event is still referred to as a "school," even 31 years later. More importantly, the TPD agreed that PGA Class-A membership was equal in value to an Approved Tournament Player card, in the sense that either one allowed the holder to play in Monday qualifiers.

To career club pros who harbored playing ambitions, that clause was significant. At least one prominent tour player of the '80s and '90s, Doug Tewell, played his way onto the PGA Tour without ever attending Q School. Beginning in 1975, Tewell simply flashed his PGA card at a series of Monday qualifiers and played well enough in various tournaments to inch his way up the money list. By the time the all-exempt system came into place in 1983, Tewell was well within the top 125 and on tour to stay. In addition to having all its Class-A cards honored for rabbit-style qualifying, the PGA also got to reserve several places in PGA Tour events strictly for its members. To this day, there are three club-pro names in the starting field of every full-scale noninvitational on the tour schedule. In exchange for these privileges, the George Baileys of the PGA agreed to conduct the first-stage qualifiers and many of the second-stage qualifiers leading up to Q School finals. In a further example of quid pro quo, the winners of sectional PGA of America tournaments, such as the 41 Assistant Professionals Championships staged across the U.S., get exempted into second stage of the annual PGA Tour qualifier.

When the TPD was formed, long-suffering tour veterans exulted at their independence, but as might be expected they took steps to raise the bar for entry into the holy domain they now controlled. As part of the Safari Hotel agreement, the TPD validated the results of all three qualifiers held in 1968 (two of which were sanctioned by its former oppressor, the PGA), thus finding itself with 66 new players in the Monday-rabbit system. That naturally put a squeeze on things the following year. Due to the numbers crunch, the record increase in applicants between 1968 and 1969 would be met with the smallest window of opportunity for new players—only 27 spots available—since the inaugural Q School of 1965. There were still two schools in 1969, spring and fall, but the first yielded only 15 cards to its 91 finalists and the second school coughed up a mere 12 cards—with 48 finalists on hand to compete for them.

Mike Reasor, who had spent the winter of 1968–69 memorizing

every bump and swale on the PGA National course, was fortunate on two counts. First, that the newly sovereign Tournament Players Division had stuck with the twice-yearly system and kept the Q School at PGA National, the redoubt of their longtime captors. And secondly, Reasor was lucky indeed that he had tackled the challenge of earning a tour card at that spring's 1969 qualifier with such dedication—the ratio he would battle being 91 players for 15 spots. The TPD's addition of regional qualifying had cut Q School's final stage in half, to a mere four rounds. Reasor's total score of 300 (one stroke higher than Johnny Miller's 299) was necessary just to earn him a spot in the six-way play-off for 13th place. According to modern protocol, Reasor's finish in regulation play would have earned him a card, but not so back in 1969. The Seattle native was thrown into a sudden-death play-off, six golfers for three spots. He managed to get one of the spots, and went on to an undistinguished eight-season pro career.

The format of Q School has been a work in progress since the beginning, and particularly since the tour and the PGA split apart in 1968–69. Like new corporate management theories, changes to the system for feeding players into the pro ranks have come and gone periodically. Economic factors dictate many of the tour school's parameters, the major factors being the number of tournaments on the tour schedule and the amount of purse money offered by the two tours, the PGA Tour and (since 1990) the Nike.

To some degree, the number of players trying out each year also influences Q School's format. But interestingly, that number has never exceeded 1,200. Even more noteworthy is the fact that the growth rate of applications stayed virtually flat from 1984 to 1993—even as the PGA Tour's purses more than tripled, rising from $17 million to nearly $55 million. As a further inducement to would-be tour pros of 1984 to 1993, the Hogan/Nike Tour was established during that period, as well. And yet, measured on a percentage basis, the applicant pool took its largest-ever one-year jump not during the cash-happy '80s but back in the fall of 1969, rising to 182 from the prior school's application total of 91. At that point, administrators perceived a clear need for regional pre-qualifiers.

They responded by setting up nine simultaneous 54-hole qualifiers prior to the 1970 final stage, which was played November 1–7 at Tucson Country Club in Arizona. This was the only qualifier the tour offered in 1970, following two straight years in which a pair of schools, one each in the spring and fall, were conducted. The introduction of regional prequalifiers streamlined the challenges of staging the finals and, for that matter, competing in them. Players with dreams of joining the tour found spending five days in their home region far less onerous than spending 12 days in south Florida. Still, for some of the newly declared professionals, these advantages were offset by the retreat from two annual qualifiers back down to one.

The Q School's breakthrough year was undoubtedly 1967, when 30 cards were granted to 111 applicants, including such eventual standouts as Tony Jacklin, Lee Elder, Bobby Cole, Gibby Gilbert, Bob Murphy, Deane Beman, and Orville Moody. Unlike the first two schools, whose medalists enjoyed three- and four-shot cushions over the runners-up, the 1967 edition was won by a single stroke. Among the 30 qualifiers, only one player, John Stevens of Wichita, Kansas, failed to break 80 every single round. Even the last-place finisher in the field, Phoenix-based Richard Taylor, turned in the reasonably respectable score of 625, which was only 78.2 strokes per round on average. The year before, a James P. Ringholz of Ashland, Ohio, had finished 30 strokes aft of the next-highest shooter. Ringholz's eight-round score of 670 began with a 90 and went no lower than one round of 79 and one of 78. As a point of pride, no organization wants to see its national qualifier infiltrated by players who are clearly incompetent, and the 1967 PGA tour school was the first one that could rightfully say it hadn't been.

Putting aside the number of cards handed out, the Q Schools conducted in 1969 by the new and fiercely independent Tournament Players Division followed the original PGA blueprint with nary a tweak. But that was simply a pause for air, soon to be followed by a dozen years of experimentation with the qualifier's formats. From 1970 through 1982, the TPD would switch back and forth between annual and twice-yearly qualifiers. It would add a regional stage and then eliminate regionals, then add them back. It would set up a 108-hole competition at the final stage, then stretch that to 144 holes, then trim it down to 108, then down further still to 72, before expanding it back up to 108.

"When I got involved in 1982," recalled the PGA Tour's former tournament director, David Eger, "we conducted a fairly extensive poll of the players and officials to try and really settle on an acceptable format, in terms of number of rounds. Six was the number that kept coming up. Four wasn't considered enough—somebody's luck could possibly hold out that long. But the good bounces and the hot putting streaks wouldn't get a player through six rounds, not going up against Q School kind of pressure. At the same time, most people considered eight rounds to be overkill. Whatever you had to prove in eight rounds you could just as easily prove in six."

Eger's poll helped bring the hectic innovation period to an end. Bill Clarke, who had sat in on deliberations concerning the various format changes, felt many of them were shortsighted variations based on subjective attitudes.

"There were always certain goals for running the tour school, but they got in the way of each other," noted Clarke. "If you add the regional stage, that makes it easier on the players in terms of travel, and it gives the field staff a final that's easier to manage. But if you try to do that twice a year, it's double the work and double the expense. So now you're back to the problem of leaving guys in limbo—making them wait a whole year to try again." For five years (1977–81) the PGA Tour did in fact stage twice-yearly Q Schools that began with a regional stage. But the final stage during those years was only 72 holes, opening the gap for a lucky player to run the table while his hand was hot. "A lot of the switching back and forth between formats was done with no rhyme or reason," said Clarke. "You'd get a new guy on the policy board, and whatever he and his friends didn't like about the present system would get changed. There was a lot of politics involved."

The tour school's 35-year annals contain innumerable format shifts and scheduling variations, but the two-year experiment conducted in 1973 and 1974 has to rank as the strangest of all. In each of those scavenger-hunt years, an original applicant pool of about 400 golfers was pared down via regional tryouts to 78 finalists. Of those 78, 23 would receive tour cards in 1972 and 19 would get cards in 1973. Both years, the field of 78 players was put through an eight-round, 144-hole marathon made all the more exhausting by a 500-mile change of venue at the halfway point. The first mass migration was from Perdido Bay Country Club in Pensacola, Florida, northeast to the Dunes Golf & Beach Club in Myrtle Beach, South Carolina. The next year, players traipsed from Silverado Country Club in Napa Valley, California, downstate to Canyon Country Club in Palm Springs. Since life on tour required that a player be able to finish a tournament, pack his belongings, drive several states, and start another tournament, the 1973–74 arrangement had a certain inner logic to it

Although administrators apparently weren't explicit about

their intentions at the time, replicating the play-travel-play reality of tour life was indeed the goal of the 1973 and 1974 schools. When the 1998 Senior Tour Championship brought several well-known 1973 Q School graduates back to the Dunes Club—some for the first time in the quarter century that had elapsed—questions naturally arose as to the origins of the double-site experiment. Cliff Mann, the club's director of golf and a part-time golf historian himself, was told by a tour official that switching from Pensacola to Myrtle Beach had indeed been a conscious attempt on the tour's part to replicate the grinding travel requirements of touring life. Among the 1973 tour school graduates who competed in the 1998 Senior Tour Championship were Larry Nelson, Joe Inman, and Gil Morgan. Out of nostalgia, Nelson brought with him a copy of a class photo that had been taken the day the 1973 Q School concluded, which was shown on ESPN's telecast of the tournament. Inman, as it turns out, had lived on club property at the Dunes for much of his PGA Tour career, before trading his tour card for a Ping sales territory in greater Atlanta, which he ran successfully while gearing up his game and waiting to turn 50.

"It's possible the tour wasn't satisfied with how well the guys coming out of school were performing," theorized Mann. "In that case, by adding the travel aspect they might have been able to graduate more players who could make the grade." Rarely, if ever, will an official or administrator forecast or estimate the PGA Tour prospects for either a graduating class of Q School contestants or (since 1990) a batch of card-earning top finishers from the Nike Tour. But it's interesting that Ben Crenshaw, along with the other big names in the 1973 school, put a stamp of approval squarely on the double-site, 144-hole concept with his stellar play. Crenshaw dazzled observers with his course-record round of 67 at the Dunes and his eventual 12-stroke margin over second-place finisher Morgan, then further validated that year's qualifying process by winning the first PGA Tour event he entered, the 1973 San Antonio Texas Open.

In the second and final year of the eight-round, two-site format, players bivouacked from the Northern California site of final qualifying's first 72 holes all the way to Palm Springs, where the last four rounds would be played. The length and intensity of the process may be partly responsible for the fact that over half the players earning cards at this final were Californians. If you have to endure a dislocating half-day drive from one site to the next, you may as well do it within the borders of your home state.

Bobby Heins, a metropolitan New York club pro who played the tour briefly in the mid-'70s, paid his $300 entry fee to take part in the 1973 Q School. Heins, like other competitors in the scavenger-hunt Q Schools of 1973 and 1974, doesn't recall school officials ever directly stating that the travel element was intended to mimic actual conditions of a tour member's existence, nor did the players directly ask. Theirs was not to question why.

"It was an opportunity, that's all we saw it as," said Heins. "Seventy-eight of us made it through the regional stage ('regional tryouts' is the quaint term used in tour records) and all 78 of us made it through the eight rounds," which included 400-plus miles of driving from Pensacola to Myrtle Beach. When the fourth round was over at Perdido Bay, Heins and his caddie, Charlie Levine, loaded their car and drove through the night to South Carolina. With the likes of Crenshaw, Morgan, Nelson, and Gary McCord strung out along the same route with them, Heins and Levine reached their motel somewhere past three o'clock in the morning.

"We drove all night, and it wasn't all interstates back then, either," said Heins. "I guess they wanted us to have a taste of what playing the tour was really like—including the travel. If that's the case they definitely succeeded." Compared to the highly seasoned young professionals of the 1990s, Heins was fresh off the turnip truck when he entered that 1973 tour school. His score for the four rounds at Perdido Bay in Pensacola was 70–70–76–70, which Heins confesses was the first time in his life he ever broke par for 72 holes.

"I had only played in three or four 72-hole tournaments up to then," Heins acknowledged. "I was at the University of Florida and the golf coach had just told me to clear my eligibility because he had a spot for me on the team. I told him no, thanks, I was turning pro and trying for the tour. But I only entered for the experience—I had no thought of actually making it." An OPEC oil crisis and rampant inflation were yet to hit the U.S. economy, which made the players' financial investment in this movable feast of a Q School entirely reasonable. "We paid $10 a night for the hotel rooms, $25 a day to the caddie. The whole two weeks cost me less than $1,000."

According to club history, the Dunes had no local caddies on hand to accommodate players who didn't bring their own. They addressed the problem by enlisting members of several local golf clubs to drive carts for the players, "serving as the 'caddies' the PGA required!" the Dunes's official club history enthusiastically relates. Heins is somehow able to recall the results of the written examination on lecture material, which in those days was still being administered. "I remember Wally Armstrong got the highest test score," said Heins, "and Ben Crenshaw, who was medalist, had the lowest test score." Bobby Wadkins, who spent two decades on the PGA Tour and won over $2.5 million in purse money, has lately been forced to go the Q School and Nike Tour route to regain eligibility. His powers of endurance were proven early when Wadkins played and drove his way through both of the road-warrior tour schools, finishing nine strokes outside the qualifying mark in 1973 and coming back in 1974 to earn his tour card with an eight-round total of 580 strokes.

The current arrangement of the Q School finals is as follows: a tournament of 108 holes (18-hole rounds on six consecutive days), with no cut, awarding PGA Tour eligibility to the low 35 scorers (and ties) and awarding Nike Tour eligibility to the next 70 finishers and ties. The low 35 who earn PGA Tour cards also split a prize purse of $1.2 million, with the winner receiving about $50,000 and even the highest-scoring survivors of the 35 card-earners getting checks for $25,000 or so. Of the 169 players who made it to La Quinta, California, for the 1998 tour school finals, 138 were survivors of second-stage qualifying, which takes place in October at six different sites around the U.S., and 31 players were exempted straight into the final stage.

There is a settled feeling to the present system, suggesting that six 18-hole rounds, following two regional stages, has become the gold standard by which would-be pro golfers can be judged. Corroborating the PGA Tour's faith in this format is its adoption by the European PGA Tour and its sheer longevity as the U.S. tour's entry exam. The once-a-year, 108-hole system dates back to 1982, the year Mac O'Grady finally got his card after 17 tries and Donnie Hammond, with a 14-stroke margin over David Peoples, broke Ben Crenshaw's eight-year-old record for highest margin of victory by a tour school medalist.

When Q School was first established in 1965, it became the only means for non-PGA members to become Approved Tournament Players. Lest we forget, however, an Approved Tournament Player was also a "rabbit." When he got his ATP card and joined the tour, he could only compete in the PGA's tournaments by competing successfully in Monday qualifiers against not only his fellow ATPs but against full members of the PGA (those who had not gained exemptions from Monday qualifying by winning major championships or finishing high on the previous year's money list) as well as sponsor invitees.

The term "rabbit" appears in golf writing as far back as 1931, according to Peter Davies's *Historical Dictionary of Golfing Terms*. It originally meant a middle-handicap amateur golfer. The sense of "rabbit" as a "touring professional who has won no exemptions and must compete in qualifying rounds for chances to play in tournaments" is cited as far back as Tony Lema's 1964 book, *Golfer's Gold*. So Monday qualifying and even the notion of a tour rabbit certainly predate the Q School era. That said, however, the 17 years from 1966 though 1982 embody the true essence of what it meant to be a rabbit on the U.S. pro tour. To hop from one tournament city to the next—leaving behind the players who would compete for the prize money so you could prep for the next Monday qualifier—to "nibble a little here, a little there," in the words of 1974 Q School medalist Phil Hancock, became especially onerous once the rabbit in question had supposedly distinguished himself in the tour's official qualifying tournament.

Ideally, a newcomer would emerge from tour school as a rabbit, Monday-qualify his way into the first few events, start making cuts in the tournaments he qualified for, and cobble together enough high finishes to become one of the year's 60 top money winners. Climbing into the top 60 would end the player's rabbit days, at least for one year. And making cuts was crucial to this process, because every cut a nonexempt player made would free him from Monday qualifying for the following week's tournament. The only catch: You had to complete play in that tournament in order to exercise the following week's exemption—withdrawing or getting disqualified on some technicality negated the privilege. Vic Loustalot, a 1970 tour school grad whose nephew, Tim, also became a tour player, made the cut in the tour's 1971 season finale event, held in the Bahamas. That made him exempt into the 1972 Los Angeles Open, which offered the chance for a bright start to his sophomore season. But some kind of bug or virus took hold of Loustalot, staggering him.

"By coincidence, they were holding a special tour policy meeting that night," said Loustalot, who shuffled slowly to the meeting room to ask if he had to play the last two rounds or lose his L.A. Open spot. "I couldn't get a solid answer, so I dragged myself out of the hotel room the next morning and made my tee time," recalled Loustalot. "I had a 102-degree fever, but people thought I was the coolest customer in the whole field. Every time we came to a hole and had to wait to hit, I fell asleep right there on the tee."

Naturally, it was unusual for a tour-school graduate from the Monday-qualifying era to vault to exempt status in one season. Among the notable card-earners from the early years of tour school, Bob Murphy got a card in the 1967 tour school and finished 10th on the money list in 1968; Hale Irwin earned his card in 1968 and took three years to finish in the top 60; Johnny Miller was in the spring 1969 graduating class and did little in 1969 but finished 40th in 1970; Tom Watson came through the fall 1971 school and cracked the top 60 in 1973; Lanny Wadkins was in the same Q School as Watson and broke through immediately, finishing tenth on the tour money list in 1972; Fuzzy Zoeller got his card in fall of 1974 and broke through to the top 60 in 1976, his second full season.

Phil Hancock, though he never attained tour stardom, was another Q School qualifier who quickly got past the uncertainty and frustration of rabbit status. Hancock, who had been a standout college player at the University of Florida, was medalist at the spring 1977 qualifier in Pinehurst. No small achievement, since that tour school holds the record—most likely into perpetuity—for having the largest field of finalists—408. Hancock's immediate goal as a tour player was to earn the $5,000 that preserved a rabbit his nonexempt tour membership, thus preventing another trip through Q School. He laid that concern to rest in his first tournament, then marked all the Mondays on his calendar with times and places, hoping he wouldn't need to show up for too many of them. For many Q School graduates in the classes of 1965–82, Monday qualifying was the tragic flaw in an otherwise well-designed system.

"You always heard about guys who were 'professional Monday qualifiers,' " Hancock recalled. "But there really were players like that. All season long, they would tee it up on Monday and earn a spot. It could be 20 guys for 10 spots or 100 guys for five spots, and these professional rabbits would get in. And once they got in, they never did anything." Hancock, who didn't consider himself particularly adept at Monday qualifying, would concentrate furiously on making cuts, thus avoiding the Monday rabbit gathering at the following week's tournament.

Jim Barker, a member of the fall 1969 class, explained the complications of the old rabbit system by likening it to "playing three different tournaments every week." As Barker saw it, his week would start with a Monday qualifier that offered spots in, for example, the Motor City Open. If he were successful on Monday, Barker would then enter a 36-hole competition on Thursday and Friday. Those 36 holes were, in fact, the official first and second rounds of the Motor City Open. If Barker played them well, it would set him up for a chance at some of the Motor City Open prize purses on Sunday. But those 36 holes were also a semiofficial qualifier for the Western Open, due to take place the following week. Barker's third tournament of the week—should he still be around—was the 36-hole conclusion to the Motor City Open, in which the 70 players who had made the cut would battle it out for one of the 45 to 60 checks to be distributed. "I was a great

Monday qualifier, but not much of a cut-maker. Wasn't much of a check-maker, either," Barker confessed.

That gap between the number of players who made the cut and the number who got paid was the great Sunday crack in the system, a crack Ken Ellsworth fell through many times during his rabbit career. "I once made seven consecutive cuts and not one single check," said Ellsworth, looking back. "Qualifying every week was really a bear," he acknowledged. "I was just a very average player by tour standards, but for some reason I was good at qualifying. So I'd have the full week's expenses—hotel, meals, caddie—and nothing to show for it." Ross Randall was another Q School graduate who played as a rabbit his whole career. But he would relieve himself of the Monday-qualifying onus at times by taking advantage of a rule in place during the '70s that rewarded any rabbit who had finished in the top 25 at a given tournament. "If you made the top 25," said Randall, "you didn't have to Monday-qualify for that tournament the following year. If you had enough of those top-25 exemptions spread out through the year, you almost felt like you were fully exempt."

One year during the hop-hop '70s, Ken Ellsworth found himself in Palm Springs at a big Monday qualifier for the Bob Hope— with nothing more to play for than first-alternate status. Despite the lack of even one guaranteed berth, the rabbits of the early '70s would show up for a Monday qualifier at popular tournaments like the Hope because by then, the PGA Tour had established a minitour of so-called satellite tournaments. From 1970 through 1974, between one and two dozen of these consolation events were made available to the overflow crowd of Monday qualifiers. That satellite series was a precursor to the more ambitious Tournament Players Series (TPS) that ran for three years in the mid-1980s, which in turn made way for the Ben Hogan Tour's appearance in 1990 and the game's most successful "developmental tour," the Nike Tour of today.

Many a column writer has lampooned the all-exempt PGA Tour, calling it fairway socialism and a gravy train for marginal players. What a writer covering the tour would probably miss most about the rabbit days are the unpredictability and colorful tales they naturally spawned. The modern tour pro draws up a logical playing schedule, fitting in time for rest, family activities, and photo sessions with his sponsors' ad agencies. Even pros fresh from qualifying school have their seasons mostly mapped out in advance, once they get past the uncertainties of the first two months. But rabbits like Barker, Ellsworth, and Vic Loustalot pinballed around the country with no compass and no set course.

Loustalot (the name's pronunciation, by the way, is just as ironically pessimistic as it appears) got his card at the 1970 Q School in Tucson, along with Rik Massengale, Jim Dent, and Hubert Green. He and Green, who would win two majors and 17 other PGA Tour events, became good friends. "If I missed a Monday qualifier or a Friday cut and I was in the Southeast," said the lifelong Californian, "I had a key to Hubert's place in Birmingham, so at least I knew I could crash there for a few days." Loustalot's second pro event was the 1971 Coral Springs Open, where he tied Lee Trevino for third. Looking back, he confessed to thinking at the time, "Gee, this is easy." But neither the golf nor the travel was easy very often for rookie professionals. Their first thought after missing a cut or a qualifier was to hop to the next site and get ready to play. But the clubs and courses getting ready for upcoming events, according to Loustalot, "didn't want to see a rabbit come in early." If these clubs weren't vigilant, he pointed out, they would find themselves hosting up to 100 would-be Monday qualifiers at a time. "It's amazing to me that the rabbit system lasted as long as it did, it was so chaotic," observed Loustalot. "But by far the toughest thing about it was finding a place to practice."

To prevent psychic wear and tear, he opted for a unique and costly travel regimen. "I played the satellite tournament at the Chrysler my first year and came in first, which meant I won a new car every year for three years," said Loustalot. "I decided to put my caddie in the new Chrysler and traveled by plane myself. Since I never knew in advance where or when I'd be playing, I always had three or four airline reservations booked at a time." Meeting up with his caddie at the airport or the next tournament site seemed to be a constant challenge for Loustalot. One of their rendezvous, at the Greater Greensboro Open, was hastily arranged and basically doomed from the start.

"I was playing with Jerry McGee and Bruce Crampton in a practice round for the National Airlines Open, in Miami," recalled Loustalot. "They were big names, so we had a good-sized gallery. A cart pulls up, two guys get off it, walk up to my caddie, arrest him, handcuff him, and ride him back to the clubhouse. When I get back there, I find out these guys are bounty hunters. Turns out my caddie, whose name is Jay, has jumped bail and crossed all these state lines, and these guys want $500 to turn him loose. I scrape up the money and they unlock the cuffs, but they tell us they'll do the exact same thing the next day if they come back and spot him."

Without delay, Jay set Loustalot up with a replacement caddie and took off in the Chrysler for North Carolina. His substitute was a tour caddie named Larry who, according to Loustalot, "was a little eccentric." The first round, they brought home a sparkling 68, good enough to turn the cut into virtually a nonissue. Then Loustalot opened the second round bogey-bogey, at which point Larry announced, to whoever was in earshot, that he had not made a cut for eight weeks. "Then he says, 'and it doesn't look like you're gonna make it this week,' " recalled Loustalot. "The rest of the way around he keeps mumbling the same thing, about not making the cut for eight weeks. Of course, I miss the cut by one. And because of how depressing it all was, I said the hell with Jay up in Greensboro hiding from his bounty hunters, and I got on the next plane for California."

Along with the odd requirement that a cut-maker play out the tournament regardless of his physical condition or lose his exemption for the following week, rabbit pros generally felt pressure to play through extended periods of injury. Terry Mauney, the medalist at the spring 1979 school, battled with tendinitis even while he was shooting a 63 at Riviera Country Club that broke Ben Hogan's long-standing record.

"I was playing hurt that week, and a lot of other weeks, too," said Mauney, who left the tour after 1982 to become a sportscaster in Charlotte, North Carolina. "Eventually I got to where I couldn't raise my arm above the shoulder. But when you're nonexempt, you feel like you can't take any time off." Any physical ailments, Mauney added, come on top of the psychic stress that extended rabbit status inevitably induced. "I struggled like a lot of players do," recalled Mauney, now a teaching professional with thoughts of playing the Senior PGA Tour when he becomes eligible. "You shoot even par, you don't make the cut, it becomes a mind trip. You feel you're not worthy to be out there."

Regrets and doubts are not part of Mauney's natural disposition, however, and in assessing his achievement as a player he took solace in finding out that after being gone from the tour for many years, he was not forgotten. Mauney qualified for a recent Nike Tour event and was warming up for his opening round, displaying the unhurried swing motion that had years ago earned him the sporty nickname of Mr. Tempo.

"I was hitting balls, minding my own business, and somebody pointed me out on the range," said Mauney, with a twinge of pride. "I heard him say, 'Hey, I know that guy. That's Mr. Tempo!' "

There was an innocence and a humble optimism among the journeymen of the original rabbit era. Innocent types were being weeded out however, as the stakes on tour continued to rise. In the decade leading up to the Q School era, purse increases averaged approximately $100,000 a year. But after 1962, when the television contracts were centralized, the next decade's average yearly bump in purse money exceeded $530,000. In 1968 alone, the purse total increased by $1.1 million, breaking the $5 million mark. Over the next 10 years it would double, to $10 million. For talented players, the decision to pursue a tour career was quickly becoming a no-brainer. American culture was continuing to glorify sports as a field of endeavor, meaning that in golf, any red-blooded male with a dreamer's chance of reaching the tour was compelled to try it—repeatedly. By the mid-70s, Q School had left its innocent beginnings behind to become the seething competitive cauldron it still is today.

5

CHAOS ON BENTGRASS

The Q School contestant and his caddie had played high school golf together back in San Jose, and for nearly eight rounds of the 1974 PGA Tour qualifier they were teammates once again. Then, on what would be the final par-5 hole of their entire 144-hole ordeal, Roger Maltbie pushed a drive into the right rough and Frank Pieper, after studying the situation, held out an 8-iron. His friend refused it.

Maltbie found Pieper to be a persuasive fellow most of the time, due to Frank's levelheadedness on the golf course and to his large, imposing physique. Frank's father, Oliver Pieper, Jr., was a two-time California amateur champion whom Maltbie (along with Forrest Fezler, the other tour-bound member of that same high school golf team) respected and admired.

This 1974 final stage of Q School consisted of 144 holes divided between Silverado Country Club in California's Napa Valley and Canyon Country Club 350 miles south in Palm Springs. With only a few holes to play and 23-year-old Maltbie at least two strokes inside the make-or-break number, the little punch shot his caddie was proposing stood as the only prudent option. Pieper pointed out a spot down the left edge of the fairway about 110 yards from the green—they would lay up to that general area then fire a wedge at the flagstick.

Maltbie wasn't listening. A free-spirited player who would go on to win five tour events and more than $2 million over his long career, Maltbie had completed his playing days at San Jose State and was making a second attempt at tour qualifying. A year earlier he had failed to make it through the preliminary stage, but this time around he appeared ready to join Fuzzy Zoeller, Bill Rogers, and Bobby Wadkins—along with 16 others—in the fortunate company of tour-school survivors. Canyon Country Club was hosting its one and only Q School final ever (splitting the honors with Silverado) and the course had yielded three 67s the day before, to Rex Caldwell, Jack Spradlin, and John Abendorth. There wasn't a great deal of trouble lurking throughout the course, but there was indeed a lone, mature palm tree standing very close to Maltbie's ball, spoiling his drive on this otherwise reachable par 5.

"The palm tree was a couple of feet in front of my ball, and about a foot or so to the left of my direct line to the green," explained Maltbie, taking a break from his NBC-TV reporting work during the 1998 tour-school finals to reminisce. "I was stymied by it—the only play was to bump it forward and try to hit the next shot close. But then I saw another option, which, if I could pull it off, would give me a chance at eagle."

What Maltbie felt inspired to do was align himself toward the flagstick as if the palm tree did not exist. Taking his normal setup and making his normal swing with a 3-wood, he would hit a shot of about 230 yards that would carry over a greenside pond and settle somewhere on the green. This would set up an eagle putt and keep his positive momentum going. There were no other shots between this point and the clubhouse requiring the use of a 3-wood—which was a relevant consideration, given the extremely high odds that Maltbie would snap his club in half during the follow-through, slingshotting the clubhead who-knows-where.

"Look, I don't care if it breaks," Maltbie said to Pieper as he reached toward the golf bag, "because I'll be up there lookin' at two putts for birdie. We're not gonna need the 3-wood after this, so hand it over and let's go."

"Hit the 8," Pieper instructed. He held out Maltbie's 8-iron and took a step backward, gripping the bag tightly. "This is no time to try some crazy shot."

"I'm hitting 3-*wood*," bellowed Maltbie.

"Roger, c'mon. Don't be stupid."

"I'm hitting 3-wood, Frank. Onto that green!"

"No you're not!"

"Goddamnit, yes I am!"

"Well, I'm not going to let you," Pieper grunted. He still held the 8-iron, only now in a vaguely threatening fashion.

"The hell you aren't—gimme that club!"

Pieper's eyes narrowed. He was a lot bigger than Maltbie, and after 10 days of the Q School grind he was foot-weary and out of patience. He let the bag flop to the turf, and the expression on his face indicated that he, like his friend, had a small act of violence in mind. The prospect of a broken 3-wood had not disturbed Maltbie, but the possibility of a broken nose now troubled him. He came to his senses and accepted the caddie's choice of club.

"That's the kind of thing that can happen at tour school," Maltbie surmised, digging out a cigarette and shaking his head. "You get goofy, like guys on a desert island." Part of the pressure, he said, was the tour's practice in those days of commencing the final stage without setting down the specific requirements. "When I played in it," said Maltbie of final-stage qualifying, "they didn't even tell us at the start how many cards were available—they just sent us out there. You played your best until they gave you the word with a couple of rounds to go." He blew a stream of smoke toward the treetops as he shook his head. "Jesus," he said. "Can you imagine another tournament where a guy would try a shot *knowing* the club was gonna break in his hands?"

Maltbie's standoff with his caddie ended with no punches thrown and the original 8-iron punch shot played. What restored Maltbie's sanity—other than realizing the sheer absurdity of brawling during a golf tournament—was his recognition that Pieper's 8-iron-and-wedge strategy offered a far less risky chance at birdie. He did as he was told and went on to earn his tour card with a three-stroke cushion.

It was certainly ironic that as Maltbie was telling this story, a rumor began circulating around PGA West that Carlos Franco, a 33-year-old Paraguayan coming off rounds of 69 and 66 the previous two days, had broken his putter and was trying to make it through this final qualifying round stroking every putt with his driver. Franco, born to poverty and bilked out of most his earnings during a 10-year contract with a conniving sponsor, was emerging as the 1998 tour school's most compelling character. The curly-haired son of a greenkeeper at one of Paraguay's three golf courses, he grew up playing golf barefoot against his brothers—just as Sam Snead had done a half century earlier in the Virginia hollows. While still unknown in the United States, Franco has been plundering the Japanese tour in recent years, earning huge six-figure sums that assure the comfort of not only himself, his wife, and their two children, but about 30 other relatives back home in Asunción.

The background story of Franco's toughness under adversity

and his unmistakable poise raised a question as to why he could
be seen on the Golf Channel's monitors making do without the
putter, which he must certainly have broken against some boulder or else chucked into a water hazard. When Franco reached
the 18th green, however, he was seen wielding his putter again.
His trademark air of calm was replaced with a slightly flustered
look, but the 73 he was polishing off was hardly a blow-up score.
Best of all, it ran his six-day total to 10 under par, or 422, exactly
the score needed to earn a PGA Tour card. As he later explained,
a three-putt par on the ninth hole of the PGA West Weiskopf
course and a four-putt bogey on the 10th had spooked Franco
into the drastic switch from putter to metal driver on the greens.
"No good feeling," he told *Golfweek* reporter Jeff Rude after the
round, when Rude asked him why he stowed his flatstick. "I need
change."

The tournament golfer's physical and psychological metabolism
is calibrated to handle 72 holes, four competitive days, five nights
in the hotel, a cut after the second round, and payouts from the
purse after the fourth. Most importantly, it is geared to a one-
week interval between whatever mistakes and misfortunes are
endured at, say, Greensboro and the clean slate that greets all
participants when they arrive in Houston. The PGA Tour qualifier, with its two additional days of competition and its 50-week
wait for the next opportunity, plays havoc with a player's sense
of time and his ability to regulate mind and body. For an experienced tour player, the school's stripped-down atmosphere is
hard to get used to. The anonymity of so many contestants in the
field gives the event an eerie, unsettling quality—akin to the
"who *are* those guys" feeling Butch and Sundance endured when
they couldn't shake their posse.

Returning to the qualifier can be like descending into a

netherworld where *The Canterbury Tales* meets *Tin Cup*. Imagine what it must have been like for a battle-tested tour veteran from the mid-1970s who happened to hit a dry spell and lose his card at the end of the 1977 season. This player would have found himself competing in the spring 1978 tour school at Albuquerque, New Mexico. And if by chance he failed to finish in the top 28, he would see as he scanned the final results that players the likes of Mike Zack, Adam Adams, Rocky Rockett, and Wren Lum had beaten him out. At that point, he would be forgiven for questioning whether life has meaning.

Q School, over its 35 years, has been a melting pot of obscure and unusual names. Unforgettables like Lan Gooch, Skip Guss, Mark Mike, Mahlon Moe, Beau Baugh, the aforementioned Rocky Rockett, and a golfer known as Buzz Fly have all passed through qualifying successfully and joined the big tour.

In the Q School that was held in fall of 1968, a pro from Campbell, California, named John Allen traveled more than 3,000 miles to Palm Beach Gardens, Florida, and completed the eight-round qualifier in 87–86–83–78–77–88–85–91—675. His score was 72 strokes above the highest qualifying score and 29 strokes higher than the next highest nonqualifier. The following year, a John Allen of San Jose, California, played in the new, four-round tour-school format, shooting 83–88–76–81—328, 28 strokes above the allowable total. When a check of PGA membership records turned up a John Allen of about the expected age living in the Northern California town of Benicia, the possibility of investigating those ragged showings presented itself. Instead it was discovered that three different John Allens, at least two of them Californians, were all playing tournament golf in and around the PGA Tour level at that time.

"They even paired the three of us John Allens together at one tournament," recalled John J. Allen, who now lives in Benicia and spoke about playing the pro tour in 1969 and 1970. For the record, this John J. Allen did not recognize the gaudy Q School scores from the late-60s results sheets. Must have been some other guy.

Keeping track of so many entrants, especially the nonqualifiers, has been a task too great for even the PGA Tour itself. Without accessible records of who entered when and how far through the various stages they made it, sorting out one player from another can be challenging. For example, the Billy Glisson who was medalist at the spring 1981 finals in Walt Disney World is not to be confused with seven-time tour winner Bill Glasson. The medalist in 1972, John Adams, is not the same John Adams we have seen on tour throughout the 1990s. In a tour-school trivia quiz, would anyone know that Spike Kelley first got his tour card in 1973 and Spike McRoy first got his in 1996? Then there is the case of current tour player Len Mattiace (pronounced *muh-teece*), who finished tied for 35th at the 1992 finals in Texas. Does Len Mattiace (or anyone else) realize that a *Ken* Mattiace finished tied for 83rd to get his tour card in the school of 1984?

The obscurity of most Q School participants combines with the sheer volume of skill and talent to produce a numbing confusion throughout the little knot of people who comprise a tour school's gallery. Some names are familiar, a few players are even moderately famous. But most of the athletes on the grounds are unknowns. If you stand on the practice tee at a time when a series of players happen to be practicing their low irons, the sound you hear is the same steady *hwuhh/cluck/hiss.hwuhh/cluck/hiss* of top-quality ball-striking. First the club and shaft swoop through the air (*hwuhh*), then the clubface strikes balata (*cluck*), then the ball bullets forward (*hiss*). That's the relentless, repeating sound of golf talent, assembled en masse.

The melange of names at tour school has been known to cause

more than idle confusion. At a second-stage qualifier in Titusville, Florida, during the mid-80s, rules official Mark Russell made a highly unusual yet legitimate ruling that allowed one contestant's error of anxiety to go unpunished.

"The starter was on the first tee, announcing players in the second-to-last group of the day," explained Russell. "He announces a player named Sills [not the veteran tour player Tony Sills], and the player tees up and hits his shot. There's one player left in the group to hit, but before that third guy can get his tee in the ground, some other, unknown player jumps in between the markers, tees his ball up real quick, and whacks a drive.

"Nobody can figure what's going on," recalled Russell, "so they signal me over. Turns out the player who jumped in was named Mills. Mills was assigned to the final group and he was coming a few minutes early. But on his way over, he thought he heard his name called. He panicked, thinking he'd be disqualified for missing his starting time. That's when he jumped in. I had never seen this situation before, so I had to react on the spot," said Russell—who hasn't seen or heard of a similar incident since. "I told the starter to have the last player in that group hit, send them off, and let the ball Mills hit stay where it was. That would be his ball in play. There's a penalty for starting late, you see, but there's nothing in the rule book about starting early."

Among PGA Tour rules officials who regularly work the Q School, one first-tee mix-up comes most readily to mind. It took place during morning play at the Bear Lakes Country Club tour school final of 1995, at West Palm Beach, Florida, and caused a healthy, contending, paid-in-full player to find himself suddenly down the road.

"He missed his tee time," explained Arvin Ginn, the ranking official at most qualifying finals. "Read the tee sheet incorrectly.

You never want to miss a tee time, but missing one at a tour school final is really awful."

The player, whose name Ginn conveniently and mercifully forgets, was expecting to go off early that afternoon. The tee schedules for Q School, and most other pro tournaments, are printed up every other day and list two sets of starting times covering two consecutive rounds. Typically, one is a morning time and the other is an afternoon time. "This guy wouldn't even have been at the golf course, except the player he was rooming with had a morning tee-off and they only had one car," recalled Ginn. "We looked all over trying to find him. Wasn't in the locker room, wasn't in the grill room. When we finally found him, he was sitting on a bench, drinking coffee. I had to DQ [disqualify] him right then and there."

At that same Titusville prelim where the Mills/Sills confusion occurred, Mark Russell was forced—for the only time in his career—to disqualify a player based on a newspaper photo. The previous day's round had been played in poor weather and Russell had slogged over the course trying to provide rulings for the entire 144-man field by himself. Wondering over breakfast just what snafus would arise in the day that lay ahead, he picked up the sports section of the local paper, shook his head and sighed out a curse word or two.

"The picture they happened to run with the story about qualifying was of a guy hitting a putt while his caddie held an umbrella over him," Russell said. "Just my luck, the picture couldn't have been snapped a second earlier, with the player just addressing the ball. At that point, it would still be okay for the caddie to be there with the umbrella. No, this photo shows the ball coming right off the clubface." When he arrived at the course, Russell sought the player out and confirmed that the player (whose name could not be recalled) had turned in his card without assessing himself a one-stroke penalty under Rule 14–2. Russell's duty at that point was to disqualify the player for signing an incorrect scorecard, which he regretfully did.

Russell was also assigned to a school that took place, to his recall, in 1986 or 1987, in which an obscure tour pro named Ivan Smith was disqualified in sinister fashion. Smith, a prematurely wizened Ohio man who had played the tour in both 1983 and 1985, was trying to qualify for a third time and playing reasonably well. But after hitting a drive out-of-bounds he became so irritated that upon reteeing, he neglected to state audibly that he was playing a provisional ball. In stroke play, that amounts to an improper substitution, which carries a two-stroke penalty separate from the stroke-and-distance penalty Smith duly assessed himself for the ball out-of-bounds. One of his two fellow competitors silently noted Smith's error and said nothing. He then waited until after Smith signed his scorecard—for a total score that was two strokes less than it should have been, given the substitute-ball problem—and reported Smith to Russell for signing an incorrect scorecard. When Russell checked on what happened, he had no option but to disqualify Smith and send him home.

"He looked at me and said, 'You know you're ruining my life, don't you?' " recalled Russell, who could see Ivan Smith's wispy white hair and transparent moustache clearly as he related the story. "I felt like I had stuck a sword in him." Bitter and baffled over the incident, Smith lingered on the grounds with plans to confront his accuser before eventually departing. A day or so later, the malevolent Q Schooler who had sabotaged Smith approached Russell again, this time with a casual question about how some other golf rule should be applied in a particular situation.

"I gave him my answer," said Russell, "then I brought up how he had turned Ivan in to me the day before. I just asked him, 'Hey, what is *with* you, man?' The guy walked away without saying anything."

Vaughn Moise, a rules official who nearly made it on tour via Q School himself, has a favorite tragicomic story of his own. It took place at a second-stage tour qualifier in Kingwood, Texas.

"There was a guy in one of the threesomes who had no business being there," recalls Moise. "He had won his club championship or something and thought he should go on tour. The guy is four-putting, hitting balls in the water, hitting them out-of-bounds, you name it. He was constantly going into his bag to get out another ball." The player would have "shot 100," in Moise's opinion, if he hadn't run into an equipment problem on the 7th hole.

"He had just knocked another ball in the water," says Moise, "and so he's got the ball pocket of his bag unzipped and he's dumping whatever's left onto the grass. I asked him if he was all right, and I can tell he's embarrassed. He's got this odd collection of yellow-colored balls and orange balls and no two of 'em match. He knows the rule that says you can't change the type of ball you play during a round, but I think he was looking for a loophole in the rule." There was no such luck. Moise asked the player— who had just paid his $2,000 entry fee to compete in the qualifier—to hand over his scorecard and head back in. Moise took out a pen and wrote, for the first and only time in his officiating career, "R.O.B.," which stands for "ran out of balls."

Ninety-five percent of all famous rules stories from the PGA Tour turn out to be heart-warmers in which players call significant penalties on themselves under circumstances in which no one else but the player could have witnessed the breach. The annals of Q School are not exactly brimming with such tales. In fact, there seems to be no classic story of a PGA Tour card that was missed by one stroke, or even by a few, after a player assessed a penalty on himself. In the 1997 finals at the Grenelefe resort, contending players got fat on the more vulnerable South course during fifth-round play, turning in a raft of 65s and 66s that positioned them well for final-round play on Grenelefe's more demanding West layout.

Of all the fifth-round fireballs at that school, Sweden's Niclas Fasth (pronounced *fahst*) burned the hottest, carding an eagle and eight birdies to shoot 8-under par 63 and motor up the standings from a tie for 72nd into a tie for 13th. Outside the flimsy scorer's tent pitched beside the South course's 18th green, Q Schoolniks waited in the dimming light for a glimpse of this wunderkind. When Fasth's caddie preceded him up the walkway and paused beside the tent, he was quickly asked for some details on the 63.

"It's not for sure yet," the caddie said quietly. "We may have had a problem on 17 with a tree limb. Niclas had to play a shot out of some woods and we're not sure if a branch broke while he was setting up." Under Rule 13–2, Fasth would not be penalized for breaking a limb or branch while taking his stance, but if he did so while making a practice swing it would have cost him two strokes. Several minutes later, Fasth emerged from the scorer's tent and walked over to where his clubs lay. "What happened with the tree limb?" a reporter inquired. "Huh?" Fasth replied. "Wasn't there some branch or something on number 17 that might have broken? Your caddie mentioned it." Fasth shook his head and began working the zippers on his golf bag. "There's no problem," he said. "No branch. I had 63." The caddie, who from the start seemed uncertain as to what had occurred, headed back to the clubhouse. If there had been a matter of doubt concerning the violation of a rule, Fasth had given himself the benefit of that doubt.

Tour schools are highly emotional yet minimally chronicled events. The record of these tournaments exists not in highlight tapes and news clippings but in human memory, for the most part. As a result, isolated moments at long-ago tour schools take on an aura of mystery as the parties involved revisit them. Sal DiPietro, the Ohio restaurateur and golf course owner who played in the 1968 qualifier sponsored by the renegade Association of Professional Golfers, spoke nostalgically about "giving the tour one shot" before returning home, regaining his amateur status, and starting up a business. All well and good, but DiPietro in fact gave the tour two shots, competing in 1966 as well as in 1968.

Q Schools are expected to produce oddities and mishaps that other tournaments don't give rise to—which may somewhat affect its tapestry of oral history. In the fall of 1990, Dave Rummells was forced to repent for his first lackluster PGA Tour season, which followed four solid years in which Rummells banked over $1 million in official earnings. His dignity bruised, Rummells set to work on the La Quinta Dunes and PGA West Nicklaus courses, compiling a 4-under cumulative score through 72 holes. Despite a 2-over 74 in round five, he kept a rein on his emotions going into the final day's play.

"That last day I made up my mind not to put any pressure on myself," he explained, reliving that afternoon's events eight years later. "I went out with a good feeling and when I came off the 16th, I was 4-under for the day, which was plenty. I was sitting in good shape."

The downside for Rummells was that he had just bogeyed 16 and the tee at number 17 was backed up with players. "I had about 20 minutes to dwell on that bogey, so I walked away and tried to clear my thoughts," he said. "When it was finally my turn to hit I had gotten my head straight and I was able to make a good swing." A good swing, yes, but a hair too hard. His ball hit 10 feet past the hole, squirted forward, and tumbled into the back bunker.

"Now I'm in a position where it's par-par or I can forget it," said Rummells. "I had a slightly downhill lie in the bunker but a lot of green to work with, and I hit a really good shot." Cozied up to the hole at 17 thanks to his fine bunker recovery, Rummells sank the putt and buttoned up the first of his two compulsory pars. Having dodged an arrow, he had "some adrenaline going" as he walked to the par-4 18th in search of that second par.

"I hit one of my best drives of the day on 18," Rummells said, with about as much outward pride as his Cedar Rapids upbringing would permit. "My caddie, Darrell Chivington, stepped off the distance and told me it was 185 yards to the pin, slightly downhill, over a pond. The green was long and narrow, so we figured anything straight and solid—even if it wasn't the perfect club selection—would put us on the green."

Rummells took the 6-iron from Chivington and lined up his shot. "I remember standing behind the ball and thinking, 'This shot shouldn't be that bad.' Then, you know, you get over it and because of the situation you start tensing up a little. My plan was to hit it 175 yards and keep it below the pin," he said. "The far edge of the water was 160, so I was going to land it about 15 yards past that spot. Unfortunately, I hit the shot a little thin."

When you have played as much tournament golf as Rummells had played by that point, and you are hitting a shot that absolutely *must* carry a certain distance, your eyes automatically turn skyward to locate the ball in flight, then flick down to the chosen landing spot, then recheck the ball, then recheck the landing spot, several times. This up-down act is especially easy to observe on par-3 approaches over water. On number 16 at Augusta National, to take a prime example, Masters contestants look straight into a CBS television camera that captures them, in tight close-up, flicking their gaze high and low after they have launched their shots toward the green. With experience, golfers and caddies are able to gauge the outcome of a shot in this manner well before it lands.

It even seems at times that golfers can study their ball in flight and—being attuned to the rate at which visual perspective causes the ball to appear to shrink in size—comprehend right at the moment of apogee whether the ball has become "small enough" to indicate a long-enough carry and a safe outcome of the shot.

If so, then Dave Rummells's golf ball on the last day of Q School 1990 was flying toward the 18th green and not getting small enough.

"It hit the wooden piling," sighed Rummells. "Bounced up, then dropped down in the water. I looked over at Darrell and he looked at me. I remember how shocked he looked. That ball going in the water was so out of the question, and yet it happened. We were both in total disbelief." Drop three, hitting four—the reality of what was unfolding staggered Rummells. He walked like a zombie down to the front edge of the water hazard, which was only 30 yards forward. He had an 8-iron in his hand. Although dazed, Rummells understood that (a) if he were going to get his tour card and his livelihood back, this shot had to go in the hole; and (b) this shot was certainly not going in the hole, so there was no reason other than basic professionalism to even drop a ball on the grass and swing at it.

At this point in the story, the facts fall into dispute. Standing by the green was a local PGA golf professional named Gary Gentile, who was a friend of Chivington's and, by this point, an acquaintance of Rummells's wife, Ira. Gentile had been standing and conversing with her as Rummells blankly whacked his godforsaken fourth shot on the par-4 18th. According to Rummells, the shot turned out be a very good one, landing near the pin and coming to rest four feet from the hole. According to Gentile, "the shot flew dead-on for the pin and the ball went *in the cup*. It went in with a bang and then it hopped out and stopped four feet away."

All parties agree that Rummells sank the four-footer, signed his card, drifted around until he was even more fully convinced that his 428 score was no good, then decided to wait in the clubhouse for the couple of hours it would take for his friends' fates to be determined and the final results to go up. What happened in the end—Rummells was called out for a play-off involving at least six players and played well enough to outlast several other competitors and indeed receive his tour card for 1991—is a matter of recorded fact. But what set of clubs did Rummells use in that play-off? And who caddied for him? According to Gentile, this is "one of the great tour-school stories ever, because Dave let me and his caddie borrow his clubs so we could go play a few holes" on some other PGA West course. "When he got called for the play-off," marveled Gentile, "he had no clubs. I'm not sure he had his golf shoes, either."

A colorful anecdote, indeed, but an apochryphal one, according to Rummells, who said he entered the play-off with his regulation equipment intact. Told of the discrepancy, Gentile, who is now a high-ranking pro in the PGA West hierarchy, seemed honestly mystified. "Ask his wife—she was there." For Mrs. Rummells, the question of how the wedge shot on her husband's final regulation hole had landed was obscured by the passage of time. But the question of missing equipment did ring a bell. "I think that's how it happened," said Ira Rummells, "because didn't Dave play the extra holes in his tennis shoes?" Some might speculate that the possibility of a rules infraction could cause self-inflicted amnesia in a golfer who entered a long-ago play-off with borrowed equipment.

Under the Rules of Golf, however, a competitive round of stroke play is over after 18 holes, and any competitor called to a play-off is entitled not only to change equipment, but to seek advice from a swing coach and hit practice shots between the regular "stipulated" round and the play-off holes.

By and large, the Tour Qualifying School's history is an oral one—documented in a hit-and-miss fashion reflecting the event's quasi-official status. While cascades of information and insightful cross-references exist for the rest of the tournaments on the Tour schedule, archive information on the Qualifying School is patchy and at times unreliable. For example, the official results of the fall 1976 qualifying school at Rancho Viejo Country Club in Brownsville, Texas, which appear in the appendix of this book on page 256, were not on record at the PGA Tour's Florida headquarters in any form—digital, microfilm, printed, or handwritten. In order to present that qualifier's results, it was necessary to look through back issues of *Golf World* magazine, which has been in existence since long before the first tour school.

The tour's official media guides are a primary source for the dates and years in which tour members have gained their eligibility, but it is fairly common for the media guide to list a player—for example, Fuzzy Zoeller—as having gained eligibility in "Fall 1974." This notation implies there was a spring qualifier in 1974, which there was not. In the case of a player like Doug Tewell, a four-time winner on the PGA Tour, the bio incorrectly reads: "Q School: June 1975." In fact Tewell never spent a moment at a Q School until he began broadcasting them for the Golf Channel in the late 1990s. He was a Class A PGA club pro who earned his tour eligibility the old-fashioned way, using his Monday-qualifying privileges as a PGA member and gradually building toward exemption. The first two seasons he tried this, 1975 and 1976, Tewell played only a few events and earned only a few thousand dollars each year. But, according to a little-known tour bylaw of the time, any PGA of America member could earn and retain a tour card by Monday-qualifying his way into tournaments and making as little as $3,000. In his fourth season, Tewell won $33,162 and was out of the club-pro ranks for good. He attributes the error in his media-guide listing to the ubiquitousness of Q School. "They saw that '76 was my first year, so they naturally assumed I went through the Q School in '75," he said, shrugging. "You can't get out of going to Q School, right?"

For years, the official PGA Tour media guide has listed the spring 1969 and fall 1969 qualifying tournament finals (both held at the old PGA National, now known as JDM Country Club) as having been played at 144 holes—the same marathon distance the 1965 through 1968 schools were played at. In fact, the 1969 school finals were cut in half by the new Tournament Players Division to four rounds. Bob Eastwood was medalist in the spring school with a score of 291, which would be 3-over par at PGA National. A pro named Doug Olson was medalist in the fall edition of qualifying with a score of 286.

Round-by-round scores are not available in PGA Tour archives for graduates of the first Tournament Players Division qualifying tournament, but thankfully the PGA, despite having been spurned by its tour players, kept even more accurate records of the spring 1969 qualifier than the TPD kept. Which is how we know for certain that Johnny Miller put together his 11-over score of 299 by shooting 74–78–73–74.

The tour school's penchant for giving rise to bizarre and unprecedented occurrences made it the natural place for the Casey Martin cart-riding controversy to erupt. Two events took place just before the 1997 final-stage qualifier to put Q School footage on network evening news. First, Martin earned a spot in the 1997 final stage by shooting a 289 and tying for 12th place at his second-stage qualifier in Seaside, California. The Stanford varsity golfer, who had competed on the 1994 NCAA championship team despite being hobbled by Klippel-Trenaunay-Weber syndrome, a rare circulatory disorder that had compromised the bone and muscle of his right leg, was pressing onward with his quest to play the PGA Tour in spite of pain that was sometimes searing and the added obstacle of reduced strength and stability in the leg. Second, a federal magistrate in Oregon issued an injunction preventing the PGA Tour from forcing Martin to walk the six long rounds of final stage.

The rumpus over whether a court of law should dictate rules of play for a major professional sport spilled out of the sports pages and onto the front pages and opinion sections of every major newspaper in the country. PGA Tour golf doesn't look like everybody else's version of the game due to two important visual differences, both of which involve legs: Nobody wears shorts on the tour, nobody rides in an E-Z-Go. These are passionately defended customs—the shorts issue will even create an uproar when caddies beg to wear them. But the requirement of long pants is a mere afterthought compared to mandatory walking. Regardless of their other beliefs and values, tour players and officials share an unshakable faith in the sanctity of self-propulsion for professional tournament players. At the least provocation, they can launch into fiery speeches in support of the concept.

But apparently the mandatory-walking dogma shared by tour loyalists never encountered anything but theoretical opposition. Forrest Fezler showed up wearing shorts in a men's tour event once, and he was duly reprimanded. But no pro golfer other than Charlie Owens ever demanded a rules waiver that would permit riding in a cart during competion. And Owens was a senior, playing the cart-friendly PGA Senior Tour on a weekly basis. His grievance involved just one event, the U.S. Senior Open, where carts were prohibited, and Owens ultimately failed in his bid for the waiver. Perhaps it would have been useful if the Owens dustup had prompted some prescient observer to ask: "What happens when a profoundly disabled golfer arrives on the scene with a golf game worthy of the tour but a severe disadvantage when it comes to walking? What will we think then?"

That hypothetical was never brought up and discussed, and as a result traditionalists were completely unprepared for Martin's arrival. No matter how splendidly the case was made for professional golf as a pure physical contest to be waged with clubs, balls, spiked shoes, and no other accoutrement but a single cabretta glove, the drive to shut Martin out appeared heartless and small-minded. At ground zero, the finals themselves, Martin's case had attracted a few additional reporters but otherwise exerted little effect on the proceedings. The 25-year-old Eugene native played fine golf throughout the week, missing his tour card by only two strokes after failing to break 70 on the more birdie-prone South Course at Grenelefe resort. Despite his hobbled gait, Martin takes a mighty rip on most every shot. He was seen cutting off doglegs and shooting at pins aggressively. When Q School ended, he had a Nike Tour card and his long-running lawsuit for the right to use a cart in tour-sanctioned play went forward, eventually resulting in a judgment under the Americans with Disabilities Act that awarded Martin his right to ride.

Q School officials, though forced to let Martin ride, did not revert to their liberal cart policies of prior years. Instead, they stripped 60 Yamahas of their roofs and windshields (to prevent riding players from receiving unfair protection from the elements) and allowed them to be used for personal transport only—no bags allowed. Scott Verplank, the eventual medalist and a player with a long history of serious injuries, snatched up the offer.

"If I can save six days of wear and tear on my feet, why not?"

asked Verplank, in the midst of his smooth ride to victory. "And when this kid wins his lawsuit against the Tour," he cracked, referring to Martin, "I'm gonna get me one with a top."

The playing privileges at stake, the throng of semi-obscure players, the contestants returning for their sixth or eighth attempt, the six days of competition—it all came together during the 1970s to enfuse Q School with a slight touch of madness. Due to its lowly status, the tour qualifier's early days are sparsely chronicled, making individual memory our only means of sifting back through the years. Asking players about their long-ago performances in tour qualifiers, an interviewer finds that time heals most, if not all, wounds. In the upcoming chapter, some of the golfers who tell their stories are able to revisit past Q Schools with a twinge of amusement. Others look back nearly in horror. Still others look back on their multiple attempts at qualifying in search of a break they surely deserved but somehow never got.

6

GOOD ENOUGH TO DREAM

Harry Taylor's compact frame and streamlined ego have graced the tour's Qualifying Tournament for nearly half its grim existence. Sixteen times Taylor has gone to the Q School finals, beginning in the fall of 1979, and seven of those 16 times he has made it through and pocketed a tour card. The prize money he has earned doesn't amount to much—Taylor's lifetime winnings on the big tour are a slender $367,000. But he has made a rousing success of his parallel career as an on-tour representative for club manufacturers and a designer of irons and woods, including such "player's clubs" as the Mizuno T-Zoid and other blade-style irons.

Any pro who has been through the tour's annual meat grinder more than a couple of times and doesn't know Harry Taylor needs to glance up from his divot patch more often. Taylor—whose record suggests that if he ever won the Qualifying Tournament he would return the following year to defend his title—is that rare actor in pro golf's repertory company who has never played lead but has kept continually busy as an understudy.

Good enough to get his card but never good enough to keep it, Taylor wasted no time after his failed rookie season in 1980 before signing on with Taylor Made Golf (no relation) and turning his lifelong interest in club-tinkering into a paying gig. Harry is the all-exempt era's throwback to those enigmatic pros who could Monday-qualify with seeming ease but could not make cuts or paychecks once the bell sounded. In 10 complete seasons on tour, his highest finish on the money list is 140th. While he may envy the players around him who've been blessed with just a hair more talent, he prefers to look into their golf bags and chat with them about woods and irons. Every player on tour—those who linger and those who last—is in need of golf clubs. And Harry Taylor has always been on the scene to consult them, cajole them, and fit them for equipment.

As a result, he is perhaps the ultimate Q School antihero. By turning the tour qualifier into his personal week-long trade show, Taylor has managed to drain the pressure from it. Playing his way to final stage—where all the important customers gather— is important to Harry. Sufficiently important, you would think, to make his throat go dry and his palms go moist along the way. But as they say in the gangster movies, this is about business for Taylor, it's not personal. He has the luxury of putting his self-image aside in favor of practicality. When ego is removed, the stakes go down, and the pressure, as well.

Another pro might return every year with a little more gray hair and be seen as a pitiful case, but Taylor is a civilian colonel in the golf world's version of the military-industrial complex. He is one of the unseen agents who travel between two diverging skill levels, helping to maintain a marketing symbiosis that allows average golfers to legitimately believe they are playing some modified version of the clubs the tour pros play. A Detroit native who has lived much of his 45 years in Tennessee and speaks in a courtly drawl, Taylor can swing a club, design one, and market it with dignity among his peers. If you're not a superstar, he can reach into Mizuno's limited U.S. golf budget and find you a modest endorsement contract for putting his company's brand name on your golf bag.

"The guys out here know me as a player, as somebody who's at least good enough to play his way in the door," Taylor explained as he spectated the 1998 finals, which he had had to pass up while recovering from disc surgery. "When I talk to them about their clubs and their game, they don't have to wonder if I know what I'm talking about." Taylor's record of seven successful trips through the Fall Classic is impressive. Most of his seven different tour cards have been won by a safe margin, while many of his misses have been by only one or two shots. He has played Q School rounds with current members of the Senior PGA Tour and with players still young enough to be seniors in college.

To an interviewer, Taylor's mixture of diplomacy and directness is both frustrating and charming. Harry looks you straight in the eye when you ask him a question and straight down at the ground while he puts that answer together. He came out of the University of Tennessee with a political science degree in 1979, and it shows. Taylor could spend an afternoon recalling the players who have teed it up with him at tour school, players who missed and those who made it through, without ever indulging in gossip. "I can't tell stories about other players," he said. "Never once done it without it coming back to bite me." The tour's grapevine of sensitive players, boastful agents, and motor-mouthed caddies has schooled Taylor in diplomacy. "It's not just with you press guys. Out here, what you say *to* anybody *about* anybody is gonna get twisted."

He is forthcoming about the freeze-ups and high drama that marked his early days in Q School competition, before Tour Qualifying School became, in Harry's words, "just, you know, what I did in the fall." Q School pressure has never caused Taylor to vomit, but it has made him cry (one time, after missing his card by a stroke) and it has vapor-locked his swing on a couple of occasions. In the 1986 final stage, split between the La Quinta Resort and PGA West, he came to the 108th and final hole with a safety margin of three strokes, perhaps even four. Somehow, some way, Harry opened his imagination to the classic tour-school question of "how badly can I screw up and still make it." Despite this breach of competitive concentration, he got off a reasonably good tee shot, which settled alongside the fairway in light rough. Having learned his lesson about defeatist thinking, Taylor made up his mind to grab a 4-wood, get set, take dead aim, and swing.

"I'm gonna get my feet planted and quick hit it—that's what I told myself," said Taylor, recalling the shot. He took his stance, got set, and then did nothing.

Attempting to clear his mind of negative thoughts, Harry had accidentally deleted all files. He stood over the ball with his mind completely blank. Golfers talk about having Zen-like experiences during competition—about getting "in the zone," but a man can carry a good thing too far. In this case, the oft-praised "zone" morphed into the Twilight Zone for Taylor. Eventually, he realized he was standing over his ball with no preset instructions for hitting it.

"By that time, my feet had been in the same place for so long, I was actually a half-inch or so lower than when I started," he marveled. "I realized that if I was going to hit the thing square, I needed to choke down a bit." This technical detail, ridiculous as it was, served as a reset button on Taylor's brain, allowing his hands and arms to begin the takeaway. "Funny thing is, when I finally did swing, it was as hard a swing as I've ever made in competition," he recalled. "And I hit the ball absolutely perfectly. Bombed it." Taylor watched in a semitrance as his shot climbed, leveled off, and descended onto the green, setting him up for an easy par. Then he turned to his fellow competitor, Brad Fabel, and meekly held his hands out to his sides. "I told Brad, 'I am sorry, man,' " said Harry. " 'I just could not swing that club.' "

According to Taylor, his most satisfying shot in 16 Q School finals came on the par-5 18th at Grenelefe West, after he drove his ball safely, hit a reasonable second shot, then blocked a 7-iron into a bunker to the right of the green. The ball landed with a puff of bogey dust that signaled the deep fried-egg lie Taylor would soon be cursing. His caddie handed him a sand wedge then jogged up to the scoring tent to see how matters stood. A minute later he was back with the skinny.

"Get your ball up and down from there," explained the caddie, "and we're in. Take three from there and we're in a play-off." All well and good, but Taylor's half-buried ball could not be finessed or feathered onto the putting surface. It responded to Taylor's decisive smack as he had anticipated—on-line but with too much air speed. Its only chance at a safe landing was to hit the flagstick, which the ball somehow managed to do.

"It stopped 15 feet from the hole," recalled Taylor, who experienced a moment of déjà vu as he stepped onto the green. "A while earlier, I had won a Space Coast tournament on that very same golf course by sinking a putt of the same length," he noted. "That was all I needed, I guess. The putt dropped and I was in, on the number. The reason it was so satisfying," Taylor concluded, in revealing fashion, "was that I never gagged. I needed to hit the shot a certain way, I hit it that way, then I needed luck, and I got the luck I needed."

Taylor swung his gaze in several directions as players went about their postround business. "So here I am at La Quinta for the 1998 Q School just watchin' from the sidelines," he said, folding his arms across his chest and slumping his shoulders. He had been cleared by the doctor to play again, "starting next week, of course, as soon as the school is over," and a reporter reminded him that he could well be back to start another streak of Q School appearances in 1999 at Doral. Taylor nodded, glanced down, and unconsciously began to crisscross his arms stiffly in front of him, then rotate his torso, simulating a golfer's warm-up. "I could. I could be back," he said affirmatively. But you could see in Harry's expression that any new tour-school streak would be considerably shorter than his first one.

In the era when Harry Taylor began entering tour qualifiers, the final stage of the process served a function it no longer serves. Young men would show up at the national final after playing a few nice rounds at the sectional stage and look for an augury of their future from the twin forces of reality and fate. Because a touring life in the 1960s and much of the 1970s was not the gold rush it is today, many players showed up simply to take a flyer. The Qualifying Tournament final would do many of them the favor of pointing out their insufficient talent. Returning home without a tour card had to be disappointing, but for the realists in the field it was far preferable to spending their adult years asking "what if?"

Andy Nusbaum, for example, was a 1967 West Point graduate who had distinguished himself as a junior golfer in his native Kansas, captained his college team, and managed some high individual finishes in NCAA national competition. Nusbaum is a slim, well-spoken man whose wavy hair has silvered with the years while his judgment and gentle wit have remained keen. His career reflects Nusbaum's diverse interests and skills, including stints as head golf professional at prestigious clubs, directorship of the Golf Digest Instruction School program, and service on the steering committee of the groundbreaking Golf & the Environment project. Nusbaum has also been active in the Northern California–based Shivas Irons Society, a small but noted sect within golf that promulgates the ethereal spirit of the Michael Murphy novel *Golf in the Kingdom*. Reminded recently that the yellowed results sheet from the spring 1968 tour qualifier includes among the also-rans "Andrew Nusbaum, Salina, Kansas," he offered a bemused smile.

"That was a long time ago," he said. "I only tried it that one time and I didn't play particularly well." If not for a freakish injury to a vertebra in his neck, Nusbaum would have been an Army officer serving the Vietnam War effort. As it was, he spent the year after college in a military hospital slowly recuperating. He accepted a medical discharge from the Army that came a mere 53 weeks following graduation. "I had committed four years to active service in the military," he pointed out, "so when I got discharged, I was faced with a question of what to do instead." He turned pro, took a job at Shady Oaks Country Club in Fort Worth, Texas, and set his sights on tour qualifying. Like any other assistant pro at Shady Oaks, Nusbaum would have been thrilled to receive a few casual pointers from the club's most illustrious member, Ben Hogan, who was only then fully retired from tournament golf and whose regimen included frequent visits to the club for lunch and golf.

"Hogan never said much to any of us, let alone helping guys with their swings," recalled Nusbaum. "About the only conversation we would have with him was when Hogan and his regular golf group were planning one of their little afternoon tournaments. They would sit down for lunch, about a dozen of them, and draw the teams. One two-man team would be picked as the 'wheel,' and that team's score would go against every other two-some. It meant you were in a six- or eight-way bet against every-body else." Nusbaum and his fellow assistants would be in charge of taking down the pairings and setting the teams up with carts—one man to a cart, for some unstated reason. "The day before they were planning one of these tournaments," said Nus-baum, "Hogan would come into the back room of the golf shop with instructions on where the pins should be set. Depending on the course conditions and how the wind would be blowing, he had certain pin positions he preferred. And that's how the greens crew would cut the cups that day."

Nusbaum's eight-round score in the spring 1968 school—which included Hale Irwin among its 15 qualifiers—was 22 strokes higher than the 592 needed to get through. "It was a week-to-week existence on the tour back then, so even if you made it through the school there was nothing you could count on," said Nusbaum. "I was like a lot of young guys who try it, I guess. You give it one shot then you go figure out what to do with your life."

That was precisely the plan of a confessed "terrible college player" named Bill Glasson as he was scraping his way through regional PGA Tour qualifying back in 1983. Real estate license in hand and no thoughts of adding a tour card to it, Glasson arrived with very few butterflies for the 1983 tour school finals at TPC Sawgrass in Ponte Vedra, Florida.

"I had a job," said Glasson, who was on hand for the 1998 Q School finals at La Quinta and found a little time to reminisce. "I had a career in real estate that I was looking forward to. The reason I tried to make the tour was to get golf out of my system and get on with life." Glasson's unexpected presence at the 1998 finals was in the service of friendship. He was there to coach and encourage Chris Tidland, a young minitour player whom Glasson knew well from Tidland's years at Oklahoma State University.

Glasson, who lives with his wife and two children in the college town of Stillwater, Oklahoma, plays frequent practice rounds with Sooner varsity golfers, who naturally seek his professional advice. After Tidland played his way through both preliminary stages, Glasson, who owns a twin-prop Merlin jet and happened to be on a family visit to his wife's hometown of San Diego, commuted over to La Quinta a couple of days to help his young friend, who was struggling with the pressure and marooned at 10 over par following the third round. (Tidland regrouped admirably to play his three remaining rounds at seven under, earning a conditional Nike Tour exemption). The first question a reporter asked Glasson was whether it unnerved him to walk among 168 golfers who all coveted his job.

"I had reservations about coming," he admitted, standing on the practice tee in jeans and running shoes, easily recognized by his wavy blond hair and the weight-room physique that belies his long rap sheet of sports injuries and surgeries. "Haven't been back to Q School since '84." Glasson paused. "I'll admit it, I feel like vomiting just being here."

Glasson said that if interest rates hadn't soared to 18 percent and thrown the real estate market into deep freeze, he might not have felt free to make his what-the-hell bid 15 years earlier. Glasson was successful in the 1983 finals, squeezing into a group of 50 card-earners that included no fewer than five players who would eventually win major championships—Corey Pavin, Mark Calcavecchia, Tom Lehman, Paul Azinger, and Mark Brooks. Rounding out that "graduating class" were eventual Ryder Cuppers Brad Faxon, Jim Gallagher, and Loren Roberts along with Kenny Knox and Gene Sauers, who each would go on to win several PGA Tour events. Glasson began the week with a wind-blown 79 but rebounded immediately with a 69. Then it was back up to 77, down to 70, and finally two 74s to end the week at 443, two strokes inside the safety margin of 445. He wasn't too stunned to accept the eligibility card they typed up for him, but neither was he prepared to be a serious touring pro.

"I made something like $17,000 all year," lamented Glasson. He would have needed more than twice that total to finish in the top 125, but somewhere in all the misplayed shots and missed cuts, Glasson must have glimpsed at least the possibility of success. Telling family and friends that this second try for a card would absolutely be his last, the long-driving Fresno native showed up at the 1984 qualifying finals, which were played at two golf courses in La Quinta and Rancho Mirage, California. Azinger, Lehman, and Knox were also humbling themselves with a return trip, and on the less intimidating desert courses the 1984 scores were significantly lower. But Glasson again played without any emotional duress. "I was either not smart enough or too smart [to experience the event's renowned pressure]," he said in hindsight. At 437 for the week, Glasson was six strokes better than his prior year's performance, but it was a borderline score that nearly became his permanent ticket home.

"There were six of us sitting at that score, which made 52 players total, and in those days they cut it off at exactly 50," said Glasson. "There was a play-off—six guys for the last four spots— and off we went. A big cold front had moved through and it was nasty. Looked like it was about to snow and you had to struggle to grip the club and make a swing. Luckily the play-off was over after one hole. Four of us made par and two guys made bogey. I can't remember who the other two guys were." Glasson never returned to tour school and has won over $4 million playing pro golf despite sometimes crippling injuries. To hear him talk is to conclude that Glasson had more belief in himself than he had in the whole notion of professional golf as a bona fide career.

"You want to know when I started telling myself I was a pro

golfer? That this was my real job?" he asked. "After I won my fifth tournament. Five wins—that's what it took for the whole thing to finally seem real. Up until then it was just a stopover between college and what I was really going to do. There aren't too many guys who come into this knowing they're qualified to do something else. I had another avenue, something I wanted to pursue. Trust me, I will sell real estate someday. I've spent a lot of years delaying it, that's all."

Jim Albus, similar to Andy Nusbaum, gave the tour one shot as a young man during the 1960s. He too put up scores that were well above the make-or-break line, and accepted the results. But unlike Nusbaum, Albus was a physically robust and intensely competitive golfer. After joining the club-pro ranks, he kept up his game and did plenty of damage against sectional competition. Albus, while working at clubs in New York City and Long Island, qualified for the PGA Championship seven times, making the cut in 1984. In 1980, he finished second in the PGA Club Professional Championship, one of eight top-25 finishes he would score against that tournament's large and highly competitive national field. He played in six U.S. Opens, finished tied for 26th in the 1982 Westchester Classic, and competed in the now defunct PGA Winter Tour in 1977 and 1978.

A college baseball and basketball jock who took up golf while at Bucknell University, Albus compiled his impressive playing record while running a business and watching his children grow up. Then, 22 years after first attempting to become a tour golfer, he joined the Senior PGA Tour and proceeded to win five tournaments and $3.3 million in the five years from 1991 through 1995. For most people, a midlife athletic triumph like the one Albus scored would offer consolation for the leftover ache of an also-ran finish at the fall 1968 Q School. But it wasn't that way for Albus, because he never let the events of that week get under his skin.

"I tried it that one year and never went back as a young man," he recalled while prepping for the 1999 senior season. "I just wasn't good enough. I had been playing golf for six or seven years and I didn't know how to play in wind, didn't know about Bermuda greens—I was a neophyte, and I had a terrible time." For all his ill-preparedness, Albus hung tough in the six-day, eight-round ordeal. A score of 65 in the final round would have earned him a card and probably changed his life, but Albus had not managed anything better than a 75 all week, and he packed it in with nine holes to go.

"I never had any second thoughts about not trying again," he said. "I had a family and a decent job. I got to play in U.S. Opens and PGAs, plus all the section events, so it's not like I didn't keep my hand in." Albus did, in fact, forward an entry for the 1983 qualifier, but true to the Q School's confusing and seemingly ever-changing formats and regulations, he soon regretted even ponying up the entry fee. The decision to exempt school survivors from Monday qualifying had been widely publicized, but with that rule change came an extreme form of a condition that still applies today, namely, the school qualifier's relatively low eligibility *status*.

As a result of the numerical pecking order into which newer tour players are grouped, the 20-plus tournaments that every exempt player is inevitably allowed to enter tend to bunch themselves in the middle to late part of the season. Albus came not intending to give up his club job. He merely wanted to play tour golf during his club's off-season. "Most of the playing that I was looking to do would have been in the winter," he explained, still sounding mildly indignant about the snafu. "It wouldn't have worked at all. I was annoyed that I had even tried."

Another player from metropolitan New York who gave the tour a shot before pursuing his club-pro career is Bill Greenleaf. In Greenleaf's case, Q School was not the monolithic force which in and of itself would either deny or permit him his goal. For starters, Greenleaf was going nowhere without sponsor money. Tour card or no tour card, he lacked the personal or family resources to head out on the circuit, even briefly. And in the event pocket money could be lined up, any ATP card he earned at tour school would carry only symbolic value. This was still the pre-1983 era, when PGA membership, plus the entry fee, ushered any Class A pro into all the Monday qualifiers he could stomach. After finishing his golf career at Arizona State University, Greenleaf, who at 47 remains slim and well conditioned, had wasted no time moving through the PGA Apprentice program, taking all the courses and tests needed for Class A status. But the tour fantasy remained foremost, and Greenleaf beat balls daily to keep it alive. Looking back, he admits that his finest, most dramatic golf shot as a professional probably occurred during the degrading process of scraping up financial support.

"Playing the tour was my life dream," said Greenleaf flatly. "I needed money, so I had to have sponsors, that's all there was to it. In 1972, I approached a guy who I thought might be interested, and he said he'd think it over." Asked if the man was prosperous enough to be bankrolling long-shot golfers, Greenleaf shot back with a classic golf-pro answer: "The guy's grandfather invented the circuit breaker," he said.

Notwithstanding the magnitude of the fortunate grandson's inheritance, Greenleaf found that he was somewhat ambivalent about dream-funding. In a casual audition of sorts, Greenleaf and his circuit-breaker heir had arranged to play 18 holes at Brae Burn Country Club in Purchase. Through 16 holes of their round, the young pro had made six birdies, and after each one he screwed up his courage to renew the request for money, with scant success. "No matter how many times I brought up the subject, we always seemed to be talking about something else," said Greenleaf, who since 1993 has been the head professional at Sunningdale Golf Club in Scarsdale.

"Finally we come to number 17, which is about the hardest hole in Westchester County—450 yards, tight fairway, elevated green, and I hit a great drive," he said. "The next shot is 180 yards, uphill, and I clobber a 5-iron. We know it has to be close to the hole, but we can't see the green, so when we get up there and don't see a ball, I start to feel a tingle. The guy looks in the cup, sees the ball, and starts yelling to me. That's when I knew this had to be one of those magical days in my life. The odds against that shot going in were so huge. I was actually wondering whether the hole had ever been eagled before—I mean, since it was built." When the clamor died down, Greenleaf had his first sponsor—although the sum his trust-funded friend put up was relatively modest.

Greenleaf's second sponsor was a total stranger whose loyalty Greenleaf captured through yet another outrageous act on the golf course. This one took place on the 18th green of the Riviera Country Club, one of golf's great prosceniums, during the first round of the 1973 Los Angeles Open, which Greenleaf had Monday-qualified for against a large—though not biblically vast, as in earlier days—field of aspirants.

"The '72 season had taught me that my tee-to-green game was good enough to get me through most Monday qualifiers," said Greenleaf, who played his way into seven straight tour events that year without making any money. "But I was a lousy putter back then, and it really killed me. By the time '73 rolled around I was nearly out of cash and I was getting desperate. My approach on number 18 that first day stopped about 20 feet from the hole, and if I could hole the putt I would be even-par for the round, which would have meant a lot going into the second round." Greenleaf paced the kikuyu grass on Riviera's 18th, lining up his putt and trying to block out the sounds and movements of the fans who were conversing and moving about the clubhouse, which sits slightly above the green. Then he stopped what he was doing. Holding his putter high in the air, he called out a loud request.

"I said, 'Folks, I need everybody's attention for just a minute. I've got this 20-footer with a tricky break in it and I really need to make it. So please, if you would, just focus all your positive thoughts on this 20-footer going in the hole. Just please do that for me. Thank you.' They all went completely silent, of course, and I stroked the putt. Believe it or not, the putt dropped in, and everybody around the green just went crazy."

After a few dramatic bows, Greenleaf walked off the green and headed straight over to the practice tee. By the time he reached it, a man who had witnessed the theatrics at 18 caught up with him. "He was a guy with a son who played high school golf and wanted to play the tour when he grew up. The father thought it would be great if his son could caddie for me in a few tour events and get a feel for tour competition," explained Greenleaf. "I told him it sounded nice, only I was out of money and getting ready to go home. I needed $5,000 right away or I was going to pack it in that week. Right on the spot he gives me the money."

Dreams of the PGA Tour that take root on the frozen sands of Brooklyn's Coney Island seem destined for a funky culmination. Jay Golden's 18-hole Q School round of 100-plus, as described by the golf-pro-turned-comedian with his hands chopping the air and his New York accent sharpening the narrative, started out to be a career round of an entirely different sort. Golden now resides in central Florida, but his original stamping grounds were Dyker Beach Municipal Golf Course and every unlikely sort of urban practice range from the off-ramps of the Brooklyn–Queens Expressway to Brighton Beach in the dead of winter.

"I looked so bizarre practicing golf on Brighton Beach that bag ladies combing the sand for quarters would go out of their way to avoid me," Golden admitted. "That's pretty bad." After high school, he attended community college in Sullivan County, north of the city. With no particular amateur success to buoy him, Golden still paced about like Hamlet, wondering aloud if he should turn professional and devote himself to becoming a tour player. One day, partly because he saw a license plate with the word "go" as part of its serial number, he decided to leave New York and move in with relatives near Miami. In his mid-20s by this point, Golden worked as a waiter and a substitute teacher while he practiced and took lessons from the eminent golf instructor Bob Toski. With calluses on his palms and a bit of money saved, Golden moved to San Diego to escape south Florida's summer heat. He signed on as an assistant at the Singing Hills golf resort and in spring of 1974 entered a series of local minitour events. In which, according to Golden, he finished "last, last, DQ, last, and second to last. My one bright spot was winning the San Diego City Putting Championship—yeah, there was such a thing."

It could only have been blind optimism that inspired him to travel to Monterey and enter a regional qualifier for the 1974 tour school. But Golden held his own against the other regional contestants, shooting 73–78–76 to keep his hopes alive in the 72-hole prelim. He was unlucky in his final-round tee assignment, however, getting stuck in the very last pairing of the afternoon. When he arrived to warm up, he found the club's entire stock of range balls already pounded into the distance, except for a few dwindling baskets soon to be emptied by the small clutch of players still practicing.

"This country club wasn't ready for a hundred guys to come through and each hit a million golf balls," said Golden, who proceeded to search for an employee who might drive the picker out and scoop him some ammunition. "There was no one around to help, and I was about to panic. Then I got a brilliant idea. I decided I would prepare for the round entirely in my head. I wouldn't use any balls, I would just picture the shot, set up, make the correct swing, and see the ball fly exactly where it should go." The term "creative visualization" was hardly current in golf coaching circles at the time, so Golden was indeed progressive. For 40 minutes, he carefully rehearsed every shot he was likely to face that day. On all the shots conceivably within range of the green, he etched in his mind an image of the ball flying perfectly up to the hole and dropping in. Working himself into an almost hypnotic state of positive thinking, Golden struck his last perfect imaginary shot. He shouldered his clubs and walked down the tee line—which was now completely empty of players—toward the clubhouse. Along the way he glanced down and spotted a range ball.

"One single, solitary ball," recalled Golden. "My first instinct was to hit it, but then I held back. I was thinking, don't spoil this perfect state of mind you're in." Golden, who has a spidery build, straight dark hair, and boyish looks, stood in his tracks until a reasonable notion occurred to him. Given his perfect state of mind, it was by all means predestined for the shot he hit with that one golf ball to be a magnificent one. He picked the ball up and rubbed it. Remaining in his mode of careful, specific rehearsal, Golden began to "dial in" the ideal drive for hole number 1, a high fade.

"I teed the ball up," he said, "and hit a wicked duck hook. High fade? Oh, no. A duck hook. Well, then I truly panicked. I started running out on the range, teeing up balls and hitting them, spraying them all over. When I got to the first tee I was a wreck. I went out there and after 12 holes I had lost five balls. The round was a disaster from the start."

Such a disaster, in fact, that Golden eventually rebelled against the pressure and began firing his shots almost at random. Nothing that the other players in his threesome were also out of contention, the street kid from Flatbush decided to show the PGA Tour what it could do with its qualifying school (bang), with its grueling pressure-cooker (smash), with its almighty American dream machine (kapow). When Golden's emotions were all spent and the round was over, his scorecard read in the triple digits. But he didn't have quite enough Brooklyn chutzpah to turn the score in at the tent. "I tore the card up," he confessed. "I didn't want to get kicked out of the PGA."

Golden's demolition-derby ride through his final 18 holes during first-stage qualifying in 1974 is a mere coda to the strikingly similar meltdown of Parker Smith. Also Brooklyn-raised (and perhaps this is no mere coincidence), Smith tried for the tour in 1968 and, after an early crisis, saw his attempt at qualifying devolve into a tragicomic odyssey preserved tersely in the record books by this line score:

Parker Smith, Memphis, Tenn.:
86–80–92–86–96–90–93–96—719

Smith is a singular figure in qualifying school annals—a one-visit wonder who appeared to have a legitimate shot of getting through, only to incur a freakish first-round mishap that led him to record one of the two or three worst performances in tour-qualifying history. That being said, Smith went on to enjoy what has been a satisfying career in the golf industry and actually looks back at his eight-round adventure in the spring of 1968 with sardonic pleasure.

"Pat Abbott, who was the head pro at Stonebridge Country Club in Memphis, got me set up to play in that qualifying school," recalled Smith, who is now 54 and lives in Lake Worth, Florida. He runs a company called Sports Opportunities International, which handles press events and media relations for companies that market golf products and services. "Pat knew me because I would sometimes play as a guest at Stonebridge. I had never played in any kind of important tournament, but I could beat just about anybody in Memphis, and in those days that was enough to make you a threat for the tour, I guess."

The rules governing what the PGA then called Approved Players put great emphasis on having respected PGA members vouching for the tour candidate. Abbott was influential on the national scene, and he detected in Smith enough natural talent to overcome the young man's paucity of experience. The two discussed Abbott's idea and came to a simple agreement: If Smith could show up the following Sunday and, playing with Abbott, shoot below par for 36 holes, they would go ahead with the plan for a Q School appearance at PGA National later that spring. Smith did just that, and the appropriate paperwork went down to headquarters. When the post office in Memphis received Smith's application and delivered it promptly to the correct address, it may have been the last thing to go as planned in his whole tour-qualifying experience.

Arriving in Palm Beach Gardens one evening a few days prior to the tournament, Smith searched without success for the motel where he held a reservation. "It wasn't at the address they gave me," he said, recalling his first night, "and it wasn't anywhere else. I never did find the place." He did find the parking lot of the PGA National golf course, where he stopped his car, climbed in the back seat, and fell asleep for the night. Though groggy from the long trip and the makeshift accommodations, he jumped straight into his preparations, playing a practice round with Cesar Sanudo and shooting a 4-under score of 68. The following day he played a practice round with Larry Hinson, a Georgian who by week's end would emerge as one of the 15 successful qualifiers. Again Smith shot 68.

Still, he remained much more in awe of his surroundings than of his own early form. Bob Dickson, that school's eventual medalist, was coming off victories in the U.S. and British Amateurs. By chance, Smith was standing near the caddie yard after his first practice round when Dickson approached him and asked Smith to caddie for him in Q School.

"When I told him I was one of the players, he got all embarrassed," said Smith. "I told him, 'Bob, don't worry about it, caddying for you would be the closest I could ever get to first place here.'" The other entrant Smith viewed with awe was Chuck Thorpe, older brother of another tour aspirant, Jim Thorpe. "Chuck would walk on the tee, drop his ball on the grass, and pound it with his driver. The guy never used a tee and he was still 25 yards longer than anybody else at the school."

Smith mustered a mighty drive of his own to start play in the opening round. His inspiration was rage, brought on by undesirable circumstances. To begin with, he had been assigned the very first starting time of the day and, by luck of the draw, was first man up in his threesome, as well. To make matters worse, his caddie showed up drunk. With a boozy bag-toter by his side and dense marine fog negating what little daylight there was to navigate by in the first place, Smith dug in his spikes. "I wanted to kill that caddie," Smith confessed. "So, I killed my drive instead.

Through all that fog and dew, it covered 310 yards. It was a par-5 hole and after my tee shot I had a 4-wood to the green." Smith parred the hole and congratulated himself for channeling his aggression. After seven holes, he was a stroke under par. There were moments of anxiety along the way, but no bungled shots. One of his playing partners, noting that cumulative scores of 16-over and 27-over had earned tour cards in the preceding two schools, told Smith to stay loose and he'd be a shoo-in.

The third player in the group had uttered nothing throughout that front nine except muffled curses at his own poor approach shots. The player, whom Smith would only identify as "Jimmy" in recounting the story, outdrove Smith on every hole but number 1 and still found himself scrambling for pars. On the fourth hole, Smith popped up his drive and had 200 yards to the green; Jimmy, meanwhile, laced a tremendous tee shot and had just a 9-iron left. Smith's 2-iron, from a fuzzy lie, flew on the green, and stopped within 30 inches of the cup, while the unfortunate Jimmy chunked his 9-iron into a greenside bunker.

"He got so pissed off he whipped his club at the golf cart he was driving, which broke the club and cracked the plastic roof of the cart," recalled Smith. "The other guy and I just looked at each other. He suggested we lodge a complaint, and I agreed, but we didn't do anything. On number 8, the same stupid thing happens. I sky another drive and Jimmy smacks one down the middle. It's a fairly short par 4 with an elevated green that has water in front and a bunker front left. I'm holding a 3-iron and playing a high cut shot, which turns out to be maybe the best golf shot of my entire life. It trickles by the hole and stops three feet away. Jimmy, who's about 6-over by now, can't stand it, and he of course dumps another one in the bunker.

"I go to read my putt," said Smith, "and I'm thinking, when this putt drops I'll be 2-under. I'm playing my head off and if I can keep it up maybe I'll just win this goddamn thing." Smith marked his ball and stepped back as his fuming fellow competitor hit an explosion shot that lifted not only his golf ball but a huge shower of sand out of the trap. The three-footer Smith needed for his birdie was above the hole, opposite the bunker Jimmy had just blasted from. All the same, a tiny pebble from Jimmy's sand plume had landed in Smith's line. Just as he was about to stroke the three-footer, Smith reached down with his left hand and flicked the pebble away. Then he returned to the ready position and drew his putter back.

"YOU'RE CHEATIN'!!" Jimmy suddenly bellowed. Smith's putter, already in motion, flashed forward at triple the intended force. His ball zipped past the hole, picking up speed as it rolled downhill, and spilled into the same bunker Jimmy had just departed. "You were testing the grain of the green!" Jimmy declared. He was still angry, but he was soon aware that his own wrath had been dwarfed by that of Parker Smith, who now held his putter caveman-style and was racing across the green in Jimmy's direction. Smith stopped short and roared a series of murderous threats. The commotion drew a rules official to the scene and Jimmy—his skull still intact—was disqualified on the spot. For Smith, there was no recourse available. "You and I both know," said the official, "that in golf there is no such thing as a do-over. So even though you probably deserve one I'm afraid you'll have to play your ball from that bunker." Parker Smith's notion of winning the 1968 tour school had suddenly and completely vanished, replaced by shock, outrage, and the growing sense that he should never have made the attempt.

"For somebody to do something like that, which to my knowledge has never been done any other time in competitive golf before or since, it had to be an act of God," Smith later mused. On the phone that night with Abbott, whom Smith knew to be devoutly religious, he put forth his divine-intervention theory, which Abbott seemed to accept. In an earlier postround call to his father, Parker had "cried his eyes out" over the incident and the stumbling 49 he had shot on the back side, for his unthinkable 86. By his recollection, Smith played reasonably well the second day, managing an 80, but by then doubt had hold of him. He was playing on the same field with Bob Dickson and Hale Irwin and Mike Hill, and he didn't belong there. He showed up for the third round and gouged out a 92.

"It got worse and worse," noted Smith. "My caddie kept showing up just as drunk as the day before. Eventually I fired him and jumped in a cart with Arnie Tining, this real nice guy from Denmark who had never ridden in a golf cart before. He was way out of it, too. [Tining's eight-round score of 670, though 49 strokes better than Smith's, placed him second to last in the school.] We made up games, like hit it off that tree, skip it over that pond. Arnie kept driving the cart in big circles up and down the fairway."

Telling this story for perhaps the first time in many years, Smith voiced regret only about his two fine practice rounds and the effect they'd had on him. If he had struggled during practice instead of shooting the two 68s, he would have been more able to simply dismiss what happened later as a freakish event. Instead, he has been forced to examine it for deeper meaning.

"Think about that," wondered Smith, "a man bellowing at you as loud as he can while you're taking a stroke. What it told me was that I didn't belong on tour. It wasn't the life I was intended for."

A week later Smith was drafted and told to await orders that would send him to Vietnam in a tank corps. That's when, in Smith's words, "Golf saved my life." He was stationed at Fort Monmouth in New Jersey, an Army base equipped with a challenging golf course. Soon after arriving on the base, Smith unpacked his clubs and walked onto the first tee.

"It was for officers only, and there I was, a PFC," he said. "Some general watched me play a hole and asked me what I thought I was doing. He couldn't play a lick, and I was hitting everything pure. I suggested we play together, and I'd give him lessons. He said okay, but to seal the deal I had to break par for 18 holes right then and there, with him watching me. If I could do that," said Smith, "the general would let me give him lessons and play the course whenever I wanted. And oh, by the way, he could probably get me out of that tank corps headed for 'Nam." Smith shot under par that afternoon and remained happily stateside throughout the Vietnam War, playing golf and producing Army newscasts and training films. Amazingly enough, he does not consider himself to be a contestant who suffered the most extreme psychological damage in the Q School of spring '68. That distinction, in Smith's opinion, goes to a player named Walter Postlewait of Homestead, Florida, whom the official results list as having withdrawn.

"From what I heard, Walter had recently won the Florida Amateur title," explained Smith. "Then he turned pro and showed up at Q School. By the time he got through 16 holes, the guy had completely cracked under the pressure. I guess he was on his way to shooting 120 or more. The officials had to carry him off the 17th tee and bring him to the clubhouse. He couldn't take the club back—couldn't hardly move. It was really sad." Parker's distant recall of this withdrawal-under-duress was checked against the recall of Postlewait's son, Walter, Jr., a PGA pro who goes by the nickname Rusty. True to the Q School irony machine, Rusty had himself made a recent attempt at PGA Tour qualifying. He reported getting knocked out in the first stage of tour school in 1995, although he felt he and Walter, Sr., still qualified as a rare "father-son combination" of tour aspirants. As for details of the 1968 school appearance by Walter, Sr., the son said only that he had not been in recent contact with his father, who could perhaps be tracked down at an auto dealership in Las Vegas.

Innocent Q School dreamers are much more numerous than barbarians like Smith's Jimmy, but Peter Jacobsen, like Smith before him, managed to run into one. Jacobsen's experience at the fall 1976 Q School stands out in his mind all the more because he has never had to repeat the process. But the behavior of his playing partner, a classic Q School interloper named Eric Edelman, is something Jake won't ever forget.

"That school was held at Rancho Viejo Country Club, down in Brownsville, Texas," said Jacobsen, winner of over $5 million in 20-plus years on tour. "They paired me with this guy Eric Edelman, who couldn't break 90 and who eventually got thrown out for cheating. That was the year it snowed, hailed, and sleeted. I think the final field was about 1,000 players. Sound like fun?" Though Jacobsen overstates the size of the field, his passage through tour qualifying did come during the brief era in which the twice-yearly finals were reinstated and regional qualifiers were temporarily abandoned. In the first decade of Q School play, the average field for a final had always been fewer than 80 players. That number had more than quadrupled, to 349, by the time of the Brownsville school, creating the confusing, throng atmosphere that pervades the event to this day—even though recent final-stage fields have been closer to 170 or 180.

Jacobsen arrived at the fall 1996 final-stage qualifier at age 22, having just turned pro following a successful but unspectacular amateur career. A native of Portland, he had spent his college years at the University of Oregon and was never financially able to go barnstorming in the summertime from one major amateur event to the next. He worked instead at the A. J. Davis & Sons plumbing-and-heating supply house, wheeling handtrucks loaded with copper pipe and thermostats. The owner of the business, Stan Davis, encouraged Jacobsen to take time off one summer for the British Amateur at St. Andrews, but otherwise Jake fell behind contemporaries like Curtis Strange, Craig Stadler, and Ben Crenshaw in tournament experience. The public would eventually come to know Jacobsen as an outstanding ball-striker, host of his own high-profile charity tournament, and lead singer for the semipro rock band Jake Trout and the Flounders. But the confidence Jacobsen exudes in all those settings was in short supply at Brownsville.

"I played scared," Jacobsen admitted. "I expected the pressure to be intense, but when you add the miserable weather and the fact that I was due to get married two weeks later, it was hard for me to play any kind of good golf."

By far the worst distraction he faced, according to Jacobsen, "was having to keep the card of a cheater for the first two rounds." Edelman appeared on the tee at Rancho Viejo for the first round with a black eye, a crust of beard on his cheeks, and a torn T-shirt as his golf attire. "I'm thinking, what is going on here? This is a pro golf tournament?" recalled Jacobsen. "Turns out Eric had spent most of the previous night at a bar in Tijuana, which is just over the border from Brownsville. I guess he wasn't much better a fighter than he was a golfer. We found out later that he got into a brawl, staggered out of the bar, and came straight to the golf course.

"What's sad is, he's got his father forecaddying for him, helping him cheat," Jacobsen groaned. "The very first hole he tees up and drives it into what looks like deep rough. When we got up there his ball is in this real nice spot and he's got a clear shot to the green. It seems his dad is up there ahead of him dropping balls down his pant leg, and by now the old man is pretty skilled at it. Finally they DQ'd my friend Eric. I found out later he had been DQ'd from Q Schools before this one, but somehow he kept getting back in."

Today, any tour hopeful with no exemption into second-stage or third-stage qualifying is required to cough up not just his $4,000 Q School entry fee but letters of reference from two different PGA professionals. By filing this entry fee and a completed application form, any player who had previously been an amateur declares himself a professional. Since it is dealing only with pros, the PGA Tour sets no maximum allowable handicap for Q School entrance. The letters of reference serve as a low-tech throwback to the Approved Tournament Player era that preceded Q School, but they do help protect the tour against embarrassingly high first-stage scores shot by deluded young men with $4,000 to burn.

In the freewheeling days before the "all-exempt" policy, many golfers entered the tour qualifier and showed up for open qualifying on Mondays basically as a lark. "Even in the early '80s, when we ran first-stage qualifying at Bear Creek in Dallas," said Gary Dee, the facility's former director of golf, "one-third to one-half the guys were there just to say they once played in a Q School."

For a player like Ken Ellsworth, who had an obscure but legitimate pro tour career, it can prove somewhat irritating to have his golf background brought up in the presence of a one-shot Q Schooler or the acquaintance of someone who barely broke 80 in his lone attempt at Monday qualifying decades prior.

"I don't bring it up very often," said Ellsworth, "but every once in a while in a group of people I'll refer to the fact that I played the tour for a few years. And no matter what, there always seems to be someone who says, 'Oh well, you must know my boyfriend, he played the tour back then, too.' What they mean is the guy played in a couple of Monday qualifiers 20 years ago. I usually just smile and try to move on.

"But sometimes they press it and say his name is Joe whatever, then it's like it's your fault you don't know the guy. You just want to turn to them and say, 'Joe? Oh yeah, Joe. Never heard of him."

7

ONE TRIP THROUGH, OR 17

Seventeen Louisville Slugger baseball bats would have cost Mac O'Grady $200 or more back in 1982, but the relief they brought him made the lumber well worth its price. After hauling the bats home from the sporting goods store, Q School's most famous repeat customer took a felt-tip marker and labeled the barrel of each one with a month and year.

"Seventeen bats for the 17 different times I went to tour school," O'Grady said, nodding calmly, when asked about the oft-told anecdote. "I picked them up in chronological order and smashed them to pieces against a huge tree. *That's* a true story," he added. "A lot of things have been written about me, and most of it has been lies, but that one's true."

Exploring the gloomy caverns of tour schools past, one naturally trains a lantern on repeat participants—and in that category O'Grady is the prime specimen. His 0-for-16 streak took place over a 10-year period when, for the most part, Q School was being conducted every spring and fall. On that basis, we could view

O'Grady's struggles as being just half as protracted as they would have been in a one-school-per-year era. Looked at another way, his Q School failures were twice as frequent as they otherwise might have been.

Contemplating the toil and trouble of a tour school returnee like Mac O'Grady, it is sometimes hard to remember there have been players who showed up to qualify, played well, earned eligibility, then rattled off 20 or 30 straight years in the champagne district of the tour money list—never to cycle back through qualifying again. Nonsuperstar players like Jay Haas, Tom Purtzer, and Bruce Lietzke are good examples. Each went through one qualifying tournament more than 20 years ago and each has retained his eligibility ever since. And unlike another nonsuperstar from the same era, Mike Reid (Reid has enjoyed 10-year exemptions two different times for winning the PGA Championship and the World Series of Golf), Haas, Purtzer, and Lietzke have renewed their credentials annually, or at most two years at a time, taking advantage of the two-year exemption players automatically receive for winning an official tournament.

But O'Grady, for more than a decade, was the PGA Tour's lion in summer, stalking the pampas grass beyond the close-cropped fields where titles and prize money are contested. Hatchet-faced, and hoarse now in a Dylanesque way, he still warms to the Q-and-A rhythms of an interview and still exerts a peculiar draw upon his listener. O'Grady on his soapbox combines an aura of priestly inspiration with a trace of the campus-radical paranoia he still nurtures. Mac's head tilts and his eyes widen with each oblique accusation, and at times they seem to shine as if flecks of neon were embedded in each iris. Financial woes, reconstructive back surgery, and time's passage have covered O'Grady with the battle scars that at last seem to justify his youthful insurrection against the PGA Tour and other forms of authority. In an era

when the tag of "rebel" has been applied to tour veterans lob-
bying meekly for recognition of their fledgling Tournament Players Association, O'Grady's ad hominen outbursts against Deane
Beman (commissioner of the tour during Mac's prime in the mid-
1980s) seem even more incendiary and over the top than when
he first launched them.

In those years, O'Grady burned with multiple ambitions. He
had redesigned his swing through an intense collaboration with
a Seattle engineer and physicist named Homer Kelley, one of several mentors and father figures Mac turned to during his youth
and early manhood, and the only one, according to O'Grady, who
repaid his trust. Kelley's 28-year study of the golf swing had cul-
minated in his arcane, self-published book, *The Golfing Machine*,
first released in 1969 to a mixture of derision and awestruck
praise.

Although O'Grady had been coached as a boy by an L.A. eminence, Walter Keller (who also mentored LPGA Hall-of-Famer
Amy Alcott), Mac's mechanics were not sound. Other pros—
Bobby Clampett most notably—have borne the label of "Golfing
Machine player." But to see O'Grady in action is to visually comprehend Kelley's post-Sputnik system of compounded levers and
retained angles. Mac thrived as a Kelley disciple and imagined
himself not only winning pro tournaments (he would win two,
the 1986 Greater Hartford Open and the 1987 Tournament of
Champions), but changing the sport of golf as he went. He aimed
to become the world's foremost authority on golf-swing biomechanics and then use his credibility as a player and teacher to
spread an alternative, noncorporate image of pro golf. Years of
Asian travel and competition had opened him up to non-Western
philosophies, and when he listed "modern times, sciences, history" under the interests-and-hobbies section of his tour profile,
he was serious.

O'Grady's wiry power and sweetly tuned swing gave him cult status among leading golf teachers and instruction-magazine editors, especially once he began his move up the money list. *Golf Digest* even published swing sequences of O'Grady's right-handed and his equally impressive left-handed swing in a splashy fold-out spread. Quoting his fiery comments also helped publishers sell magazines. In recent years, however, O'Grady has been inclined to connect his erratic behavior to a dysfunctional, abusive upbringing rather than to a legitimate philosophical cause. "It was a defense mechanism on my part to act crazy," he acknowledged. "I spent a lot of time as a kid being scared. I grew up in an oppressive environment." He cuts himself a pass on the baseball-bat smashing, however. "I had to get that tour-school frustration out of my system," he said, "and I'd say that was a clever way to do it. It was kind of cute, really."

Around 1986, O'Grady began promising that his own forthcoming treatise on the physics and biomechanics of the golf swing would render all other instruction manuals obsolete. Nearly 15 years later, he is still touting his manuscript and projecting future publication dates for it. At the 1996 Greater Hartford Open, a tournament he plays regularly as an exempt past champion, O'Grady spoke in stirring fashion about his decade of tour school disappointments, and about a breakthrough moment during one of his many failed attempts at qualifying in the mid-1970s.

"It was the fourth round and I was inside the cut by a couple of shots with a few holes to play," he recalled. "I had a three-footer for par and it power-lipped on me. That left me with another three-footer, and I choked on it. Couldn't breathe as I was addressing the ball. The next hole, I wasn't together, and I made double-bogey. Finished with a par somehow and missed the cut by one shot.

"I went off by myself and cried. I bawled out the tears for 30 minutes straight. Then I stopped crying, and after a few seconds I heard a voice that calmed me. The voice said, 'Greater things have I in store for you.' It was then that I developed my total passion for golf," said O'Grady. "My love for learning and for playing was never as strong before that day as after it." Even before his epiphany with the divine voice, O'Grady's pure love of the game had made it possible for him to endure the repeated trials of tour qualifying.

"People have always asked me, 'How could you go back that many times and try to qualify?' " he said. "The answer is, I was able to do it because I never developed a phobia about Q School. Q School was just a test I had to go through if I wanted to play golf at the top professional level." Golf, according to O'Grady, had already shown itself to be the hardest to learn, the least attainable of games. Suffering as a child in what he has called "an abusive family environment," Phil McGleno (that was O'Grady's original name) was at first gratified to discover that sports like football or track and field came easily to him. Not so with golf, which he speaks of as a proud, demanding goddess.

"Golf tested my faith from the beginning," he explained. "I gave it everything I had for so long and had no success. Friends and family gave up on me. I would go to sleep at night and in my dreams I was beating everyone. But the game demanded more."

O'Grady's breakthrough took place at the 1982 tour school, which was held at the Tournament Players Club in Ponte Vedra, the PGA Tour's much publicized new headquarters facility, complete with its backbreaking Pete Dye golf course. No fewer than 50 tour cards were handed out at this qualifier—a dozen more than at any of the previous 16 Q Schools O'Grady attended. But by no means did he finally hop the bar simply because the tour decided to temporarily lower it. Despite a dismal opening-round

79, O'Grady rallied to finish tied for fourth, right behind Nick Price and far ahead of players like Loren Roberts, Ken Green, Jeff Sluman, and Blaine McCallister. One of the four other players who tied O'Grady for fourth, Bob Boyd, ended up being paired with Mac at some of the 1983 season's early events.

"There was no reshuffle back then," explained Boyd, referring to the tour's practice of refiguring the pecking order of Q School grads based on their early-season performance, "so Mac and I found ourselves paired together a lot."

Boyd, a Carolina gentleman who would not in his wildest dreams call the PGA Tour a soulless, multinational corporation and its commissioner a fascist dictator, had great admiration for the nonconformist who would publicly utter these accusations. "Mac was a guy on a search," observed Boyd. "He was well schooled in the golf swing and his own swing was beautiful to watch. But he was very tough on himself. He demanded absolute perfection." As for the stigma of having washed out of 16 tour schools before finally gaining exemption, Boyd said it eventually became a plus.

"The fact that he was a 17-timer at tour school was always coming up in interviews," said Boyd. "Mac actually relished the fact that he had tried so many times. He was proud that he hadn't quit, and people picked up on that. He got almost a celebrity status out of his Q School story."

There was poetic justice in O'Grady's 1998 appearance in Sutton, Massachusetts, for the last-ever playing of the New England (aka Bank of Boston) Classic, an event that is finally gone from the PGA Tour schedule after years of bad feeling between the PGA Tour and the Mingolla family, which owns the Pleasant Valley Country Club and spearheaded the tournament for over three decades. His day of practice completed, Mac was engaged in a solitary cool-down exercise. He stood spread-legged about

18 inches from a waist-high spectator rope, amusing himself by flipping sand-wedge shots lightly over the braid of yellow nylon. During his update on the State of O'Grady he lifted his golf shirt up in back to reveal a skid mark of a scar down his spine.

"They did a four-bone fusion on me," he said. "I couldn't swing, couldn't do anything, my left foot was basically paralyzed. Now I'm back to where I was two years ago." Amazingly, O'Grady has set off on a major comeback from his exile to the teaching ranks by sailing through the 1998 European PGA Tour qualifier and, at age 48, gaining a full exemption. If he was not a golfer-without-a-country before 1999—if his wanderings on the Asian and Japanese tours, his Japanese wife, his name change, his complete ambidexterity as a golfer, his public repudiation of Beman and company weren't eccentric and alienating enough—then O'Grady's relocation to the European men's tour so late in his career clinches the deal.

O'Grady's next tour school in the United States, if he enters one, will be for the senior circuit. From that perspective, he views the qualifying process in terms that remain clear and simple. "It's more about ability than about anything intangible," he argued. "You just have to be good enough. You take the top 125 on the money list from any year, and send them all back to Q School, I would say 110 would requalify. They have the skill and the experience, and they'd make it through."

Having been asked so many times about his 17 trips back, O'Grady is prone to mention some of his fellow returnees, players like R. W. Eaks and David Peoples. To O'Grady, Peoples is an intrepid kinsmen, a warrior who found himself stuck in the qualify/lose-the-card cycle while O'Grady was enjoying his half-decade of success. Fittingly enough, Peoples earned medalist honors and the $15,000 first-prize money in the last of the nine qualifiers he entered from 1981 to 1989. He built on that breakthrough by finishing comfortably in the top 60 of the money list for several years. Then Peoples ran dry again, and while sponsor exemptions helped keep him active, the qualifying process loomed anew in 1998. On yet another pass through the qualifying mill, Peoples posted a four-round score of 290 in second-stage qualifying at the Grenelefe Resort in Haines City, Florida. The score needed to survive second stage at Grenelefe was 287, so Peoples, nearing age 39 and with only $70,000 in earnings over the previous three seasons, found himself on the outs for 1999.

But at least he never shied from the challenge—that's the view O'Grady takes. Mac is fond of turning the how-could-you question around and asking about players who could have and maybe should have gone back to requalify, but chose not to, writing for sponsor exemptions instead of braving the scrum.

"How about players like Jerry Pate, Howard Twitty, Peter Jacobsen?" he asked rhetorically, lifting an eyebrow. "They lost their cards and we didn't see them coming back through. What about those guys? Why couldn't *they* go back?"

Then there are the players who never had to go back. For them, tour school is still a scary ladder to climb, but they have the privilege of picturing it in a far-off place and their own careers as surely beyond its creeping shadow.

Ben Crenshaw shot 68 to start out the 1973 school, got his card, and still hasn't given it up. Fuzzy Zoeller was medalist in 1974 and hasn't had to requalify in the quarter century since. Fred Couples fired a 67 at Fresno in the first round of the fall 1980 tour school, made it by a single shot and never looked back. Mark O'Meara, a member of that same "graduating class" (to use the PGA Tour's own quaint expression), now looks like a lock to complete his career as a one-time-only qualifier. "At the end of my second year I filled out the application and sent my money in for tour school," O'Meara recently commented. "I was so close to the 125th spot [he would finish 118th on the money list in 1982] there was no way to be sure I'd stay exempt." Hal Sutton and Larry Mize are in the same general category as O'Meara, having qualified together at Huntsville, Texas, in fall of 1981 and kept their exempt status ever since.

Mize, Sutton, and O'Meara are prominent players who caught the tail end of the Monday-qualifying era. Mize shot 77–71–72– 75 at Huntsville for a score of 295 that was well over par but one stroke better than needed to get in. "I made it by the skin of my teeth," said Mize when asked to recall the week. "I wasn't worried about where I finished, I just wanted to get my card and get out here." His year as a Monday qualifier was a "wonderful experience," according to the 1987 Masters champion. He went the full West Coast swing without getting into a tournament, then proceeded to make 13 cuts out of 28 starts and scrape together nearly $29,000 in purse money.

Hal Sutton went from his standout college career at Centenary in Shreveport, Louisiana, to the fall 1981 School at Waterwood Country Club. He qualified that year and quickly became a star on tour. Sutton's 1983 PGA Championship title made him exempt from tour qualifying through 1993, a decade-long waiver that in the end became something of a sword of Damocles for him. He was a regular top-30 finisher for the first eight of those years, and never lower than 88th until 1992, when he finished deep in the weeds at 185th. The next year, his last of the 10-year exemption, Sutton faltered again, finishing 161st. He then exercised his right, as one of the top 50 all-time career money winners, to be classified as exempt under that status. This bylaw remains in effect but has been restricted to the top 25 career money winners. Playing in 29 tournaments during the 1994 campaign, Sutton mounted a stirring comeback that earned him $540,162 and returned him to the top 30 money winners for the season. He had dallied with the prospect of repeating tour school, but by the late 1990s his continued success made that prospect seem immaterial. "I was able to put tour school out of my mind and just move ahead with my career," he said, in retrospect. "But I'll never forget the shot I had to hit to get my card in the first place."

Sutton, still thick-haired and thickly muscled at 39, easily recalls Waterwood's number 17, a par 3 that plays 230 yards from the back tees over water.

"It's essentially an island green, because it's got water in front, water left, and a bunker with a stone wall next to it on the right. If you hit it there, you're dead." When Sutton and his playing partners reached the hole for their sixth straight competitive round, they were well aware of the trouble around the green. What stunned them was the trouble around the tee: five groups waiting. It is something of a tour-school tradition for rules officials to let pace-of-play regulations go unenforced. To begin with, the field is too large for a few officials to cover, so by definition the few players who might be singled out among the slow-moving masses would be justified in charging unfairness. Secondly, the officials simply can't bring themselves to put any added pressure on a contestant.

"Where I stood in the field, I figured I was safe by two shots and there wouldn't be any trouble making par on number 18," said Sutton. "I took out my 1-iron and said to my caddie, 'Eighteen is not the problem—it's this shot here. My whole next year is riding on it.'" Forty minutes later, he began practice-swinging that 1-iron in earnest, searching his imagination for some way to keep his composure. When it was his turn, Sutton took his stance, swung the club, and knocked his shot 10 feet from the hole. Two putts later he had his par and a 72-hole score of 294, which was two shots inside that year's number for PGA Tour eligibility.

When Billy Mayfair came to his one and only Q School, the 1988 tournament at PGA West and La Quinta Resort, he was widely expected to make it through with ease. Mayfair's résumé included victories in the 1987 U.S. Amateur and the 1986 U.S. Amateur Public Links. At La Quinta, he had rounds of 66 and 69 in the course of the six-round school, and those two low rounds carried him safely to his tour eligibility, which he has kept ever since.

But day one of Q School was anything but a breeze for Mayfair. Feeling a hint of the jitters, he hit his tee shot on the first hole out of bounds. Still lamenting this classic opening blunder, he motored down the fairway in his golf cart, strategizing about how to save bogey. These thoughts were interrupted by the smell of smoke coming from his cart. Mayfair dismounted from the buggy and watched as flames began appearing through the seams in its melting fiberglass body. He grabbed his clubs from the back of the cart and stepped away. Shaken, he nonetheless finished out the day with a respectable 73. Within two years, Mayfair would find himself 12th on the tour money list and on his way to a stellar career.

Back in 1968, when the talent gap at tour school was still fairly large, a true natural like Jerry Heard could honestly live by the old saying "you don't have to play great golf to get your card at Q School." Amid the players who chafed and trembled, Heard yawned through three straight 71s in the eight-round event's early going. By midweek, he was so far inside the safety zone he could scrape out a 76 and a 77 and barely lose his spot on the scoreboard. In rounds six and seven, Heard tidied up his act and carded 74–73. When heavy winds and rain greeted the field on the eighth and final round, Heard went into rocking-chair mode and squeegeed out a healthy round of 80. That was good for 593, a full 10 strokes inside the make-miss line.

"I was kind of a hotshot from my area," admitted Heard, whose pride was not wounded in the least by his 8-over final round. "After eight rounds, we were all a little frustrated and tired. Plus, I just knew I had it made. You could look at the board and pretty much figure what it's gonna take." All week, in fact, Heard had the sense he would not have to go through this tour-school thing a second time. Anxiety and tour school are practically synonomous, but Heard brought a distinctly California attitude to the event.

"It was actually a nice trip," he said. "I did more fishing than I did practicing that week. Ken Ellsworth and I would head over to this great little inlet and fish for blues. That fishing hole," said Heard, "was right on the spot where Jack Nicklaus's house is now. Kenny and I went down there all week. We had a lot of fun at tour school that year."

Mark McCumber is neither a one-time wonder nor, obviously, a captive of Q School Purgatory. His story is one of lofty success that somehow wrestled itself out of what looked like protracted failure. The spring 1978 qualifier at Albuquerque, New Mexico, was McCumber's sixth trip to the tour's casting couch, and after rounds of 70–69–73 he appeared ready for a role in the big show. On close inspection, McCumber's temperment—a mix of sincere humility and high personal expectations—is well suited to the pro-golf existence. In 1954, when Mark was three years old, his father moved the family to a house in Jacksonville, Florida, that bordered a public golf course. Neither parent was a golfer, but they liked the notion of exposing their sons to golf both as a game and a place of employment.

The McCumber boys, who grew up to become golf course owners and managers, started out digging weeds by the bucketful to earn a summer day's playing privileges—and eventually became regular members of the maintenance crew. Later, to fulfill their duties as members of the Seventh Day Adventist faith, they would dress in dark suits and walk door to door through the Florida heat spreading the faith. McCumber arrived in the New Mexico heat that June morning knowing even a middling score would get him through. He even projected the maximum score he felt he could balloon up to without scuttling his chances. That estimated number was 81 or 82, and as things turned out an 82 to go with his 70–69–73 start would have been exactly good enough to make it.

"I was in a better frame of mind that tour school because I knew I had improved my game. I was more ready," he recalled. "I had been the medalist at my regional qualifier, which gave me some more confidence. But even with a big cushion on that last day, you can't help being nervous," McCumber admits. "I managed to hit a decent drive off the first tee and keep myself out of trouble through the early holes. Then I got to number 8 and made a bogey. I three-putted."

McCumber walked off the eighth green feeling suddenly spooked. Negative thinking is just as treacherous as sports psychologists say it is, but it's also the seed of some dramatic flights of imagination. McCumber's pessimism had been kept in check through the first 62 holes of the 72 to be played, but when it broke loose it did so with a flourish of creativity. The thought actually crossed McCumber's mind that his bogey on number 8 was perfectly timed, if he were planning to bogey in from there, shoot an ungodly 82 and put himself "on the number," as the players say.

"Here's where it all falls apart—for a second that's all I could think," he says. But this bolt of fear somehow focused McCumber, and he rattled off a pair of birdies to find himself under par on the back side. When the milk horse sees the stable, he tends to loosen his gait and make better time. McCumber let himself ex-

Carl Paulson, a onetime Q School medalist, returned to the annual qualifier in 1999. Paulson, far right, joined a few fans at the PGA West scoreboard to take stock of his progress. (Photo courtesy of Mitchell Haddad)

Having wives and children with you for a Q School final serves as either a happy distraction from the grind or a telling reminder of the breadwinner's burden. This child's innocent toddling at the 1999 final surely offered some form of inspiration. (Photo courtesy of Mitchell Haddad)

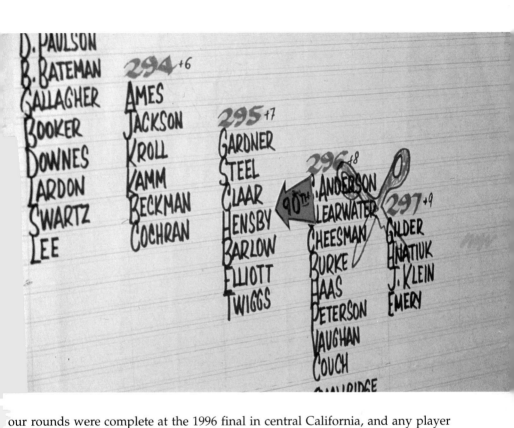

D. PAULSON
B. BATEMAN 294 +6
GALLAGHER AMES
BOOKER JACKSON 295 +7
DOWNES KROLL GARDNER
LARDON KAMM STEEL
SWARTZ BECKMAN CLAAR 296 +8
LEE COCHRAN HENSBY ANDERSON 297 +9
BARLOW CLEARWATER GILDER
90TH
ELLIOTT CHEESMAN HNATIUK
TWIGGS BURKE J. KLEIN
HAAS EMERY
PETERSON
VAUGHAN
COUCH

our rounds were complete at the 1996 final in central California, and any player with an average score of 74 or higher was cut from the field. The dreaded scissors con—retired the following year when the four-round cut was eliminated, can be seen over the recognizable name of former star Keith Clearwater, among others. (Photo courtesy of Mitchell Haddad)

Every lipped-out putt and incorrect club choice gets replayed in the mind of a pro who is "on the number" at Q School finals. Surrounded by fans who are intrigued by the entire field's ups and downs, this aspiring tour player pensively assesses the fate of one contestant only. (Photo courtesy of Mitchell Haddad)

Beginning with junior tournaments and on through high school, college, and to the pro level, parents of a would-be tour player do their best to encourage and support without making themselves conspicuous. This couple at La Purisma Golf Club in Lompoc, California, endure the scoreboard-watching ritual as Q School 1996 winds to a close. (Photo courtesy of Mitchell Haddad)

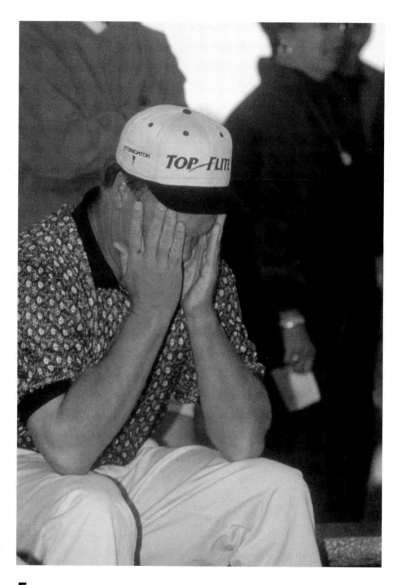

For about one-third of its forty-year history, tour qualifying was conducted on a twice-yearly basis. Beginning in the early '80s though, one chance a year is now all you get. For this exhausted Q Schooler, the prospect of twelve more months on the sidelines appears difficult to bear. (Photo courtesy of Mitchell Haddad)

Calligraphy with a dash of cruelty covers the Q School scoreboard as an assortment of fans, players, family, and caddies drifts in and out of the scoreboard pavilion. At the 1996 finals on California's rugged central coast, rain delays and Q School's only weather-shortened final added to the anguish. (Photo courtesy of Mitchell Haddad)

Mike Standly, who had been a frequent contestant at tour school finals throughout the 1990s, was forced to return again in 1996 despite having "broken through" and becoming a tournament winner on the PGA Tour. Standly survived his 1996 final exam, as well as finishing four strokes inside the number. (Photo courtesy of Mitchell Haddad)

Surely the most dramatic back story to Q School in 1998 was the requalifying mission embarked upon by Dave Stockton, Jr., who had left the PGA Tour early in the season to see his expectant wife through a harrowing pregnancy and stay with her as their premature baby fought back for months against extreme post-natal trauma. By the time mother and child were finally home and well, Stockton had golf firmly in perspective. With his famous father watching, Junior took care of business in Palm Desert and earned back his tour card. (Photo courtesy of Mitchell Haddad)

With its cast of obscure characters and late-November or early-December dates, Q School finals, ruefully called "The Fall Classic," receives scant press coverage. In 1998, however, Haines City, Florida, became the dateline for a series of national news stories covering the unsuccessful qualifying efforts of Casey Martin. Martin, who suffers from a progressive circulatory condition in his lower leg, won an injunction against the PGA Tour just before arriving at Grenelefe Resort to compete for his tour card. The legal victory, which allowed Martin to ride in a golf cart, was widely cheered by advocates for the disabled. (Photo courtesy of Mitchell Haddad)

When Q School was first conducted in the mid-1960s, touring life
was difficult and purse money relatively small. Many players pos-
sessing unusual amounts of raw talent, including New York native
Jim Albus, gave Q School one or two tries then found steady work
at a country club or elsewhere. Albus, who went to Q School once
as a young man, waited a generation later before emerging on the
Senior PGA Tour as a bona fide star. (Photo courtesy of Paul Lester)

Another rare player with the ability to generally defuse the pressure of a Q School final was Bill Glasson, who said of himself in hindsight that he was "either too smart or too stupid" to let the six-round grind get to him. (Photo courtesy of Andres Sone)

With enough talent to compete with the best but not enough to beat them, Harry Taylor became one of several Q School constants during the '80s and '90s. Through sheer repetition, Taylor was able to turn Q School from a cauldron of pressure into—in his words—"just, you know, something I did in the fall." (Photo courtesy of Andres Sone)

Three decades after the original PGA Q School of 1965, the name that jumps out from the short list of qualifiers is Jim Colbert. Colbert's career on the regular tour was far more successful than that of his classmates, but merely a warm-up act for the stellar years he would enjoy as a senior tour player. (Photo courtesy of Paul Lester)

Hal Sutton represents a level of tour talent that would require only one pass through Q School but not quite translate into superstardom. For a few seasons, Sutton was one of golf's top players, then problems with his swing nearly finished him. In the late '90s, the Louisiana native—who had to wait forty-five minutes to hit the 1–iron shot over water that earned him his card at Q School—has regained his original championship form. (Photo courtesy of Paul Lester)

A member of the graduating class at the largest and perhaps most chaotic tour school finals ever—at Brownsville, Texas, in 1976— Peter Jacobsen never looked back. For Jake, the worst part of the cold, windy, mosquito-plagued Brownsville school "was having to keep the scorecard of a cheater for two rounds." (Photo courtesy of Paul Lester)

hale. "I did relax at that point," he confesses. "I was playing with Wren Lum, the eventual medalist, and I remember thinking that from there on I was just playing against Wren to win the thing." Lum diddled home with a 73 while McCumber cooked up a 69, but it came up two strokes short of first prize. End of story, except McCumber's imagination wouldn't let go, at least not during the uncensored hours that come with deep sleep. He composed, in his unconscious, a classic Q School nightmare.

"In the dream I kept having, the thing I was afraid of really happens," he explained. "I blow up and make a string of bogeys and I end up shooting that 82. I walk off the 18th and I can't hardly speak. I'm sure the field has caught me and passed me so I flip my card on the table without saying anything. A while later I'm walking around in a daze and a guy asks me what did I shoot. I tell him my total, and he congratulates me. I'm like, 'for what?' The guy says, you know, 290 or whatever the score was, 'that makes it!' "

College students who have dreamed they totally forgot about one of their final-semester courses until the week before graduation can empathize with what comes next. "I start running like a madman back toward the scorer's tent. I have to find that scorecard and sign it so it's official," McCumber narrated, his eyes widening. "When I get up to where the officials are, there's a big crowd around and I'm just fighting to get through it. 'My scorecard's in there,' I'm yelling. 'Let me get through, let me through.' " Naturally, this is where McCumber would wake up, stare into the darkness, and—especially as the seasons went by—begin laughing at himself.

"I never lost my exemption after 1978," said McCumber, whose undersized frame would eventually succumb to a passel of golf-related injuries, at the same time his course-design-and-management business was flourishing and thus requiring more time. "But I had that awful dream three or four times a year for about a decade. Eventually I'd laugh about it because I had all these successful seasons and yet part of my brain was still stuck back in the qualifying process. Now if that doesn't tell you how big an impression tour school makes, I don't know what does."

8

FIRST DAY OF SCHOOL

On day one of Q School's final stage, a reporter carrying a notepad finds himself in a position comparable to the apartment dweller who keeps a high-powered telescope by his window. Is that telescope for studying the constellations, his friends wonder, or for peering into apartments across the way? The Q School crowd on day one has a diverse, fairgrounds feel to it, but 99 percent of the people who show up are there because they have to be. Anyone who arrives voluntarily comes under automatic suspicion, like a *Playboy* subscriber who says he values the magazine's political coverage, or the hockey fan who claims to prefer a finesse game over vicious body checks and bloody brawls.

On day one, the Q School stage is set for eventual misery— not the kind that loves company, either. Other golf tournaments, from the Anderson Consulting Match Play to the U.S. Open to the PGA Championship, get under way merely hoping to deliver fateful twists and turns and a dramatic ending. But you may re-

call that when the first Anderson tournament ended with Jeff
Maggert playing Andrew Magee for the title, critics declared it a
dud. When our U.S. Open champ turns out to be a player like
Andy North or Scott Simpson, the gallery moans. Likewise with
the PGA, when someone like the talented, hardworking, but relatively unexciting Vijay Singh comes in first. There are only four
majors a year, and we're always hoping for, you know, Tiger-or-
somebody.

But the final stage of tour school has zero chance of fizzling.
Victims are guaranteed; heroes, too. Among its losers and survivors there will be overconfident veterans and frightened first-
timers and every kind of pro in between. Most of the Sturm
und Drang will take place in the final round, but along the way
there will be road kill every few miles, beginning on day one.
And while Harry Taylor may be the only player who approaches
Q School as though it were a single 108-hole tournament that runs
continuously except for six eat-and-sleep time-outs, his approach
makes sense. A foolish double-bogey on Wednesday morning
costs a player just as much as the one that happens on Monday
afternoon.

On day one of Q School 1997, Tommy Armour III had arranged to meet his caddie at what turned out to be the busiest
spot in the entire Grenelefe West golf complex. As time ticked by,
Armour came to regret the decision. Tall and powerfully built,
with a square jaw and a mane of brown hair, Armour has the
looks, the famous name, and the lengthy tour tenure that suggest
he has lived a charmed life. Anchored in one place and easily
distinguishable from UFO golfers named Joey Gullion and Jimmy
Gilleon, Chris Stutts and Jerry Foltz, the approachable Armour
found himself greeted by a stream of reporters and local golf fans.
Asked his thoughts on the first day of Q School 1997, he half
smiled and half winced but gave a straight answer.

"This isn't where I want to be, especially after 17 years," Armour said, "but it's not like I'm going to wear a paper bag over my head. It's the hand I've been dealt, so I'm here to play it."

The namesake of his champion grandfather, Armour had the luxury of knowing his 1997 Q School effort was just a booster shot designed to improve his eligibility status within the PGA Tour's computerized pecking order. He had finished in the 126–150 bracket on the 1997 money list, which already granted him a back-of-the-bus eligibility for 1998 events. When this day ended, Armour would be 1-over but poised for a three-day tear of 66–70–70 that foretold PGA Tour reinstatement. Then, sadly, he shot a fifth-round 77 on the less difficult South course that effectively scuttled his week's mission. Asked how he could have produced such a ragged showing after all those fine rounds, Armour, stoic to the end, replied: "I hit it 77 times."

Day one of any Qualifying Tournament offers an eerie mix of hope, free-floating dread, coiled-up energy, and the knowledge that certain plot lines are destined to play themselves out. You know two or three pedigreed players will show up, shoot low numbers, and ramble through the rest of the week with tour cards waiting for them and no need to ever requalify. Davis Love III's 66 in the first round at Grenelefe in 1985 is a prime example. Love shot a 2-over 74 the next day, but rolled home to a 6-under 423 that tied him for seventh place out of 50 qualifiers. It's also a given that some diligent, deserving gentleman of the links will lose his composure on the final day and find himself one stroke outside the magic number. Clark Dennis, at that time a 10-year veteran with a one-year-old son and a second child on the way, suffered through a humiliating 77 after four rounds of 70–72–70–72 in the rain-shortened 1996 finals and missed regaining his card by a stroke.

If form holds, there will also be a rules controversy, à la the

Casey Martin dustup of 1997, or else a chaos-causing rain delay, or complaints about tee times that stick one bracket of players with two straight windy rounds while the other half of the field gets to play in calm conditions. If the officials are lucky, they won't have any disqualifications based on faulty scorecards or a rules breach that went unnoticed during play but was called in by a Golf Channel viewer who should have been out raking leaves or Christmas shopping in the first place. Tour rules official Mark Russell thanks the golf gods every time a tour-school round ends without incident. He knows the next message over his walkie-talkie could be some ticklish situation that will lead to heartbreak for one of the players in the field.

"Working the tour school as a rules official," Russell once said, "makes me think of what the airline pilots say about their work: 'Hours of boredom, moments of terror.' "

Not every Q School finalist arrives with the same "PGA Tour or bust" motto. Many of the raw youngsters, in their hearts, are angling for fully exempt Nike Tour status and a year of seasoning at tournaments in Gainesville, Odessa, Boise, and Wichita. Meanwhile, players in their late 40s—the Bob Gilders, Bruce Fleishers, and Allen Doyles—have shown up at recent tour schools looking to feather their beds for the Senior PGA Tour. For these golfers, a "big tour" card would offer the chance to stay in top competitive form and take some swings—blind or not—at the great piñata of PGA Tour purse money. In Gilder's case, another advantage of additional PGA Tour time would be to keep himself high enough on the PGA Tour lifetime earnings list that he could avoid a dance with the senior tour's qualifying school come 2001.

On a first visit to Q School's final stage, even a knowledgeable golf fan is struck by two thoughts: (1) most players in the field are unrecognizable, and (2) the ones you recognize deserve a little sympathy.

By week's end, some of the pros forced to requalify will have done so, much to their relief if not their elation. But along with the merely relieved and thankful players who have gained back their livelihood, there are bound to be newly minted PGA Tour members whose last day of tour school is Christmas, New Year's, and the Fourth of July all rolled into one. Since the young ones seldom qualify in a cakewalk, it usually takes an hour or more of postround recovery before the early signs of delirious joy show themselves. But if you miss that moment of ecstasy, not to worry. Relapses are easy to induce.

"This is *the* tour," sighed Ron Whittaker after receiving his engraved PGA Tour money clip in 1995 and getting a taste of the big leagues. Whittaker, nephew of Lanny Wadkins and a veteran of both the Nike and South African tours, dug deep for a 67 on the windblown final day of the 1995 qualifier in West Palm Beach. "The first-class way they run it, the free clothes and equipment people give you. Nothing else compares."

Esteban Toledo, who grew up malnourished in a Mexican slum and—perhaps worse—played the Nike Tour for five years, glows with gratitude whenever he steps on the grounds of a PGA Tour event. "This is heaven, this tour," Toledo whispered during a practice round for the Buick Classic in 1998. After a decade of scuffling, he had just won $105,000 at the BellSouth Classic the previous month. "I paid for my house with it," he exclaimed. "Before that my biggest check in 12 years as a pro was $18,000."

On opening day of the final stage, a journalist is forgiven for lamenting in advance all the stories and stats of the upcoming week that will disappear with the close of play. Only major facts and highlights of a final-stage qualifier make the historical record. A dozen or so players who earn cards and perhaps a half-dozen near-miss cases will be written up in the golf weeklies and spotlighted on the Golf Channel's wrap-up show.

What's more, there is already a curtain of obscurity in place come day one, covering up the worthy events of second-stage and even first-stage qualifying. From Northern California to south Florida, there are approximately 20 preliminary qualifiers and over 900 players swarming through them. Among tournament officials and players, it has become fashionable to claim that "all the pressure of tour school is at second stage now, because if you miss there you've got no tour at all to play." Given how high the PGA Tour purses have risen and how miserable a life the Nike Tour is for a veteran player, that comment smacks of over-statement. But surviving one of the half-dozen or so second-stage tour qualifiers has indeed become a rugged business, especially since the Nike Tour's ascendance in the mid-90s.

One natural source of information about recent doings at second stage is the caddie corps. Not all tour caddies are willing to work the Q School. Compared to the predictable, professional atmosphere of a regular tour event, early-stage qualifiers, and even the final stage, have a honky-tonk, bus-station roughness about them. When Ty Armstrong emerged from the 1993 finals with a share of first place and PGA Tour privileges for the 1994 season, he parted company with the caddie who had been with him for six rounds of qualifying, Scott Brokaw. "He brought his brother out on tour with him," grumbled Brokaw. "What's the point of caddying at tour school if you aren't going to end up on tour with the guy?"

Then there are caddies like Jay Kincannon, a tour regular who enjoys the qualifying rigors so much he once worked three different second-stage events in a single year. A fair-skinned Texan with a beard the color of nylon guitar strings, Kincannon appreciates the quiet heroism he has witnessed at first and second stage. That courage-under-fire outweighs the incidents of unprofessionalism a preliminary qualifier sometimes brings forth.

"When they used to let the players have carts," Kincannon recalled, "I always seemed to get paired with some kid who had his father driving him around. The dads wouldn't have any tournament experience, so once they realized you were a professional caddie they'd stick to you the whole day, asking question after question. I remember one guy's dad drove over the kid's ball in second stage back in 1993. Cost him a two-stroke penalty." Kincannon caddied for one second-stager who misplayed a 7-iron shot on one of the home holes in the second-to-last round, only to drive his ball to that very same spot in the final round. "It was the same distance and the same wind conditions, and it called for the same club," recalled Kincannon. "So he tries the shot again and botches it again. Then he screams at me, 'You cost me a year on the PGA Tour.' Like it was my fault he couldn't hit the shot."

Countering that unpleasantness for Kincannon was a performance by journeyman pro Bill Britton in the second-stage qualifier at Deerwood Country Club, Kingwood, Texas, in 1993.

"That was the best round of golf I've ever caddied," Kincannon declared. "The weather was misty and overcast, and Bill was way down the standings. He needed a low number. He didn't seem nervous, but he didn't say much, either. I remember we paid a lot of attention to keeping the clubs dry and keeping his hands dry, and he just hit the shots. It was classic grinding. When it was over I think he had one bogey and about eight birdies, for a 65. It was low score of the whole week at Deerwood. I won't ever forget how Billy played that day."

About 80 percent of the final field will have competed at second stage, with 30 or so exempted straight through to the final. (These include high finishers on the European, Japanese, and Australasian tours, plus players ranked 126 to 150 on the PGA Tour and 16 to 25 on the Nike Tour for that year.) Of the 170 or so in the final field, at least 50 or 60 will have made it through all the way from first stage. That figure is somewhat amazing, given that virtually any professional golfer in the country can pay his $4,000 and suit up for a first-stage tournament. Some measure of dignity is preserved by those 500 or so applicants, including most of the recognizable ones, who get to skip the Ellis Island atmosphere of first stage and advance their token to the second preliminary round. There are 10 different categories of player, from former PGA Tour members to Nike Tour winners to "the low 25 scorers from the last-played PGA Assistants Champion-ship" who receive this privilege.

Gary Grabinski was the Northeast New York PGA Assistants champ for 1997, and that credential ushered him into a second-stage event in Gulf Shores, Alabama. Jay Williamson, a once and future member of the PGA Tour, took the medal in that event, shooting an 8-under 280 for 72 holes. Tour vets like Andy Bean, Brian Tennyson, and Barry Jaeckel also competed. Grabinski was out of his league. He shot 84–77–73–83, to miss by 24 strokes. "I had no swing at all the first seven or eight holes," said Grabinski, who works at a club called Mohawk Valley. "I once Monday-qualified for the B.C. Open, and when I played the B.C. Open there was pressure, but it was good pressure—if you know what I mean. The pressure at tour school was different. I felt intimi-dated."

Grabinski had the disadvantage of refrigerating his golf game in upstate New York before descending into Gulf of Mexico warmth for his second-stage qualifier. Due to the traditional placement of tour qualifying between Thanksgiving and Christ-mas, that's a fairly common scenario. For Jerry Kelly, a Madison, Wisconsin, native who has closed out the 1990s with several fine years on the PGA Tour, Q School proved an impossible route to the big show. He earned his big-tour card by finishing first on the 1995 Nike Tour money list. Not surprisingly, he considers that long Nike season a truer test than six days of anxiety between the holidays.

"The tournament being in late November or December makes it tough on any player who doesn't live in Florida or someplace else warm," commented Kelly, who missed getting his card at Q School by one shot two years in a row. "I knew exactly both times what I needed to do to make it," he said. "Once it was a 10-footer, the other time it was a 15-footer. Neither one dropped. So I've never gotten a tour card at Q School." Staying true to his hometown roots put Kelly at what he considered a disadvantage. "I was always up in Wisconsin," he said, "wishing I had the money to stay in a hotel in Florida for two weeks and practice. Instead I'd go out and hit 7-irons for 15 minutes into the snow, then run back inside to warm up. In Wisconsin in December, a good 7-iron flies about 110 yards. You better hit it solid or you'll break your fingers."

For many final-stagers, the Fall Classic may as well be listed as the final event on the Nike Tour schedule. Coming down the stretch of the Nike season, the players in or around the top 15 of that money list play hard for the chance to avoid the big Q. Only 15 make it, and final money rankings are greatly influenced by what happens in the season finale, the Nike Tour Championship. Naturally, the 10 pros who finish from 16th to 25th on the Nike Tour money list are going to arrive at the Q School finals (these 10 are exempt from first-stage or second-stage qualifying) feeling like first-class passengers suddenly kicked back into coach. True, their solid play on the Nike Tour positions them well for a Q School run at the big tour, but did it have to come to this? Nike Tour players who finished in the 26 to 55 spots on the money ranking will only be found at the Q School final if they were able to survive the rigors of second-stage tour qualifying.

When the merits of Q School versus the Nike Tour are debated by PGA Tour aspirants, the younger players tend to favor the Nike route and the older, more battle-scarred players will usually favor Q School. One group needs the seasoning the Nike Tour offers, the other group doesn't. Because the pro-Nike group is composed of patient-sounding men who are just a few years out of college, their arguments are naturally persuasive. Players who are pro-Q School (sounds odd just saying it) almost always are older, more road-weary, and slightly dinged-up physically. Their careers tend to include dry spells, if not droughts.

Because of when tour qualifying takes place, it brings together a scattered constellation of pros who have been off for at least a few weeks from whatever tour or minitour they spent the year playing or whatever club job they worked at. Jeff Woodland, a Queenslander who won three Nike Tour events in the early 1990s, showed up at the 1993 tour school finals in Palm Springs with typical Australian nonchalance.

"He came off a 17-hour flight the day before he had to play," recalled Bob Chaney, an athletic-looking, middle-aged caddie with a tanned, shaved scalp and clumpy white whiskers encircling his mouth. "His flight landed in Los Angeles something like 20 hours before his first tee time at La Quinta. He drives straight over there, gets a little sleep, and shows up on the tee. I remember the temperature that first morning was 45 degrees, so Woodland puts on the one sweater he has with him. He's got no rainsuit, no windbreaker. The average person takes at least 24 hours to recover from that kind of flight before they're even functional, but this guy's right off the plane and playing for a tour card." Woodland, who had arrived late in order to play in one last Australian event, shot two 68s, two 69s, and two 71s that week to finish tied for fourth and earn a PGA Tour card with 10 strokes to spare.

John Elliott, who had succeeded in the 1995 school but made

little hay during that tour season, may have been on mental overload at the 1996 Q School. The long-hitting Elliott was nearly late for his tee time the first day because, according to his traveling companion, he drove to the golf course without his contact lenses and had to go back to the hotel room to get them.

"So, you mean he wore his glasses and didn't realize he was wearing glasses instead of contacts?" the young woman was asked.

"No, he didn't have any glasses. Or contacts."

"But how can you drive to the golf course without one or the other and not realize—"

"I really, I don't . . ." She shrugged. "I don't know."

When the tour school final of 1998 began, one player strikingly conspicuous by his absence was John Wilson, a 38-year-old father of four who lives in the Palm Springs area and had only turned pro 10 years earlier. Wilson played in the previous two Q School finals held at La Quinta, earning his tour card each time, and certainly should have played in the 1998 edition, as well. With his 17th-place finish on the 1998 Nike Tour money list, Wilson would be VIP'd straight into the final stage, needing only to have forwarded a check for $4,000 and his application to PGA Tour headquarters by September 18, the absolute deadline for entry. Unfortunately, Wilson—en route to a $112,000 season on the Nike Tour—didn't have the $4,000 to send in.

"He called 15 people asking them to lend him the money," one sports agent familiar with the situation disclosed. "None of them was able to do it. Then, when the school began and people who knew him didn't see his name in any of the results, he got 15 phone calls from people saying, 'You should have just asked me, I would have been glad to lend you the money,' the agent said. "I guess he called the wrong 15 people." Wilson's own agent, Dallas-based David Parker, confirmed this information. "I was one of the 15 people who called him afterward," said Parker. "His own agent, and I don't hear from him when he needs the money to go forward with his career. But for John it was an issue of pride. He wanted to take care of it his way."

Of course, Wilson had to be thinking in mid-September that he would, by the grace of God, maintain his top-15 ranking on the Nike Tour and thereby earn PGA Tour status without a trip to Q School. Two weeks before the September 18 deadline he was ranked number eight on the Nike with $108,000. A half-dozen events remained on the schedule, including the Nike Tour Championship. As the tour moved through the Pacific Northwest and down to San Jose, Wilson was losing traction. He shot 71–71 in the opening rounds at San Jose and missed the cut by two shots. With one more full-field event to play, the Inland Empire Open, before the season-ending tour championship, Wilson ranked 14th on the list, ahead of Sean Murphy by some $1,300. He arrived at Moreno Valley Golf Club for the Inland Empire event needing a few hot rounds. Opening with 70–69, he made the cut easily. But his next two rounds were 76–73. Wilson finished in 54th place, which paid him a meal-money check of $540.

Murphy, meanwhile, had finished in a tie for 17th, earning $2,591 that vaulted him over Wilson into the top 15. The Nike Tour Championship in Mobile, Alabama, became Wilson's personal Q School. A brutal 7,154-yard layout called the Crossings Course at Magnolia Grove was selected for the event. Only two players broke 70 in the first round, and John Wilson, with a solid 71, stood sixth. Then his ladder started to sway. Wilson's second-round score of 77, from a pure standings perspective, was no disaster—the rest of this select field was struggling its way to a 76.5 scoring average for the day—and after 36 holes Wilson would still find himself tied for 11th place. But he had not played any good golf on the weekends since his Q School deadline had passed, and that pattern was not about to break. Wilson carded a pair of 76s to close out the Nike Tour season, finishing tied for 33rd in the Nike Tour finale and earning prize money of $1,995. He had needed to move only one spot on the list, and he did just that—in the wrong direction.

There are only two kinds of players on hand for the opening round of tour school finals, the ones who've proven they have what it takes to break into the PGA Tour ranks and those who have yet to prove it. First-day nerves are worse for the unproven players. In the case of a veteran who is requalifying, it usually takes an injury or an illness or a notably poor streak of play coming in to make the first round a white-knuckle trip. If that's how it felt for eight-year tour vet Patrick Burke at the 1998 final, you could hardly tell. Burke had been diagnosed with a torn tendon in his right wrist after hitting from the rough during a PGA Tour event in the summer of 1997. It was a painful moment, but Burke later sustained a fall through the cracks in tour policy that hurt even more.

"I picked the wrong time to get injured," he said, referring to the "major medical extension" clause that might have solved his eligibility problem if he had sustained his injury earlier in the year. "I ended up on the outside looking in."

A hydrant-shaped golfer whose off-course activities include ice hockey, Burke had skated close to the edge of tour eligibility throughout the early '90s. In 1995, his fifth year on the circuit, he kept his card for the first time by finishing 119th on the money list with earnings of $162,892. A year later the Florida native found his stride, making 14 cuts and pocketing $265,083, a money total that placed him 79th overall. His success opened the way for appetizing endorsement deals with advertisers like Reebok and Marriott Courtyard.

But Burke's earnings were a mere $89,000 at the halfway point of the 1997 season, leaving him well in need of a rally. Instead, he went to Hattiesburg for the Deposit Guaranty and dinged the wrist. He played with increasing soreness the next week in Hartford, and a few weeks later in Vancouver called it quits for the year. "The problem was, I had played in over 20 events in 1997, which means I didn't qualify for a medical exemption in '98," explained Burke. His wrist pain didn't prevent Burke from going on a letter-writing campaign, in which he requested some latitude from the PGA Tour Policy Board for having missed 14 weeks of competition. His contention was that he could have well made up the $90,000 it would have taken to remain exempt for 1998.

"I'm known for my late-season rallies," Burke pointed out, and indeed his one-month total of $55,000 in October of 1995 testifies to that point. With a file of medical records under his arm, Burke flew from his Southern California home to Tour headquarters in Ponte Vedra to plead his case. At that point, his story could be expected to dissolve into a cliché—corporate suits and marquee pros prove cold and merciless in the face of a journeyman's troubles. Especially when the journeyman has openly criticized PGA Tour operations in the past. (A former greens superintendent, he has complained on the record about substandard turf conditions at the Tour's own TPC courses). But Burke found the tour bureaucracy initially reasonable.

"I was pretty cynical about how they'd treat me," Burke admitted. "I'm one of those Tour players most people have never heard of, so I expected very little in the way of compassion or understanding. But they listened." According to Burke, the tour staff worked hard chasing down the player members of the Tour Policy Board—stars like Tom Lehman and Mark O'Meara, whose late-year invitations had scattered them to all points on the globe. Burke's original request was to be exempted into the final stage of 1997 PGA Tour Qualifying, but when a quick ruling failed to materialize, he showed up for a second-stage qualifier at Fort Ord, California. Ten minutes before his tee time at the qualifier, Burke faced the fact that his wrist was still throbbing and withdrew to make room for an alternate.

His case was decided at the March meeting of the policy board, where Burke was granted a "minor medical extension." Players granted that status have to wait in line behind at least 150 others, which means they don't get in many tournaments. Burke entered all of two PGA Tour events in 1998 under his so-called extension, but even with a free ride into every tournament on the calendar he would not have been successful. The injury, after further examination, turned out be joint damage rather than a tendon problem. Either way, it was slow to heal and easily aggravated. By the fall of 1998, Burke's bearded cheeks could be glimpsed at the Q School finals once again.

"I'm not fully healed, but I guess I can swing a club," he said, shrugging. "I'm going to have to one-arm it around the track if I'm going to get a card." There were no Marriott Courtyard or Reebok logos on his person—both advertisers had declined to renew Burke's endorsement contracts once his eligibility fell into jeopardy. The Courtyard ax fell during the holidays, days after Burke had returned from a conference held by the hotel chain's corporate staff in Phoenix.

Recurring through the Q School's 33-year history is the familiar scenario of an adrenaline-stoked rookie or journeyman who lights up the leaderboard in the first round, then (when he realizes what he's done) abandons his smashing offense for a determined defense. Sometimes he goes into a death spiral, sometimes he hangs on to qualify by one or two shots. At La Quinta in 1993, Paul Stankowski and Jesper Parnevik screamed out of the blocks with scores of 66 and 65, respectively. Stankowski, having sprinted to 6-under, played for the middles of the greens and never shot lower than 71 the rest of way. He finished at 5-under and made his card by three strokes. Parnevik played aggressively in shooting 65–66 to start out, then broke stride badly with a stunning 79. Regaining his composure, the Swede with the trademark upturned cap visor zipped home with rounds of 67–67–72 to earn exemption.

Jeff Sluman's experience at the '82 Q School in Ponte Vedra Beach is a classic of the hot-to-cold genre. After one round, the 22-year-old Chicagoan stood at 5-under par, tied for second and trailing only the eventual medalist, Donnie Hammond. "I felt confident that week," Sluman said in retrospect. The next day he played a solid round of 73, which left him at 4-under. The next day he shot another 73. Now he was 3-under, and comfortably in the middle of the pack. In round four, Sluman shot 76—not so comfortable, but he had survived the four-round cut. In round five the Chicagoan wobbled in with 78, and in a blaze of desperation he brought home a 79 for the sixth and final round.

If that Q School hadn't ended, Sluman may have eventually worked up to an 18 handicap. "Sometimes you get through easily, sometimes it's a learning process," is Sluman's summation of the week. He returned to the qualifying process two years later at La Quinta, this time keeping his score within a few shots of even par all week and finishing at 1-over 433, four strokes above the safety margin. "I haven't seen a system yet," he surmises, emphatically but with no way of actually proving it, "that can keep a talented enough player from getting to the top level of competition."

The wildest first round in Q School history took place in 1983, the second and last time the event was held at the Tour's home golf facility, the TPC at Sawgrass. With a December wind blowing—a "norther," as they're sometimes called—and the course laid out in all its original Pete Dye glory, no fewer than 34 of the 57 players who ended up receiving tour cards began their week with a score of 76 or higher. Two players, Mick Soli and Mike Cunning, opened with scores of 8-over par 80, but still went on to get their cards. Tour school veteran Greg Farrow remembered that windblown afternoon in 1983 and the 77 he was happy to stagger home with.

"I was paired with two very good players, Ronnie McCann, a South African, and Rod Curl, who had won several times on tour," recalled Farrow, now a club pro in New Jersey. "I've never seen any two tougher opening rounds of a Q School or any other golf tournament than those two guys had that day."

All the trouble happened on one hole, number 17. "Of course, that's the hole with the famous island green," said Farrow. "And it was famous even then. Our group had started play on number 10, so for us it was just the eighth hole of the entire tournament. The wind was blowing the hair off your head—I'm guessing there were 40- or 50 mile-per-hour gusts. They had the tee markers set at 125 yards, but instead of the normal wedge I took out my 5-iron, made a three-quarter swing, and made the ball die in the air over the green." Farrow would go on to two-putt for his par, but it would be some time before he got the opportunity to do so.

"McCann played next, and he couldn't find dry land. Two short, one left, one way right. After four tries, he turned to a rules official and said he was 'just tryin' ta ge' past the bloody hole before dark.' But back then there was no drop area up near the grandstands, as there is now.

"The green had a red line around it, meaning you had to cross the margin of the hazard," explained Farrow. "You had to get your ball into that air space over the green—and if you did that you could actually drop one in the little patch of rough on the island itself." Eventually, McCann took a 2-iron and rifled it as hard as he could over the green, to earn himself the drop. Curl suffered the same type of embarrassment, hitting three shots in the lake before taking a low iron and blasting it straight over the green.

"Ronnie made a 13 and Rod made an 11," Farrow mused. "It was a 108-hole tournament and after eight holes they were blown out of it." As a postscript to his day-one adventure, Farrow notes that he himself played 126 Q School holes that week. On the morning of day five, he went out in a steady rain and shot 73. As he and his fellow competitors came in, the storm strengthened, washing out play before enough of the field had completed their rounds to make it official. His 73 was tossed out, but Farrow kept his composure and finished 74–75 to earn his card with one shot to spare. When Farrow competed for the final time in Q School, it was four years later in Palm Coast, Florida, and his sixth-round score was once again a 75.

"But that 75 was one of the best pressure rounds I ever played," he claimed. "On the first hole, I hit my tee shot and it ended up in a sandy lie. To make sure I didn't catch any sand I hit it a little thin, and even though the ball reached the green I had put a fair-sized cut in it, so I took it out of play. On the next tee, I duck-hooked one into the water. So I reteed, and drove into another one of those sandy lies. Same thing as number 1—I hit the shot thin, knocked it on the green, but again the ball was cut so I took it out of play. Reached in my bag, and come to find out I had one ball left," he said. "I had about 12 dozen back in my locker, but somehow I only took four balls out there with me. And the guys I was with were playing a different type of ball, so I couldn't borrow one, either," he explained, referring to the tour rule that prevents players from shuttling different types of balls in and out of play depending on their need for distance, control, high spin, et cetera.

"Matanzas Woods, it's kind of a funny routing—you don't

reach the clubhouse until after the 10th hole. So I used only irons on the next eight holes, trying to protect my ball. If I'd lost it or ruined it, those first five rounds would have gone down the drain." Farrow made it to the 10th green with his last ball, grabbed a fresh box, and went on to earn yet another PGA Tour card.

One of the many 79s that first day of 1983 belonged to Grier Jones, who despite his fine success had wearied of the tour grind several years earlier and was only in the field at Sawgrass because of a recent change to the eligibility rules—one of the many policy changes in the 35 years that tour qualifying has been tinkered with, but one of the most profound and lasting changes, as well. "When I left the tour in '76, they were still letting a former winner come back whenever he felt like it," said Jones, now a college golf coach at Wichita State University. "You didn't have to qualify on Monday, just let them know you wanted a spot. Then they went to the all-exempt tour [former PGA Tour winners who aren't otherwise exempt now receive tournament spots on a 'fill the field' basis, after a couple of hundred other players have had their opportunity to enter]. So I practiced a little, showed up, played the first day in a big wind, and shot myself a 79."

Jones showed his experience by coming back with two 74s, and hung on to regain his card. "I made it in by one shot, and I needed driver, 2-iron to reach the 18th green and two-putt for par to do it." But the weeklong struggle turned out to be a waste of Jones's time and effort. By finishing way down the pecking order in a tie for 50th place, he emerged from the 1983 Q School in a numbers squeeze. In order for Jones to gain entry into one of the early tournaments, a majority of the 40 or so tour school graduates ahead of him would have to pass up the chance first. "That tour school was in November," Jones moaned, "and I didn't get offered a spot in a tournament until five months later, on two days' notice, in Texas in the middle of April. By that time I'd lost interest again."

Out of such obvious unfairness came the "reshuffle" policy. Under this tweak to the system, the first-to-last ranking among Q School card-earners is in force for the first few tournaments of the year, then the order is reshuffled based on performance in the early going. The reshuffles occur every few weeks, to prevent a player from getting trapped in a disadvantangous spot on the pecking order. Of course, in order to get a boost from the reshuffle, it's necessary to get into at least a couple of tournaments.

"They told me, 'We think you'll get into San Diego,' " recalled Jones, "but that fell through. Then Johnny Miller, who was a good friend, helped me get a sponsor's exemption into the Crosby, but I didn't make the cut. I felt bad about taking it, anyway. When you've been out there earning everything that came your way, it doesn't feel right to get some kind of pass." Jones, having gone to the trouble of attending Q School, continued to request exemptions into upcoming events.

"They'd call and say, 'You're the fifth alternate,' meaning I could travel to the event and see if a spot opens up," said Jones. For a player who had quit the tour in the first place mainly due to a dislike for airports and hotels, this was a poor offer. "Finally they called me the Tuesday night before the Houston Open. I hustled over there and didn't play worth a darn. Shot 76–73, missed the cut by plenty." Jones had not intended to come back full-time, but his dance with the first Q School of the "all-exempt" era proved what a misnomer that term was when it was first coined.

Today when a player earns his PGA Tour card at the school, his orientation materials list an estimate of the number of official PGA Tour events various graduates will find their way into. In 1997 for example, the medalist was able to play in 33 of the 39 cosponsored official events. The 15th-place finisher made it into 31 of 39 and the 30th-place Q Schooler made it into 29 of 39. But the last-place survivor, unless he did some fancy letter-writing to gain sponsor exemptions, got much less of a shot at keeping his card than one might have expected. Only 16 of the 39 official stops had a place for that finisher. It's no wonder the orientation materials also contain instructions for how to "Monday-qualify" for one of the three or four spots still allocated to this ancient practice.

Clark Dennis has been a familiar sight at the tour qualifying school since he turned professional in 1987. After missing out on a PGA Tour card by one stroke at the rain-shortened 1996 finals, the Houston native looked in the mirror and—his boyish features notwithstanding—realized the Texas State Junior Champion he had been in 1983 was a stranger from another era. It is a rare 30-year-old who hasn't found that his 20s passed with stunning quickness, and tour pros living season to season are no exception. Dennis accepted his Nike Tour card and had what others might consider a decent year in 1997, finishing 21st on the money list and missing a 20-foot birdie putt on the 18th hole during a tournament in St. Louis to shoot 60. As the Nike Tour season wound down, he realized Q School would have to be his ticket back to the big leagues. He also realized that an unfamiliar sense of urgency had welled up inside him.

"I said to myself, 'You're 31, going on 32. It's now or it's never.' " Dennis had been privately ashamed of himself for surviving the four-round cut at the 1996 finals only to wake up on the day of round five with very little physical or mental energy. The physical toll of Q School is no secret—players have been known to lose 10 or 15 pounds through fatigue and nerves, and many seem to develop pale or even ashen complexions, despite being out in the sun constantly. Dennis had come out flat for the fifth round at the 1997 finals, and the problem was conditioning.

"I wasn't sharp," he admitted later. "I wasn't physically prepared for what I had to do." He adopted a strategy that would deliver him to round one of the 1997 finals less like the old Clark and more like Superman.

Every day of the seven weeks before his trip to Grenelefe, Dennis pounded through a daylong routine that included twice-a-day gym workouts, morning and evening, with golf practice sessions in between. Hitting balls and practicing the short game turned out to be the daily break, but Dennis rarely minded his 8:30 P.M. return trip to the treadmills and weight machines of the fitness club. "I was more determined to succeed at the '97 Q School than at anything I had ever attempted in golf," he said. When the training period was over, Dennis could feel new reservoirs of energy and physical stamina in his five-eleven frame. His wife, Vicki, who had loyally walked the tour school fairways throughout her husband's trials, was left off the traveling squad this time.

"We talked about her coming along, whether it would be a positive or not," Dennis said. "She's always been my support to help get through these things, but this time I told her I would go down there by myself and take care of business." True to his vow, Dennis made a slick, downhill 20-footer on his final hole to finish inside the number by one stroke.

Sometimes the Q School can be lost before day one even happens. The eve of the 1977 school more or less marked the end of the line for a contestant whose face would eventually work its way onto the covers of golf's biggest magazines. Jim McLean, a University of Houston star during the glory years when John Mahaffey, Bruce Lietzke, Keith Fergus, and Bill Rogers were also varsity players, prepared for the 1977 Q School with the care and precision that would mark the stellar teaching career that Q School 1977, in absurd and merciless fashion, consigned him to.

"In preparation for that tour school, which was going to be

held at Pinehurst, I worked closely with Ken Venturi for months," McLean recalled. "Kenny was and still is a great teacher. Together we got my swing and my game into its top form. Well before the week of the tournament, I arranged with Jeff Burey, who was director of golf at the resort, to stay at his house during tournament week. Jeff was a friend and he had a beautiful house right there on the golf course."

McLean moved into Burey's house and went about his business, hitting balls on the range and playing several practice rounds.

"I played my last practice round the day before the first round and shot a good score," he said. "I remember taking my shower that afternoon and feeling so great about my preparation, how under control everything was. All that was left to do was get my golf clothes at the cleaners and pick up some steaks at a market for the cookout we were going to have that night. The plan was to get the steaks grilling about sundown, eat dinner, and get me into bed early."

McLean, who had been whittled out of the bizarre 1974 Tour School by three shots after playing 72 holes in San Francisco and then continuing on to Palm Springs in that year's two-site, 144-hole marathon, was primed for success. Rogers and Lietzke, whom he played even with all through college, were already on tour and successful. Their old teammate, whose swing was technically as good or better than theirs, should by all rights have been on the circuit with them already. In his second-stage qualifier a few weeks earlier in Tampa, McLean had finished second to Mark McCumber, outplaying a field of seasoned mini-tour players.

Walking out of the dry cleaner's in the courtly Southern town's center, McLean—primed and ready—would have been excused for feeling a swagger in his step on the eve of the 1977 qualifier.

He hung his clothes in the backseat of his late-model Dodge Charger ("silver with red pinstripes," McLean said nostalgically. "It was the first car I ever bought new") and motored six blocks to the grocery market. He parked, went in, waited while the sirloin was wrapped, then walked back out to his car. As he went to get in, a large man in a white shirt intercepted him.

" 'Is that your car?' he asks me," McLean said. "Then he says, 'Because if it is, you got a problem. I caught you doing 60 in a 30-mile-per-hour zone.' "

McLean was a decade or more removed from his mannerly upbringing in Seattle and still had the translucent blond hair and boyish looks that might persuade a small-town Carolina sheriff to put away his ticket pad. But there were New York plates on McLean's car and, worse yet, a tinge of big-city attitude he had picked up while working for the distinguished pro Bob Watson at the ritzy Westchester Country Club.

"I had a radar detector in my Charger, so I get the bright idea to tell the cop the radar detector hadn't gone off, and therefore how did he think he caught me doing 60 in a 30," said McLean, rolling his eyes at the thought of his own impertinence. "The cop says, 'I was parked over on the shoulder and I estimated your speed.' I'm hearing him say all this, and I'm holding my steaks and thinking about playing for my tour card with an early tee time the next morning and I'm not believing it's all really happening, so I look at him and I say, 'Well, you know what, that's *bullshit*.' Great negotiating, right? The next thing I know he's telling me to put my stuff in the car and lock it up and we're going to jail."

The tour's annual entrance exam is grueling on its own. It doesn't require a night in a rural North Carolina jail with winos and hubcap-stealing delinquents to make it any tougher. But that's where blue-eyed, innocent Jim McLean, the man who

would one day be one of America's most respected golf instruc-
tors, found himself. Four hours, one mistimed phone call to the
Pinehurst golf shop (Burey was unavailable), a wee-hours wran-
gling about the $300 bail bond, and McLean somehow found him-
self on the tee.

"No dinner the night before, no sleep, and I shoot 77," he said,
reliving the galling events of that night. "The next day I have to
drive back to the Southern Pines jail with the lawyer and take
care of a bunch of paperwork. I make it to my afternoon tee time,
play the round, shoot 73, and miss the cut by three shots." In
keeping with the tour school's annals of frustration, McLean to
this day feels a deeper grievance with the policies of the PGA
Tour than with the Pinehurst constabulary. "They're only playing
72 holes, in a tournament that's always been known as an en-
durance test, and they make a cut after 36. And the cut was at
147," he groaned. "That was the rule that year, and everybody
who was right around the number went crazy. We didn't really
think about it going in, but when it happened it suddenly seemed
so wrong. They were giving out 30 cards and the cut was down
to like 50 guys. Ed Fiori, who made the cut barely, shot 66 the
next day and moved up to something like third place.

"The Tour made a mistake and they knew it and they never
did it again," said McLean. "But that was it for me. I was 26 and
I said forget it. My teaching career began that day."

Since 1982, the PGA Tour has barely tinkered with the format
for Q School's final stage. As a result, players like David Peoples,
Loren Roberts, and Harry Taylor, who made all their many return
trips through qualifying during the post-1982 era, experienced
groundhog-day monotony in its most extreme form. As the qualifiers these multiple offenders played in got under way, the
contestants dutifully took their places in the 170-man police
lineup otherwise known as the field. Joining them each time were

the fresh-faced college boys and the veterans alike—players old enough to comment dryly about wearing a paper bag over their heads.

But if they looked at the bright side, they would see that they were paid up, safely past the preliminary stages, on site at the final and ready to compete. With any luck they could expect a reasonably good showing in the first couple of rounds. At that point, the less-experienced Q Schoolers might begin to think they are in for a fairly smooth week. Better instead that they look to the days ahead and think of them in terms of what Mark Russell said about the working life of a pilot or a rules official: "Hours of boredom, moments of terror."

9

GROUNDHOG DAY

In the western horizon, a Palm Springs sunset was dividing near and distant mountain ranges into jagged strips of color that brought to mind a tacky dorm-room poster from the 1970s. Ignoring the scenery and pointing their guns east, the Q School class of 1998 strafed the dimming sky with practice balls. Four rounds were complete and a broth of mixed emotions simmered along the range at PGA West, giving off a stronger scent of failure than it had the night before. Reporters, business reps, and sports psychologists prospected the firing line, sniffing out success-stories-in-the-making.

Until 1997, day four of the tour school finals was cut day, which meant anyone hitting 3-irons in the twilight could count himself a survivor. For the agents, writers, and performance-enhancement folks, that made everyone still swinging a club worth approaching. After the rule change (which was designed to properly sort out the full and partial Nike Tour exemptions), players in the middle bulge of scores lost an advantage. The new no-cut policy burdened them with the psychic weight of 80 bona fide stragglers still in their midst. In Q School's merciless atmosphere, whatever helps break the groundhog-day repetitiveness is naturally cherished. So when tour officials decided they would no longer use a four-round cut to thin the qualifying herd of its old, young, feeble, and incapacitated, they upped the oppressiveness another notch.

When a day of tour school competition finally ends, reporters are able to squeeze in perhaps a half-dozen worthwhile interviews before dark. On the afternoon of round four, there is no time available for consoling a player who is hopelessly out of it or flattering one who is a lock to get his card but too sensible to start gloating early. Problem is, neither the range nor the putting green is equipped with computer scoring monitors. Unless a player is upending water coolers or dancing a jig, there is no way to discern his fourth-round score and his cumulative standing, other than legging it over to the scoreboard or media center, during which time the player or players targeted for questioning might quit the premises.

It's human nature to search out the breakthrough cases, the slightly older players who have never played the PGA Tour and are threatening to get their first crack. Geoffrey Sisk, occupying roughly the same rectangle of hitting space he had occupied 24 hours earlier, seemed after 72 holes to be neither grumbling nor gloating. Sisk had played well enough in the first few rounds to position himself for a dash up the ramparts. With scores of 67–74–69 beside his name, the three-time Massachusetts Open champion and former assistant pro at Marshfield (Massachusetts) Country Club had begun round four at six under par. It was a fairly safe neighborhood to be in, but this was Q School in the 1990s, meaning an innocent three-day run of 71–72–70 would likely end the week in misery. And if the round just concluded had been another 74, that Nike apprenticeship would surely be extended another year.

The night before, he had shown satisfaction with his three-round total. In keeping with Q School's relatively lax dress code, Sisk wore a crust of whiskers on his face and a baggy golf shirt that had fitted properly seven months and 15 pounds ago, before a long Nike Tour summer and an altered diet slimmed him noticeably. Asked how he felt after three solid rounds, the 33-year-old scratched the grit on his neck and reflected for a while on his trudging progress in pro golf over the past decade. With his pilgrim features and self-effacing manner, Sisk didn't especially look like a PGA Tour golfer. His résumé wasn't from central casting, either. More than 10 years had passed since his return home from Temple University in Philadelphia with a degree in finance. In the time since, he had resisted the obligatory relocation to a Sunbelt locale, preferring to tune his game in regional events around New England. Sisk had played the Nike Tour once before, in 1991, making only seven cuts in 21 starts. His PGA Tour career consisted of three events and no money won.

During a week in which "staying in the present" is every sports psychologist's first rule, it seemed wayward of Sisk to reflect at length on the path of his career. But the first stars were in the desert sky and I had broken the ice by pointing out two characteristics we had in common—both natives of Massachusetts and each the father of a girl with the poetic name of Hannah Elizabeth. Having been born on the night of December 5, 1997, a few hours after round three of the 1997 final-stage tour qualifier ended, Hannah Elizabeth Sisk is a bona fide Q School baby. Her timing had earned her father a paragraph in the notes column of every publication covering the 1997 tour school. For as long as there is such a thing as Q School, the girl is destined to have her birthday fall during or very close to it—one more reason for her old man to duck the Fall Classic.

Sisk left that 1997 qualifier with a Nike card he claimed would serve him well, and despite a poor showing in the Nike Tour Championship, he seemed to make great use of the experience. But the constant separation from his wife and new daughter proved nearly intolerable, and having reached the early middle age when tour hopefuls and their sponsors tend to split up, he had no insulation from the financial strain, either.

"I made about $80,000 in '98," he had mused, putting aside his preparations for round four. "That's $72,000 in prize money plus a few endorsements. But to earn that $80,000 I spent probably $50,000. And my wife stayed back home and worked. That's our big sacrifice—having me on the Nike Tour by myself. Other players have their families traveling with them, but that means bigger expenses and no way for the wife to earn any income. So mine stays home, and we put off buying anything but the necessities. And still we've got so much debt."

Now, 24 hours later, Sisk had hauled himself to a compelling crossroads. When his caddie turned to fill up a water bottle from the huge Igloo cooler 20 steps behind the players, he was hit with the pressing question: "How did it go today?"

The caddie, Michael Reistetter, arched an eyebrow. "Quite well, thanks," he answered, in his faint British accent. "Sixty-seven, on the Weiskopf course. So we're 11-under now."

The numbers hung in the air like chamber music even as Reistetter turned away. Sixty-seven. Eleven under par. Two rounds left, and a safety margin established. Sisk now had a chance of getting to the big show without moving even a single stroke farther under par—he might even be able to give one up. Despite his 38th-place finish on the 1998 Nike Tour money list and his competent play at Grenelefe over the final three rounds of the 1997 qualifier, Geoff Sisk had nothing in his portfolio to power-fully suggest he had gone out in today's fourth round and managed anything better than the 72s shot by tour veterans Dave Barr, Robert Gamez, and Kelly Gibson or the 73 scraped out by Clarence Rose. But with 67 he was practically a made man. Same place on the range as the evening before, same swing, same personality, but Sisk's life was different. It was changing in front of your eyes.

Sisk would outdo himself the next day with a fifth-round gem of 65, featuring a chip-in birdie and chip-in eagle. He would conclude the week triumphantly with a 70 and a six-round total of 412, 10 strokes lower than what was needed and only four strokes behind the medalist, Mike Weir. But that 67 in round four on the Weiskopf course at PGA West is the one he will point to when his PGA Tour career is in full bloom and his wife has money in the checkbook to put new linens on the beds and new tires on the family car. Friday night, you could look at Geoffrey Sisk and say, "Club pro who played the Nike Tour a couple of years." Saturday night, come what may, he was something different. With his fourth-round 67, Sisk caused the agents and golf-club company reps to put checkmarks beside his name. With the next day's 65, he would have them on his elbows, discussing attractive offers.

There is nothing quite like the Descent of the Agents and Reps that takes place after the midpoint of tour-school finals. Suddenly, a gritty, unrelenting golf qualifier turns into a trade show. Wherever the players gather, businessmen and -women are suddenly present, wearing a modified office attire and looking for openings. The etiquette of approaching a new player is carefully observed by most reps, totally ignored by others. Among the smaller and more established agencies, presence at Q School is considered a show of support for existing clients, never a canvassing effort in search of new ones.

"By the time a player has reached final stage of tour school," explained Mac Barnhardt of Virginia-based Pros, Incorporated, "we know if we want him as a client or we don't. We've never signed anyone that we met coming off the golf course with a qualifying score." Barnhardt's boss, Marvin (Vinny) Giles III, is a clubhouse oil painting sprung to life—skilled lawyer, honest negotiator, and a former U.S. Amateur and British Amateur champion, as well. Rubbing elbows on the competitive amateur circuits, Giles and his associates build relationships that steer most new clients to Pros, Inc., via direct contact or through a firsthand referral from a mutually trusted intermediary. A newly exempt PGA Tour member, seeing Lanny Wadkins, Davis Love III, Justin Leonard, and Tom Kite among the Pros, Inc., stable, may even contact the agency directly. But he will have to elbow past the hungry young agents on his way.

"I see guys that have no idea what is out there for a tour-school player promising them things that spook me," said Barnhardt. "They tell these players about $10,000-a-day outings, $75,000 shoe contracts, pie in the sky, basically." Barnhardt saw the money in the cyclical golf-equipment industry become plentiful in the early 1990s then dry up, at least as far as the typical Q School graduate is concerned. "Used to be if you got your card, you were guaranteed a set of deals that would cover the year's expenses, no problem. Then the money started flowing away from the new players and going all toward the top."

The established agents shake their heads when they see the annual mating ritual of agents and card-earners. A player arrives at the scoring area during the final few rounds of tour school and five business types sidle close enough to cop an ID, then scan the scoreboard to ascertain his score. If he's 4-under, the charm gets turned on. If he's 4-over, pass. David Parker of Texas-based Links MMG is another agent who attends Q School to show the flag rather than engage in cold prospecting. Without the luxury of a full client stable, Parker would be obliged to take a scrappier approach—within certain limits.

"Congregating around the scoreboard, going up to this player, that player," remarked Parker. "It's a kind of behavior I wouldn't engage in. These guys are getting ready for the biggest rounds of their lives, and here you've got unreferred agents coming up to them before they tee off—sometimes even between nines—introducing themselves."

Minding his own business at La Quinta in 1998 was Tim Shannon of Affinity Sports, whose friend and client, John Riegger, was motoring along toward acquisition of his third PGA Tour card since turning pro in 1991. Riegger, who had made it back onto the big tour with a high finish at the 1997 tour school, ended up 162nd on the 1998 PGA Tour money list. At age 35, Riegger was well traveled in the U.S. and Asia but nowhere near burned out. Tall, trim, and taciturn, he appears to study his way around the golf course, sticking to a plan and accepting the outcome. When a situation calls for Riegger to make some revealing gesture or comment, he will usually just towel off his glasses or absently light a cigarette. Appearing comfortable at La Quinta, Riegger shot 70–72–67–71 in his first four rounds and was 8-under par, nicely on track for PGA Tour exemption.

His fifth round, at the Dunes Course, began with an up-and-down 37 on the front nine. But the one shot Riegger lost to par would be more than countered by his eagle on number 10. That turnabout buoyed the Illinois native, and with the clubhouse in sight, and his agent, Shannon, making mental notes about possible endorsement deals, Riegger fired a drive straight down the fairway of the par-5 15th. Having struggled to find the right layup spot on this hole in earlier rounds, he decided to aim for the front left bunker, a fairly standard pro strategy in such cases. It worked, but the wedge shot Riegger played from the sand was badly thinned. Behind the 15th green at La Quinta Dunes is a looming mass of craggy rock four stories high, and John Riegger's ball flew into it. He was forced to declare an unplayable lie in the crags and hit again from the sand. This wedge shot came up short of the green, and the ensuing chip, while just about hole high, finished 12 feet from the hole. Two putts later, there was a triple-bogey eight disfiguring Riegger's scorecard.

"I should have maybe gone up to him on the next tee, tried to settle him down," said Shannon later. Left to his own devices on number 16, a medium-length part 3, Riegger hit a decent tee shot into medium rough just off the green but failed to get it up and down. And the par-4 17th at the Dunes, as anyone knows who has played it, is no place to get well. Long, with water down the entire left side, and water fronting the green, as well, the hole offers two classic hit-and-hope moments. Riegger drove gamely, but his tee shot found a fairway bunker on the left side, hard by the lake. From there, anything but a dainty layup was almost bound to be wet, but Riegger went for the green. His iron shot spit forward like a watermelon seed before disappearing underwater. If memory serves, he then dropped in the bunker, and found water again. Amazingly, Riegger finished the hole with a triple-bogey 7, then looked around for a rules official to whom he could announce his withdrawal from the tournament. Not finding one, he walked in. Officially, he was disqualified.

"That was a meltdown," Shannon said with a shrug. "It was building. Thursday John played this course beautifully and he couldn't get a single break. If you watched it, it was a 64 kind of round, and all he got out of it was 72." All Riegger got out of his year on the PGA Tour in 1998 and his anger-shortened Q School appearance was a long walk into limbo. He had played the Nike and the PGA Tours sporadically during the 1990s, but the decade would close with Riegger ineligible for either.

That fifth round of the 1998 tour school witnessed what must have been a record number of withdrawals in a single day's play. Four of the 168 players quit in the middle of their rounds; three due to physical injury—Bobby Wadkins, Gene Sauers, and R. W. Eaks—and one, Riegger, from wounded pride. What happened to Riegger underscored the prison-movie atmosphere any Q School takes on by about the fourth or fifth round. Every inmate in the exercise yard seems to be waiting for one guy to crack and start tackling guards in a hopeless rush to strangle the evil warden. When this flash of drama is over, a bitter calm settles over the lockup.

But a wig-out like Riegger's probably affects tour-school onlookers more than it affects the average contestant. A field of 168 Q Schoolers doesn't share a common fate the way celluloid convicts do. It would take an unthinkable number of withdrawals and disqualifications for any one contestant to feel he was lifted closer to the final goal. A typical threesome will, if anything, tend to pull for each other. The alternative to mutual rooting is to simply ignore those playing alongside you. At the 1998 finals, Dave Stockton, Jr., Patrick Burke, and Craig Barlow played together in the third and fourth rounds and seemed to develop a chain-gang camaraderie. After they made their turn on the PGA West Weiskopf course in round four, Burke took note of the scarcity of front-side birdies in the group and made a declaration.

"Okay guys," he said, unsheathing his driver, "let's quit fuckin' around."

Barlow seconded the motion. Stockton cast the three players' scoring in group terms. "Yeah, let's go," he said. "Our best-ball isn't beating anybody right now."

As one groundhog day follows another, players and caddies wonder privately how aggressive or cautious to be with each shot. The two other players in one's group provide the only real-time context for those judgments. In threesomes of tour-school players who are each playing solid golf, the shot-making can come to resemble that odd phenomenon in which college women sharing a campus apartment all begin to menstruate at the same time each month. One Q Schooler's drive goes out to what looks like a tough, risky landing area, and suddenly two more balls hit the same spot, even though the other two players are a fader and a right-to-left man, respectively. They come to a par 3 with only minor trouble on the left and the first player to hit steers his ball way to the right, setting up a long downhill putt. Two swings later, he is joined in no-man's-land by the other two. In the Stockton–Burke–Barlow threesome at PGA West, there was an unspoken suggestion that one of the three should get hot, in order to spur the others on.

But encouraging others to do well isn't the same as congratulating them when they do—especially if a lightning bolt of luck seems to be involved. At La Purisma in 1996, Michael Clark II, a compact 25-year-old Georgian, began his second round by bogeying La Purisma Golf Club's opening hole. Up on the second tee, Clark smoldered with anger as he teed his ball. He batted the sole of his driver on the grass a few times, then blistered a perfect drive down the left side. That set up a 130-yard knockdown wedge that landed four feet from the cup, bounced once and dropped in.

For eagle. A sober, silent, joyless Q-School eagle.

"Great shot," croaked his playing partners mechanically. Clark inwardly congratulated himself and walked with his caddie to hole number 3. He ended up shooting 361 for the rain-shortened event, missing the winner's circle by one agonizing shot. If you're counting road kill on a cumulative basis, you'll want to know that Clark returned to the qualifying mill in 1998 and once again missed getting his card by a single stroke.

Some fellow competitors are easier to ignore than others. At the Sandpiper–La Purisma final of 1996, a promising young San Antonio professional named Anthony Rodriguez hired a local caddie named Larry Johnson, whose nickname was Penny, or Little Penny, based on his resemblance to the comic character in a Nike commercial featuring hoop star Penny Hardaway. Johnson even sounded like the Little Penny character, exhorting every shot Rodriguez played in a full-throated shout that echoed through the foothills.

In round three, after a Rodriguez 7-iron from 160 yards ("Go ball!" called Penny) hit in the front of La Purisma's elevated 7th green ("Release!" Penny barked), then skipped ahead 80 feet ("Settle!" the caddie demanded), and came to rest within a few strides of the hole, a fellow competitor's caddie turned to Johnson with a half-serious request. "Hey, Penny," he asked, "can you talk to our ball like that?"

Not every player paired with Rodriguez was able to make light of Johnson's lusty cheerleading, however. They were hardly disappointed when the caddie was summarily fired on the morning of round five. Little Penny, entrusted with his player's golf spikes and duty bound to show up well in advance of the tee time, shirked both responsibilities that Sunday morning. With only 20 minutes to go before tee-off, Rodriguez found himself trying on Foot-Joys in the La Purisma golf shop and wondering who would carry his bag that day. When Johnson came around the corner sputtering apologies, Rodriguez accepted the shoe bag from him and declared their partnership over. Anthony then picked up an idle caddie whose employer had been cut after round four and hustled to the tee. He shot 75 that day, his worst round of the week, but earned a tour card with no strokes to spare.

Six is a lot of days and 108 is a lot of holes, but not when the margins separating the medalists from the players who just missed are taken into consideration. At La Quinta in 1998, Mike Weir won with a 408 total while 10 players at 423 missed by a single stroke. At Grenelefe the year before, Scott Verplank lapped the field with his 407, but if you toss out Verplank's total as a statistical anomaly, Blaine McCallister's runner-up score of 413 doesn't look so different from the six 424s that missed cards by a shot. At La Purisma, where only five rounds were played and where Michael Clark endured his one-stroke disappointment, the field was packed like commuters in a Tokyo subway. A total of 49 players received cards, and 13 of them shot 358. Another 13 shot the high qualifying score of 360. Allen Doyle and Jimmy Johnston were comedalists, only eight strokes better at 352.

That tour school's scoreboard had the atmosphere of a commodities pit, where instead of trying to figure out the natural price of soybeans or silver, the task was to calibrate what the price of survival would be.

"Not one player up there is safe," a young pro near the scoreboard said quietly to his caddie during the 1996 school. The scorer switched pen colors and squeaked a few more numbers on the board. The last dozen scores of the day go up quickly, and those gathered by the board speak less and less. It's as though a huge Polaroid picture of the future were developing in front of your eyes.

"The leader isn't even safe," continued the same young pro.

"He's 7-under, and the cut's gonna be like, even-par. He could easily shoot his way out of it. Anybody could shoot their way out of this thing. Look up there. Tell me one guy who's safe. There's nobody." The leader was Paul Claxton, a laconic redhead with a rural Georgian accent. Claxton's dry, self-deprecating humor would be his only consolation the following day, as a 7-over score of 79 plunged him to within an inch of elimination. All the same, it was a happier sixth round than the one Claxton experienced the following year at Grenelefe, when he shot 74 to pass from his safe standing inside-the-number to the bitter depths of 46th place.

To find a previous Q School qualifier where the scores were as tight as in 1996, you have to hark back to the finals of the '70s and early '80s. Mick Soli, who shuttled on and off the tour during that era, missed getting his card at Pinehurst in 1980 by one stroke. The proverbial One Stroke I Missed By can be elusive and haunting for a Q Schooler, or it can be unmistakable, as it was for Soli in 1980.

"My strongest memory of a Q School—like a lot of players— isn't any of the years when I qualified," commented Soli. "What I remember the clearest is the final round of my third attempt. It was at Pinehurst, and I missed getting in by one shot. On the first hole of that sixth round, I hit a good drive and had an 8-iron left. I hit it just right, and the ball went in the hole. But it hit either the lining of the cup or the bottom of the flagstick and ricocheted out 50 feet into some light rough. If it had missed the hole by two inches I would have had a tap-in. It took three to get down from that rough and I ended up missing my card by one stroke. That was a difficult phone call back home—explaining that kind of thing to your family and your sponsors," said Soli.

No tour-school finalist prepares for his ordeal without lecturing himself on the need for patience. But soon the pace of play gets glacial, and everyone's 72-hole brain clock takes over. Blaine McCallister had not been to a Fall Classic in over a decade when he found himself competing at Grenelefe in '97.

"Tour qualifying is all about how patient you can be," said McCallister. "Still, when you finish the third round, it's a shock to look up and see you've got three more to play. You're out there for five or six hours and if you lose patience you'll make a big number that's gonna hurt you."

Jimmy Johnston, a teammate of David Duval's at Georgia Tech, was comedalist at the 1996 Q School in California but hasn't been able to stick on the big tour. Back at school in 1997, he suffered a one-shot week-wrecker on the second-to-last hole of the second-to-last day.

"Jimmy had a 2-iron shot over water on 17," recalled tour caddie Bob Chaney. "The group in front of us lost a ball, I guess, but we couldn't figure which player it was or really what the delay was. Then one of their guys walks back to replay from his original spot. That took five minutes, on top of the few minutes we had already waited. I should have taken the club from him, made him sit down, done something to break the tension." Chaney never did. When Johnston went to play his 2-iron shot, his focus was badly blurred. "The ball went about 150 yards," Chaney said. "Right in the middle of the pond." At the time he made that swing, Johnston was "inside the number." That night he had to sleep on the flubbed shot and sleep on the fact that he would have to start round six by repairing the damage from it with a birdie or two. Whatever delicate balance Johnston had been in was destroyed, apparently. He shot 79 the last day to finish nine shots over the magic number.

The long waits on tees and fairways can turn a slightly flaky fellow competitor into a helpful asset. At the 1998 school, Briny Baird, Jay Delsing, and Chris Smith came to the second tee of the

Weiskopf course, each having parred the first hole and each thus reasonably relaxed. Baird, a born grinder, stalked the perimeter of the tee, but Delsing and the caddies listened with amusement as Smith discussed his shopping expedition of the previous night. This was the Saturday of the annual Ohio State–Michigan football game and Smith, an Ohio State graduate, tugged on his Buckeye cap as he discussed his preparations for the game.

"The condo I'm renting with my agent, Mac [Barnhardt, of Pros, Inc.], has this nice big TV with a VCR hooked into it," explained Smith. "As soon as I saw it, I said great, I'm taping the game. The thing worked fine—we rented a movie one night and tested it out. So I got a couple of blank tapes and went to set everything up last night.

"Only, it turns out the thing doesn't record—doesn't have the buttons or anything."

"It's just a player unit," one of the caddies suggested.

"Yeah, exactly, it's just a player," confirmed Smith, recalling his astonishment. "So what was I gonna do? I had to go out to Wal-Mart and buy a real one."

"You *bought* a VCR?" smiled Delsing. "So you could tape one game?"

"Yeah, Mac and I went out about 10 o'clock and got a good deal on one," answered Smith, a true fan's passion in his voice. "Got it all hooked up to start at kickoff."

"And then what? You're bringing it home? Don't you already have one?" a caddie inquired.

"Yeah, but it's old," Smith assured him. "We've been needing one for the downstairs TV anyway."

Sufficiently distracted by Smith's tale, his playing partners crushed their drives straight to Position A on the second fairway, where Smith soon joined them. All three ended up getting cards at the school. The only question that remained in the minds of

Smith's companions that day was why, if he wanted to avoid at all costs learning the outcome of the game until he could see it on tape, he had chosen to walk past hundreds of similarly football-minded people wearing the Ohio State cap. The next day I ran into Barnhardt and asked him if his client, along with shooting a glorious 67, had successfully avoided hearing the final score.

"Well, somebody in the gallery called out the first-quarter score to him," said the agent, "but he didn't hear anything after that. I saw him at the end of the day getting in his rental car and by this time he's got an Ohio State jersey on, plus the cap, and a bag of nachos on his lap. I wanted to congratulate him, but he waved me off. He said, 'Don't tell me anything, Mac,' and he went squealing out of the parking lot."

Not every player can muster the innocent nonchalance of a Chris Smith when their livelihood is on the line. In such cases, false bravado makes a useful alternative.

Robert Damron, a young PGA Tour player who earned his playing privileges during the chilly, rainy 1997 Q School in central California, admitted later that the sight of his 90-hole total sitting on the scoreboard immediately above the cut line undermined his natural warrior spirit.

"They kept trying to get us on the course to complete the full 108 holes, and every time we went out the rain would get heavy and they'd call us back in," recalls Damron, who had been through the wringer of final-stage tour qualifying twice before without success. Knowing how hard it might be rekindle his competitive fires should play resume, Damron tried to make his outward behavior influence his innermost emotions.

"I kept walking around the grill room and the locker room saying to people, 'We're gonna play, we're gonna get it in,' " Damron explained. "And inside all I could think was, 'Keep raining. Oh please, just keep on raining.' "

10

ON THE NUMBER

For five hours, Bob Friend had regulated his emotions like a London stage actor. Now nothing was in his control. From mid-morning through mid-afternoon, he had positioned his golf ball like a chess piece along the tight zigzags of Grenelefe South. Now his historic, 9-under-par score of 63 was a lowly pawn ready to be knocked aside.

"Who can bump me?" Friend asked between shallow breaths, shifting his gaze in the cramped press room from a computer scoreboard to a final-round telecast of the 1997 PGA Tour Qualifying Tournament. Scott Verplank's wire-to-wire, record-setting 407 topped the TV leaderboard, and Blaine McCallister's nearly record-tying 413 stood beneath it. But those achievements were old news to reporters who surrounded Friend, alternately interviewing and reassuring him.

Out on the course, the "bumpers" were Patrick Lee, Iain Steel, Charlie Rymer, and Craig Kanada. These four players were tied with Friend for 34th place at 6-under or were one back at 5-under and still had holes to play. If just two of them were to make the finishing birdies necessary to join the 7-under group, it would banish the entire minus-6 contingent from the cherished status of top-35-and-ties. Friend's string of 14 birdies over his final 27 holes would be for naught. Focusing on Lee and Steel at 6-under, Friend gulped at a bottle of spring water and implored his peers: "Par in, guys, just par in and get your cards."

Steel, who had shot 67 the day before, added a final-round 69 to finish at 423, the same score Friend had posted. Kanada, playing the par-72 West course, crafted a 67 to come in at 424. But 424 turned out to be a buck short, as Rymer holed a long par putt on 18 to finish 66–424 himself, and Patrick Lee disappeared from the 6-under ranks by botching his 108th and final hole, beginning with a pulled drive into some trees left of the fairway.

The very last piece of the Q School 1997 puzzle was a late bogey that dropped Tim Loustalot to 75–423 and rounded out the sextet of players who tied for 33rd. These 38 grads—almost one-third of whom would be rookies—set their sights on the courtesy cars, endorsement contracts, and burgeoning purses of the PGA Tour. Verplank's cannonball run past Mike Standly's previous 108-hole record of 412 (set at Grenelefe in 1991) was the week's headline story, but Friend's heroic 63 on the par-71 South at Grenelefe has to rank among the gutsiest performances in Q School history.

"My back was against the wall," said Friend, who had scuffled on the PGA and Nike tours for nine seasons before accepting a teaching job at the prestigious Inverness Club in Ohio. "Any athlete, from any sport, when he's in that position, has the ultimate chance to prove himself. I came in here playing well, then for some reason I started the week [76–69–76] playing like garbage.

"But look what happened," he said, referring to final-round pairings that put the high half of the field on the 6,700-yard South course. "I played my way over to the South course for the final round. Without that, I couldn't have shot a number low enough to get my card. Looking at the scores last night, I knew I had to take it low. Not just shoot 67 or 66, but lower than I've ever gone. That 63 today is my lowest competitive round ever." Friend's 63 also went into the books as one of the three or four lowest competitive rounds in Q School history.

There was an important policy footnote to Friend's week: If the qualifying field had been cut to the low 90 players and ties after four rounds—as it had been since 1982—he and his plus-4 score of 360 would have been cashiered. Grenelefe 1997 was planned by the PGA Tour as a radical antidote to the misbegotten 1996 Q School in the stormy canyons of central California. Instead of 198 players, a more manageable 168 were let through second stage. Instead of a cut, policy in 1997 was let-'em-all-play-108. Instead of the clunky sight of would-be Tour pros buzzing around in golf carts, a no-ride policy was drafted, to simulate PGA Tour conditions (that particular wrinkle would later be scuttled by the Casey Martin lawsuit). Instead of two dramatic golf courses located 40 miles apart, the plan in 1997 was to put the field on two perfectly fine golf courses a half-mile from each other. And instead of an afterthought purse of $175,000, there were 500,000 real dollars to play for.

"Whew. Guess he needs the money," one middle-of-the-pack player said when he looked at the scoreboard and saw Verplank stake his defiant claim to first prize with a blazing 66–64 start. By Saturday morning, the Tour was typing up Verplank's PGA card and his check for $30,000, while the field jostled for second-place money of $21,000. For this week, anyway, Verplank's elbow operations, his diabetes, and his general lack of luck were pushed to the background by virtuoso ball-striking and solid putting. His salad days as a U.S. Amateur champion, and an NCAA individual champion, and an amateur winner of the Western Open, felt somehow less remote.

"Winning feels good," Verplank commented when it was all over. "It's been a long time. Ten years ago, I was winning quite a bit. I haven't had great luck the last six to eight years. I came to Q School feeling I could play good and get my card or play real great and have a chance to win. Once I got going, I'll be honest, I wanted to win by 10 or 12."

Ironically, Verplank the front-runner received his highest praise from the last player in through the back door. "Take away the medical problems," said Friend of Verplank, "and you're looking at a big-time PGA Tour winner. I played against him in college, and along with all his talent, Scott was a fierce competitor. The guy is tougher than a nickel steak."

When the six-day grind of Q School finals begins, players lust for the moment when they are out on the course in such good position and so close to finishing that to fall below the cut line would be virtually impossible. With very few exceptions, this moment only comes during the last round. At the 1987 finals in Palm Coast, Florida, Bruce Zabriski earned his PGA Tour eligibility for the second time. Heading onto the back nine in final-round play at Matanzas Woods Golf Club, Zabriski was tied for third place, a lock to receive one of the 54 cards granted that year.

"I came to the 18th," said the six-foot-four Long Island native, "and for some reason I hit my best drive of the day and my best drive on that hole all week. Must have been too relaxed, because the ball rolled out to the 210 marker. I was cussing myself, because the hole has an island green with a long carry over water, and now I was too close to do anything but go for it. From that yardage, what could I do? Finish out tour school by hitting pitching wedge-pitching wedge? I'll tell you something, I wanted to. But it would have been too embarrassing.

"The guys I was playing with were hitting their layup shots, and there I was in the middle of the fairway, shaking," said Zabriski. "But while I was waiting for the green to clear, I decided to count how many balls I could hit in the water and still get my card." Zabriski, who went on to become a teaching professional at Westchester Country Club outside New York City and a national PGA Club Pro champion, actually tallied his maximum safe score for the hole, a 16. "I'm glad I did that arithmetic because it freed me up to make a swing," he said. His subsequent 3-iron shot not only hit the green but left him with a makable birdie putt, which he holed.

Thanks to the Internet and the Golf Channel, gory details of a tour-school final are much better known than they used to be. But even before television coverage and Web site updates, the player who suffered a long, drawn-out collapse in a Q School final became an instant anti-legend within a wide circle of players, caddies, officials, and media. The scarlet C for choking can be pinned on a pro golfer at all sorts of venues, from the U.S. Open to the Honda Classic to Quad Cities. And in those venues, one swing can brand you. All it takes for infamy is a single climactic shot that's ugly enough, or a two-footer to win that yips far enough off-line.

But Q School finals are an ocean of strokes and holes in which one gasping player is not so easy to spot. To observe the flock of players laboring under the greatest final-round pressure you have to look somewhere about a dozen strokes off the lead. Therefore, critical strokes that get thrown away due to a single bolt of fear—no matter how greatly the player is staggered by it—tend to keep from passing into tour-school mythology. Due to the sheer scale of the event, the stories that get passed around are of players who get through 99 or 100 holes in great position, then fall apart for keeps, scattering strokes all over the final homeward nine. Behind these easily spotted tragedies are the untold stories of players whose courage ran dry at an isolated moment, doing swift but permanent damage that the player alone can appreciate.

And if you look at it that way, perhaps notoriety and infamy are preferable.

Jim Carter, a slender six-footer whose freckles and thatch of blond hair keep him youthful-looking at age 38, had been described—with nods and winks—as someone who may not want to talk about Q School. Instead Carter warmed freely to the subject, leaning on his putter after a practice round for the 1998 Canon Greater Hartford Open and recalling his "famous choke stories" at La Quinta, California, in 1990 and The Woodlands, Texas, in 1992. It certainly eases the sting for Carter that his career has gone well in recent years. After regaining his PGA Tour privileges by finishing fourth on the 1994 Nike Tour money list, the former Arizona State walk-on has steadily improved his PGA Tour ranking, from 102nd in 1995 to 71st in 1998. But it's also clear from his comments that Jim Carter—not unlike Mac O'Grady—accepts and even embraces the reality of tour qualifying, acknowledging that he may never play his way beyond its tentacles and aware he is one of many who lost their nerve under its strain.

"At The Woodlands I was 4-under for the tournament through 14 holes on the last day," he confessed. "Then I made four straight bogeys on the last four holes to miss by one. They were all tap-in bogeys," Carter pointed out with a shrug. "The last hole, I had a 10- or 12-footer for par. My caddie and I both knew I had to make it to get through and get a card. The putt didn't drop," he mused.

Carter took a few phantom strokes with his putter and gazed around the practice putting green of the TPC at River Highlands, ringed by weekday spectators two and three deep. Although only a few of these fans were likely to know Carter by sight, most had firm notions about what his life must be like. "That was tough, playing so badly down the stretch and missing by one stroke," he said. "But hey," he added, almost brightening, "it was the second time in two years it happened, so it wasn't that much of a shock."

Two years earlier at La Quinta, on the Nicklaus Resort golf course of PGA West, Carter had a run of double-bogey, par, double-bogey on the back nine to finish one mournful stroke outside the number. "That one really hurt," he said of his 1990 crack-up. "I can't even remember what happened on some of the holes. On the second double-bogey, I missed the fairway by a bunch. I had to hit a layup shot, just bump it forward. Then I hit my third—a pitching wedge—into the bunker." Carter paused to think how 17-handicapesque that narrative sounded. "It was really pitiful," he concluded. "Mentally I wasn't even there. I think I was two holes back, replaying the other double-bogey."

What followed were three years of wilderness wanderings, split between the Nike Tour, a few guest appearances on the big tour, and one year, 1992, when Carter won only a few thousand dollars, perhaps wondering at that point if he should dust off his ASU business degree and quit the grind. Then he went out and won $142,000 on the Nike Tour to regain his PGA Tour exemption. Given this set of circumstances, it's only natural for Jim Carter to be a Nike Tour booster and a Q School detractor, correct? He claims that isn't the case.

"The Nike Tour and tour school are both excellent tests," observed Carter. "But I hate to see them chopping away at Q School and giving more and more places to the Nike Tour. I've made it to the big tour both ways, and I almost feel like the guys who come out of school are tougher—especially someone who plays second stage. You have to put your balls on the line every step of the way in tour school. If you can make it through, it's a great accomplishment, it makes you stronger."

Eric Epperson, according to many players who competed in the 1995 finals at Grenelefe—and many who did not—emerged from that qualifier as a symbol of classic tour-school disintegration. "Every year there's a poster boy, some guy who chokes his guts out on the last day," tour school regular Ron Whittaker explained. "The year I made it, Eric Epperson bogeyed six of the last nine holes. He was in good shape before that last nine, too. So he was poster boy."

Since his flameout in that 1995 school, Epperson has rattled around playing U.S. minitours and trying his luck overseas, as well. He hasn't been seen at a subsequent Q School final, nor has he shown the least interest in discussing his dark day at Bear Lakes Country Club in West Palm Beach. "We saw in the paper how well he was doing going into the last day," said Stacy Jordan, a friend of Epperson's from Eastern Hills Country Club in Garland, Texas. "Everybody said, 'Hey, looks like Epp's going to make the tour.' Then he had his crater."

Having a "crater" on the last day of tour school is a tradition that dates back to Roger Kluska's 80 in the eighth round of the fall 1968 qualifier, which caused Kluska to miss by two shots. Final-round balloon jobs were as common as plaid pants in the early days of qualifying, but back then you could survive one. Gary Preuss finished with an 80 in the spring of 1969 and still took second place. John Shackleford's 81 in the final round of the spring 1968 school didn't keep him off the tour—and that particular school only gave out 15 cards. The fall school in 1968 saw eight out of the 30 tour cards go to players who failed to break 80. The weather was miserable, granted, but today's players would be a lock to score far lower under similar conditions.

The tour-school fields of the 1980s were only starting to show the depth we see today. In the 1982 qualifier at Ponte Vedra, Florida, there were 16 players among the 50 qualifiers who finished with scores of 76 or worse. In 1984, another 50 players made it through and five of them had 78s the last day. In 1986, the medalist finished with a 75 and 12 other card-earners either equaled him or ballooned higher. But other than Paul Claxton's 79 in 1996, there are absolutely no volcanic final-day scores among card-earners of the last five years.

But recent tour-school history does reveal isolated mistakes— brutal, unthinkable errors born of fear—that turn competent 70s into catastrophic 73s. Dave Eichelberger's 75 in the closing round at Palm Coast, Florida, in 1987 looks fairly innocuous in the record book, but Eichelberger, who had five tour victories in his career, finished his round with double-bogey, double-bogey, double-bogey. He had been lingering in the secure zone between 10th and 15th place, but this last-minute bungling dropped him into an eight-way tie for 47th—last place among the qualifiers.

Kenny Perry's score on the last day of the 1986 tour qualifier at La Quinta, California, was a perfectly respectable 72, but it ended with a disastrous gag job of a double-bogey on Perry's final hole—number 9 on the PGA West Stadium course. Perry had spent six years on the minitours and was navigating Q School finals for the third time. He had won at every level, but had never truly believed he was worthy of a PGA Tour exemption.

"I had a dream, and I never gave up, but I had kind of a crazy swing and for a long time I was this guy in a shell," Perry said, looking back from the security of his $4 million career earnings mark. "My dad, who taught me to play, was the one person who had no doubts I could make it." Perry's father was an insurance executive who specialized in motivational training. He was also an excellent amateur golfer who liked to place the snap-on cover of his leather golf bag in the middle of the lawn and hit pitch shots at it until he and Kenny had filled the pouch with shag balls. At La Quinta, the senior Perry piloted his son's golf cart for six days, clenching an unlit cigar in his teeth most of the way. When the 108th hole finally came into view, Team Perry was aware that even-par, their standing for the tournament, was "right about on the number, maybe a little inside it." Kenny Perry revved up his self-described crazy swing for one more tee shot and let fly. His drive was snared by a fairway bunker on the right side.

"I had 170 to the flag, all over water," recalled Perry. "I hit 6-iron."

He hit it fat. The ball floated achingly toward its target, died in flight, and splash-landed. It wasn't a matter of Perry doubting his strategy mid-swing and having the "abort" light flash on in his brain. It was a simple flash of fear. The golfer's brain is a lot like any cluster of computers and printers plugged into a single AC outlet—it needs a surge suppressor to keep momentary overloads from scrambling the software. In this instance, Kenny Perry had no such protection.

"I committed myself to the shot," he explained. "My problem was purely nerves. I got a little quick, came in a little steep. Hit behind it. Man, how I would have loved a mulligan right then." Perry walked ahead, dropped a ball, knocked it on, and two-putted. He and his father stowed Kenny's gear, drove into town, and ordered burgers at a Wendy's. Peeling open the little ketchups and punching straws through soda lids, they spoke haltingly about things they could have done differently somewhere in those six rounds. But the fat 6-iron at the bitter end hung over their conversation. Father and son drove back in silence toward the club to review the final results. When they reached the scoreboard, they saw Perry's even-par 432 in an unlikely position. It was riding two whole healthy strokes above the final cut line.

"Whoa, there I was, inside the number," Perry recalled. "My dad and I went from misery to a feeling of pure joy," he said. "I called my wife, called my two sisters. It was the greatest feeling. But I was kicking myself a little, too. I knew I should have wedged it out of that bunker. Learned a good lesson that day."

Gaining a tour card against heavy odds and doing it with the help of a highly supportive father is biographical material Esteban Toledo could just about copyright. Toledo predates Carlos Franco of Paraguay as a true PGA Tour story of ashes to affluence. Broad shouldered, with coarse black hair and a nut-brown complexion, he grew up in Mexicali, Mexico, as the youngest of 10 children with an AWOL father and too little food to go around. The man he refers to as his father is a wealthy American named John Minnis who prospered in the concrete business. When the two met in 1982, Toledo was a 20-year-old tournament golfer, former professional boxer, and part-time driving-range employee. Over time Minnis became the young man's sponsor and surrogate parent, helping him relocate to California and focus on his career full-time. Minnis was with Toledo at Grenelefe in 1991, the scene of Toledo's most heartbreaking tour-school experience among all 12 of his attempts.

"When I came off the course the last day," he said of his misbegotten 1991 tour school, "they told me it was a 90-percent chance for my card. I was excited—90 percent." Before long, Toledo saw the scorekeeper pare his name from the final list. The projection had been incorrect. "I cried all the way from Orlando to San Francisco that night," he admitted. Toledo would earn his card for the first time at the 1993 qualifier in La Quinta, then fail to keep it. "After all that struggle to get the card, I didn't realize it would be so hard to keep it," he mused.

Toledo shot 71–72–70–70–66 over the 1997 school's first five rounds. He arrived at Grenelefe West for the final round determined to avoid a Black Monday. Toledo had barely slept the night before, which neither surprised nor troubled him. His 66 on the South course in round five had been the result of "playing aggressive and playing intelligent," a one-two punch the former prizefighter often refers to. Starting the final round minus-8, he could expect from the perfect weather and the depth of the field that about minus-7 would be enough to get the job done. If so, Toledo's target score would be par 72, perhaps even 1-over 73. Despite needing only a ham-and-eggs number, he found himself feeling "very aggressive" only at the beginning of the round. "On the last nine holes, I was not so aggressive," he said. "On the last two holes, I was the most nervous I've ever been in my life."

Toledo played the 17th without incident. Standing on the last tee at plus-1 for the day and minus-7 for the tournament, he could see every contour of the uphill par-5 18th of the West course without opening his eyes. Today's closing round on the West had been a wary, tingling march through the Bermuda-grass minefield. It was shaping up to be a safe 73, one over par but still good enough to earn him his PGA Tour eligibility for the second time in 10 tries. The vow he had made 10 days earlier to his wife, Colleen ("I am going to Florida tomorrow, and I am not coming back without my tour card"), was five strokes and 15 minutes from fulfillment.

Esteban bumped his driver on the grass and prepared to hit his last tee shot ever in a Q School. He drew the club back, powered it forward, and split the fairway. First-tee jitters had been warded off, but tension can creep into a tournament golfer through as many little holes as field mice find in a cabin floor. The layup shot Toledo needed to hit had an awkward feel to it. He committed to the same club he had used for this shot in prior rounds, his 2-iron, but failed to finish off the swing. "A bad lay-up," he said, reliving his rush of panic. "The second I hit it I knew I had blocked it right," he said, wincing.

His ball was playable from the stand of trees along number 18. Toledo's punch shot out of there flew well and settled in decent shape about 20 feet from the front of the green. As so often happens, the need to play with some creativity had produced a settling effect. Now the uphill-then-downhill chip shot Toledo faced called for more invention, and a well-calibrated little stroke, as well. The tension crawled back through Toledo's thick shoulders.

"I get up and down for par, I'm a lock at 7-under," he thought to himself. "Bogey, and I'm down the road. I know it," he said. His hands shook as he waggled a 59-degree wedge. Toledo put it back and took out his 55-degree wedge. He chipped it cleanly, and the ball decelerated at about the spot it needed to. Toledo was striding behind it now, asking his shot to die near the hole, not six or eight feet past, where trembling hands would be unlikely to finish the job. Then his repeated plea for the ball to slow down suddenly switched to a new directive: *Go in*. The ball bumped the flagstick and disappeared. Birdie-4, and 8-under for the tournament, good enough to make it by two strokes.

"My dad and I were so happy," Toledo said as he relived the moment. "We made plans to celebrate. We each had flights going to two different airports from Orlando, but we had lots of time so we decided to go to the airport and celebrate in the bar at the terminal. Except we were so excited and talking so much, we missed the exit for Orlando Airport. It took a while to realize it, and by then we were way out in the country somewhere. Instead of having all this time to celebrate, we each had to run to our gates to catch the flights."

Toledo had not even told his wife the news. When he caught his breath and fastened his seat belt, he called her from the phone on the plane. After a few jubilant minutes of conversation, she asked where he was. When he explained, she said he should get off the phone, the air-phone bill would be so high. Toledo was charmed by the suggestion. "I said to her, 'Colleen, what are you worrying about? I'm on the PGA Tour!' "

Round six. Back nine. On the number. At that point, "groundhog day" is an obsolete concept. Q School is no longer monotonous, repetitive, or numbing. Adrenaline dances into the bloodstream and all weariness is flushed away. The ultimate paradox of Q School is the toe-stubbing player's sudden wish for more holes beyond the stipulated 108. The contestant who is playing well but slips outside the number with a late bogey on the last day instantly becomes the cheating sitcom husband who swears off bimbos and begs his wife for one last chance, if only she'll unlock the apartment door. At La Quinta in 1998, Jay Williamson had a lasso around his tour card and let it slip with two holes to go. Seventeen and 18 at PGA West's Weiskopf course were all that remained of the 1998 finals after the former college baseball and hockey star dumped one in the water on 16. After all the days and hours, that bungled iron shot had made Williamson a man out of time.

He had begun the day 12-under with conventional wisdom whispering that either 12-under or 11-under would be "the number." At age 31, having earned a PGA Tour card at the 1994 Q School and then lost it, having overcome his late start in the game, having pulled up his and his wife's roots in St. Louis and grudgingly moved to Orlando, Williamson walked to the tee for round six feeling something was owed him. When he got to 16, a reachable par 5 with the second shot over water to a wide green, he was 1-under for the day, 13-under for the tournament. Marnie Williamson, his former classmate at Burroughs High School and his wife since May of 1997, shaded her eyes as Jay lined up a 3-iron that, if it landed right, could carry the two of them to a fresh start. He hit the shot solidly, but with a draw instead of the straight or fading flight called for. His ball struck the far bank and curled into the pond.

Bogey, which Williamson eventually made, was not even a consideration on the par-5 16th of PGA West Weiskopf. The 480-yard hole was such an easy par for these professionals that Dave Stockton, Jr., when asked the day before by his famous father what 16's par was, immediately answered "Four." Williamson fought to keep his wits about him as he cleaned up the mess at 16 and prepared to play the 220-yard par-3 17th, no birdie hole on this day thanks to a merciless pin placement. He managed a three at 17 and moved to number 18 still incredulous at what had occured just a few minutes earlier. The stroke that disappeared in the water at 16 was not to be recovered. This finishing hole was set up like a fortress, with the tee markers back and the pin cut far right—next to a water hazard and in the shadow of a dramatic swale that runs from front to back of the green.

Williamson drove long and straight. He had 165 yards remaining, and he pulled his iron shot slightly, just as everyone in the field with half a brain had done before him, taking the right-side water hazard out of play. Up at the green, the threesome heard information to the effect that, given the current leaderboard, 12-under would be okay. Wonderful news, but to finish at 12-under Williamson would have to execute a scoundrel of a two-putt. From the gallery side of the green, he looked like a man putting 25 feet along the length of a municipal stormwater pipe. He drew back his odd, cut-down minigolf-looking putter and put the ball in motion. It crawled on exactly the pace he wanted, first dying on the ridge, then stirring to life and oozing down the slope to within 30 inches of the hole. Williamson curtained his emotions behind a frozen, ashen mask of a face and made the two-footer. He was in at 12-under. Walking stiffly to the scorer's tent, he heard Golf Channel spotters reassuring him: "Eleven-under's in, 11-under makes it," they declared.

Three minutes later, Williamson emerged from the tiny tent and plodded a few steps toward a hardpan cart path where Marnie stood waiting for him. She had heard plenty of talk that 11-under was the number and at least some part of her knew their battle had been won. Their effort to embrace looked like two clenched fists attempting a handshake. Both were unsteady, although Marnie now appeared to be getting her land legs back. Waiting for Jay to sign his card, she had been panning the scene around her indiscriminately; now her eyes were regaining their focus. But her husband was off somewhere else, enduring a painful spasm of the soul. He straightened to his full height as if touched with a cattle prod and whipped his head back, gasping out a curse or a confession or both. Tears popped from his hazel eyes and covered his sunburned cheeks.

"God, I thought I lost it when I went in that water," Williamson sobbed, squeezing his wife's shoulders. Apparently hyperventilating, he panted out a series of half-sentences as the two of them leaned together, walked a few steps, then paused in another awkward hug. The Williamsons made balky progress down the crude dirt trail, probably glad to be surrounded by gnarly desert ground cover and a row of sky-blue portable toilets rather than somewhere more public. "That was the dumbest, dumbest shot I ever hit," Williamson gasped. "The 3-iron. I hit it on the right line and then it started to draw. I couldn't believe it. It hit the bank . . ." He had ceased crying abruptly and had begun a staccato replay of the events of the last 40 minutes. Because of the water ball, his final two holes had been played in a manic state of fear and deep humiliation, emotions he had somehow managed to hide from everyone watching. "I embarrassed myself," he admitted. "I was fine up until that shot, then after it I got so nervous. Never, ever been that nervous."

Two golf carts rumbled past, packed with television equipment in scarred steel cases. Williamson stopped on the hardpan and took two deep breaths. At that moment he seemed to realize, for the first time, that he had indeed earned his PGA Tour exemption for 1999. Marnie pointed in the direction of the clubhouse, and Jay seemed to remember there were still comforts in this world—there was a sinkful of cool water waiting for him to douse his sunburned, tearstained cheeks, and a table in some corner of the plush, carpeted PGA West grill room where the two of them could sit down with something cold to drink. He didn't seem to mind that reporters had witnessed his emotional siege. Possibly, he had used their stream of questions as proof that tour school was over, that he was inside the number and free to go.

"Why this tour school mattered so much to me—the real reason," he explained later, "is that I've reached a stage where I can win on the big tour. I'm certain of it. Once you have that feeling, then Q School turns into just a thing sitting in your way, which probably makes it even harder to get past, if that makes any sense."

Makes a lot of sense. A person comes to a realization regarding certain achievements he or she is capable of, and that realization starts them down a potentially wonderful path. However, along that path, there is often one obstacle that overwhelms all others. PGA Tour qualifying school is a classic example, a roadblock—a nuisance, really—impeding the steps of someone who knows they have great deeds to accomplish further along, and the fortitude to accomplish them, as well.

Which is why the perfect Q School story is of someone like Bill Ziobro, a PGA club pro in New Jersey who played the tour for seven years in the 1970s with a degree of success, then left it to settle down and live a normal life. Ziobro grew up in the town of Scotch Plains as an undersized but more than competent athlete. After graduating from the University of Maryland, he went straight to the fall 1971 qualifying school.

"I had to get through what they used to call the Eastern regional," he explained. "That got me into the final field of about 75." Ziobro's final-stage field at the old PGA National in Palm Beach Gardens included Tom Watson, Lanny Wadkins, David Graham, and John Mahaffey. The format was 108 holes at final stage, with 23 eligibility cards to be distributed. Ziobro, now head professional at Atlantic City Country Club, opened with a 76, then followed it with rounds of 72, 75, 74, 72. He was falling approximately three strokes a day behind the two or three players at the top, but keeping close to the coveted top-23 status. He set off on his sixth and final round with a sense of mission, but his scoring remained in the same rut it had occupied all week.

"I remember I came to the 107th hole and I was within one shot of making it," said Ziobro. "The whole week I hadn't played a real good round. No big mistakes, but I was on the border the whole time. Anyway, I made a 10-footer on that second-to-last hole for birdie, which gave me some insurance. It put me in a position where I could bogey the 18th and still get my tour card."

Ziobro looked down the par-4 18th and contemplated the water hazard to the left and the bunkers to the right. Basking in his small but strategically critical cushion, he aligned himself away from the water and drove down the right side. His ball landed in a fairway bunker, 215 yards from the hole. From there, he only needed a wedge escape and another wedge over the pond that fronted the green, followed by two putts. Ziobro looked at his lie, looked at the green, then looked inside his soul.

"I pulled my 4-wood out of the bag," he said. "Of course, I could have laid up, but here I'd played 107 holes without doing anything." It dawned on Ziobro that he would soon be admitted to the top ranks of golf, without showing that he truly deserved such an honor. He took the headcover off his fairway wood.

"I thought the caddie was going to faint, but I wasn't changing my mind," he recalled. "I just felt like it was my time to *make the shot*. You know, you can live on the number, but at some point you've got to break through. All my life, I had been the small guy from the public links who did more than people expected. It was my nature to be aggressive, and down at this tour school I'd done nothing but play safe."

Ziobro dug his spikes in the sand and whooshed his 4-wood lustily through the ball, gunning it out of the bunker, up over the water, and onto the green. The ball hopped once and stopped 15 feet from the hole. Ziobro followed his display of valor with a touch of discretion, lagging the 15-footer to tap-in range, then holing out for a 443 total—one dramatic and decisive stroke inside the number. He had lived on the number, but in the end he had broken through. There are many Q School stories equally as dramatic—or more so—but this one was uniquely climactic. Having recounted it, Ziobro was asked a question that appeared to have an obvious answer: The golfer who walked out of that fairway bunker on number 18 at PGA National—was he a different man than the one who had stepped into it?

Ziobro thought for a second. Then he answered, with the same conviction he had shown in launching that 4-wood shot 27 years earlier.

"Not exactly," said Ziobro. "You know who walked out of that fairway bunker? The guy I always knew I could be."

11

THE RESHUFFLE

Billy Ziobro's tour career, jump-started by one bold decision in a fairway bunker on number 18 at PGA National, continued uninterrupted for seven years. At that point, still in his 20s and having traveled the U.S. in competition with the game's best players, Ziobro closed out his tour career and became a club pro. He admits that if the money back then had been anything like what it is now, he may have decided differently. But leaving the tour when he did was an easy call to make.

"I did it until my heart told me it was time to quit," Ziobro said. "I never had to go back to Q School and requalify, but just to stay on the tour took all my effort. It turned me into a one-dimensional person. I didn't have enough talent to be a tour player and do anything else."

Sifting through 35 years of Q School history, we don't encounter many neat, clean endings to tour careers. Journeyman golfers keep packing suitcases and following the sun. Comebacks from illness, injury, marital breakup, and youthful carousing are commonplace. Attempted comebacks, anyway.

Ziobro's qualifying story—his one decisive shot on the ultimate hole—is proof that the final moments of the last day of Q School can be a decisive juncture in a young man's life—it can usher him with a flourish into an adulthood full of challenge and achievement. That's not the typical case, however. Since 1990, only 27.5 percent of all Q School "graduates" have played well enough in the ensuing year to keep their PGA Tour exemptions. When the dust settles on a Q School final, the people who experienced it are hard-pressed to accept that—statistically, anyway—card-keeping in the year to come will be three times more difficult than card-earning had proven to be.

Repeating tour school is a way of life for most pros who are good enough to make it through the early stages. For some, it becomes an annual ritual—as Harry Taylor admitted, "tour school is just what I did every year in the fall." Which is why, when a player's make-or-break four-footer lips out on hole number 108, you can't truly say, "There goes Joe's career," not if this is his fourth tour-school final and he's destined to play in several more.

Thirty-five years of Q School history have tried to fold themselves into these pages, but the revolving-door nature of the tournament prevents the record from ever being closed. As this book rests on a shelf, a player like Chip Beck or Andy Bean might be preparing for a successful reimmersion in the qualifying process. Only when a pro golfer reaches his mid-40s could you rightfully declare him a nonfactor—at which point the great redux of Senior PGA Tour qualifying enters the picture.

When Q School is over, the new inductees undergo a daylong indoctrination by the PGA Tour's player relations department. The information presented bears more than a faint resemblance to the seminar material offered at that first 49-man convocation back in 1965. Players are handed carefully prepared database printouts of all the mailing addresses of noninvitational tournaments on the PGA Tour calendar, along with corresponding contact names, addresses, and phone numbers of the PGA of America section offices that conduct open qualifying for these events. The seminar actually begins with a reception and a couple of presentations on the night play ends. After that session breaks up, some players reconvene at the hotel lounge. You can spot the ones who stayed the latest when it's time to get down to business the next day.

"Over the years there have been a few guys who enjoyed themselves that last night, and why not?" says Dave Lancer, the tour's director of information.

On the final afternoon, when play is complete, the big outdoor scoreboard is more crowded with players than at any other time. Even players who missed getting PGA Tour cards are out in force, looking on the bright side or seeking out a kind word from their associates. In one knot of people at the La Quinta school of 1998, Pat Burke, who had missed by a couple of shots, was grumbling about the Nike Tour card he would soon receive. "I don't like that tour," Burke said. "You go through all this travel and expense trying to do one thing—get your PGA card back. Q School's a much better deal—six rounds instead of six months."

Another player, overhearing Burke's comment, turned to his own circle of friends and dissented.

"I know how some guys feel about the Nike Tour," the player said, "but I'm a professional golfer. That's what I do. Wherever they give me a chance to play, I'm gonna play."

Burke surveyed the scene at the 1998 finals. There were card-earners, card-missers, agents, reporters, manufacturers, and assorted onlookers. From one small knot of people to the next, conversation came in flurries, congratulations offered to one player, consolation to another. Then each flurry would end, giving way to an odd silence that someone in the group would have to break.

"I've got another year of exemption down in Australia—that's an option," Burke said. "If I didn't have this wrist injury I'd probably head down there tomorrow. I have to think of something, anyway, got a family to support." He swigged the last of his beer and spoke the nearly unthinkable.

"Yeah, it might be employment time for me."

I have never lingered at Q School's final-day scoreboard scene long enough to notice which player was the last one left standing there, the last guy to put his hands on his hips, scan all the names and numbers a final time, then turn and walk away. The closing scene of golf's pro qualifier reminds me faintly of the opening scene in Theodore Dreiser's acclaimed Depression-era novel *An American Tragedy*. The book's opening pages introduce us to Clyde Griffiths, the novel's hero, as young Clyde stands burning with shame on the streets of his small Midwestern city, singing church hymns with his parents and siblings while passers-by drop coins into their collection box. Clyde, enterprising by nature and already feeling footloose, smolders with humiliation when forced to sing on the street corners. His mortification agitates every molecule of ambition within the boy, propelling him eastward toward opportunity, social advancement, and his eventual dark end.

PGA Tour Q School swings back and forth between tedium and tension during its six days of play, and only when the curtain falls can the cumulative embarrassment of it all sink in. Despite its 35 (plus ties) happy endings, the tournament has a dance-marathon bleakness to it. If the PGA Tour is Broadway or Hollywood, its qualifier is a gritty vaudeville tryout that plays all week to a mostly empty theater. Some performers leave with a small prize and a chance to go somewhere better, but the experience of having sung for their supper has to stick with them for a while. Not that the career of journeyman can't be pursued with a sense of purpose and honor, but if it leads the player back to qualifying school again and again, mental scar tissue is naturally going to accumulate. Mac O'Grady survived it by finding a perverse nobility in the quest. Harry Taylor turned Q School into a business convention for his tour-rep operation. Loren Roberts, who qualified through the school five times, had an excuse—his NCAA career had ended prematurely when the college he was attending shut down its golf program. He also had a singular, superior skill—his putting—that cried out for patience while a suitable tee-to-green game could be built around it.

Roberts, last seen at Q School in 1987, has gone on to become a star. Since then, the player who is the paradigm for early failures followed by huge success, David Duval, has been someone who paid his dues as a Nike Tour player, not as a repeat Q Schooler. According to one recent Nike Tour alumnus, John Maginnes, "The Q School is a tradition, but it's become antiquated." Maginnes's comment runs against the grain of Pat Burke's observation that six rounds of Q School is more bearable—and certainly a more efficient use of time—than six months on the Nike Tour. It is that time factor, and perhaps nothing more, that will keep Q School in business for the foreseeable future. As Jim Carter has pointed out, you can't reasonably send a five- or 10-year PGA Tour veteran coming off one bad season on a forced march through the 30-plus tournaments of the Nike Tour simply to gain back his big-tour privileges.

That being the case, there is an increasing sense of legitimacy and solidness surrounding players who earn their PGA Tour card

via the Nike Tour, and a corresponding sense of flukiness surrounding Q School grads. One qualifying process is slow, steady,
and built to resemble the regular tour as much as possible. The
other is quick and messy and, let's face it, more vulnerable to the
vagaries of momentum and streaky play. If nothing else, Q School
suffers the indignity of being (cover the children's ears) the only
unsponsored event on any pro schedule. Would the Callaway or
the Taylor Made or the Titleist PGA Tour Qualifying School get
more respect? It's unlikely we'll ever find out.

In the meantime, anyone with a sentimental attachment to the
Q School tradition might check to see that its recent graduates
are faring reasonably well on the big tour. Among the recent
Q Schoolers discussed in these pages, Bob Friend, Clark Dennis,
and Esteban Toledo are managing to stay "inside the number"—
number 125 on the tour money list—on a regular basis. Jay Williamson got himself off to a very solid start in the first dozen
tournaments of 1999. Geoff Sisk started 1999 poorly. Among the
recent medalists at tour school, Allen Doyle, Scott Verplank, and
Mike Weir have all performed well, with Doyle—who turned pro
and qualified for the PGA Tour as a 46-year-old, then earned
comedalist honors at the 1997 Q School—winning the coveted
PGA Seniors title and a check for $315,000 in early 1999. Medalists
Jimmy Johnston (tied Doyle in 1997), Carl Paulson (1996), and
Woody Austin (1995) have been up-and-down.

Ironically, Q School's sorriest possible fate would be its conversion into a qualifier for Nike Tour membership only. Reduced
to feeding players into the tour that replaced it as a PGA Tour
entryway, Q School as we currently know it would cease to exist.
The whole bitter beauty of a year's hopes and dreams being
packed into a single gut-grinding week would be erased. The
transformation every fan yearns to see, the stunning and sudden
conversion of a rural assistant pro from complete unknown to

PGA Tour member, would no longer be possible. It would be replaced by the demand for plodding success on the so-called developmental tour, where purse money will probably become generous enough to make the waiting and the grinding reasonably comfortable, even for an older player with a family to support and a mortgage payment to make.

Of course, the stunning or sudden appearance of a competent PGA Tour professional seems to have become less and less a feature of pro golf. Junior golf and the college ranks keep expanding and gaining exposure, tipping us off to the identities of future tour members. Meanwhile, computer-tabulated statistics that precisely track player performance are becoming more and more available. These charts and tables have the potential to strip the mystery out of who has the skills and who doesn't.

One good example is Phil Mickelson's putting and chipping performance. Anyone who has watched Mickelson over a period of time has witnessed his liquid stroke on the greens and his unrivaled touch and creativity from all varieties of greenside trouble. Over the last couple of years, however, Mickelson's day-in, day-out statistics as a chipper and putter have been spotty, allowing TV broadcasters who are up on their numbers to report a missed eight-footer on Mickelson's part without expressing any shock. Rotisserie-leaguers and other stat mavens have ways of uncovering this nitty-gritty information, thereby exposing lofty reputations to an occasional drenching with the cold water of numerical reality. Before the trend toward computerized stats began coming on strong, following pro golf had been mostly "ooh and ahh" and "look at that," without many specifics to back it all up. But statistics that add a good deal more predictability to the proceedings are on their way. And whatever adds predictability will tend to reduce the population of dreamers and chip away at the mythology of Q School.

Could the Q School tradition disappear entirely? That question harks back to what PGA of America officer Max Elbin has said about the origin of the annual qualifier in 1965. Elbin explained that the old application-and-recommendation method of adding players "wasn't very businesslike." Essentially, the PGA officers in south Florida were being given a number each year, a number indicating how many Approved Tournament Players hadn't made the grade and would be losing their status. The annual batch of washouts would then be replaced by a batch of new players whom PGA brass would have no opportunity to lay eyes on prior to the start of the new season. It wasn't businesslike, Elbin and his colleagues thought, and there wasn't much opportunity to know who you were dealing with. Sounds a lot like Q School—at least when one compares Q School to the Nike Tour.

In the meantime, pro golf's private little week of hell remains in business. And if the great experiment known as Q School one day falls out of fashion, at least it has a chance to go out in a blaze of glory. Because if the decision-makers got a notion about scrapping the current system, their likely course of action would be to phase out of the annual qualifier by gradually cutting the number of playing privileges it grants. The school's card allocation of low-35-and-ties would be cut first to 25, then 20, then 15, and so on, while the Nike Tour's allocation would be bumped up commensurately. And if that scenario were to happen, the value of the Q School tour card would increase relative to its scarcity.

For a player, getting himself "on the number" would then be all the harder. Staying there as round five gave way to round six would be harder still. The sense of despair among players who missed getting tour cards by one stroke, which is currently profound, would only deepen. Among contending players, the nights would be more sleepless, the moods testier, the breakfasts and lunches harder to keep down.

It would be a perfect story-within-a-story—the Q School, the Fall Classic, golf's cruel and unusual test of survival, itself struggling to survive. This would be a harrowing test for the annual qualifier, the golf oddity we've come to know and almost love, but surely not a fatal one. What doesn't kill the Q School, logic dictates, can only make it stronger.

APPENDIX: FACTS AND RECORDS

Year annual tour qualifying began: 1965

Number of tour schools played, 1965–1998: 44

Highest number of applicants for one playing (1997): 1,200

Lowest number of applicants for one playing (1965): 49

Number of finals played at PGA National Golf Club (now JDM Country Club), most-used site: 8

Highest winning margin ever: 14 strokes, by Donnie Hammond in 1982

Repeat medalists: Robin Freeman, 1988 and 1993 (comedalist in 1993)

1999 finals site and dates: Doral Golf Resort & Spa, Miami, FL

1999 purse: TBD

1999 entry fee: $3,500 to $4,000, depending on status

1999 PGA Tour cards to be granted: TBD

1999 Nike Tour cards to be granted: TBD

YEAR BY YEAR SUMMARY OF PAST QUALIFYING
TOURNAMENT FINALS

1965
PGA National Golf Club
Palm Beach Gardens, FL
October 28–November 4

John Schlee, Phoenix, AZ	70–69–73–74–71–77–76–73—583
John Josephson, Asheville, NC	69–73–73–74–73–73–78–73—586
Richard Canon, Dallas, TX	71–75–73–74–77–71–74–77—592
Ronald Gillespie, San Bernardino, CA	75–71–77–76–74–75–73–74—595
Bob Rose, Toronto, Canada	70–72–74–77–76–78–76–73—596
Richard Killian, Houston, TX	71–74–78–71–75–75–78–74—596
David Marad, Milton, MA	76–76–76–73–69–79–77–71—597
David Philo, Gainesville, FL	69–74–76–76–75–75–79–75—599
Randy Petri, Austin, TX	75–73–75–71–77–74–77–77—599
Jimmy Fetters, Port Arthur, TX	67–77–77–76–77–79–73–74—600
Laurie Hammer, Sarasota, TX	72–76–75–76–74–73–75–79—600
Frank Whibley, Waterloo, Ontario	72–75–74–82–76–73–73–76—601
Stanley Brion, Orchard Lake, MI	69–72–75–84–79–75–73–74—601
Roy Siegel, Jr., Fort Lauderdale, FL	70–73–80–76–72–75–77–78—601
William A. Giese, Glen Ellyn, IL	72–77–77–76–77–76–72–79—606
James Colbert, Prairie Village, KS	76–76–77–74–74–76–78–75—606
James Langley, Salinas, CA	71–74–78–79–72–79–77–76—606

Among nonqualifiers, the name of J. C. Snead, Sam's nephew and an eventual eight-time winner on the PGA Tour, stands out. The record book reports that Jesse C. Snead, playing out of White Plains, New York, shot 624 to miss by 18 strokes. Another nonqualifier in this field, John Joseph, shot 610 to miss qualifying by four strokes. His name is worth mentioning for the fact that it helps get the long history of Q School name confusion off to a rousing start. Along with John Joseph in the first field of 48 was a player named John Josephson, who would shoot 586 and finish as the number two qualifier. One of the more controversial figures in the annuals of pro-golf qualifying, Harry Toscano, is also part of the original Q School convocation. Toscano, who would eventually file a $36 million antitrust lawsuit against the PGA Tour for, in his opinion, unfairly limiting the number of Senior PGA Tour qualifying-school berths, shot 615 in the inaugural Q School, missing the final cut by nine strokes. He would make up for that disappointment the following year.

1966
PGA National Golf Club
Palm Beach Gardens, FL

Harry Toscano, New Castle, PA	69–74–71–70–72–72–74–70—572
Robert J. Stanton, Sydney, Australia	74–71–71–74–73–69–74–70—576
Allan Henning, Johannesburg, South Africa	73–75–71–73–76–68–70–71—577
Jim Wiechers, Atherton, CA	74–71–72–69–72–76–73–70—577
William R. Emmons, Wethersfield, CT	70–76–70–72–72–72–74–74—580
Robert J. Lunn, Sacramento, CA	72–79–68–72–73–80–72–67—583
Charles H. Greene, Knoxville, TN	72–83–73–73–72–74–74–68—589
Jerry McGee, Lake Worth, FL	71–78–73–73–73–72–77–72—589
James McPhate, San Bernardino, CA	70–79–71–76–71–79–71–72—589
Richard Martinez, Laguna Beach, CA	73–75–72–74–78–74–74–69—589

Wilf Homenuik, Winnipeg, Manitoba, Canada	71–77–73–70–74–78–71–77—591
David Jimenez, Dorado, Puerto Rico	73–73–73–75–79–75–72–73—593
Ettore Della Torre, Harrison, NY	73–74–74–73–72–72–78–78—594
Charles F. Lewis, Little Rock, AK	74–74–81–72–77–73–74–69—594
Bob Boldt, Lake Oswego, OR	74–80–76–75–74–73–70–73—595
Ray R. Botts, Los Angeles, CA	72–79–72–76–74–74–75–74—596
Martin D. Eichelberger, Waco, TX	75–79–74–75–74–73–74–72—596
Bruce Cudd, Portland, OR	73–76–75–69–76–77–74–77—597
M. C. Methvin, Baton Rouge, LA	73–80–73–76–70–75–74–76—597
John Mark Hopkins, Texas City, TX	78–78–74–73–74–72–74–75—598
John Joseph, Newark, CA	79–76–75–73–75–74–72–74—598
Walter Zembriski, Montvale, NJ	74–80–74–75–74–76–74–71—598
Dave Cumlin, Crosby, MN	78–77–73–73–77–71–74–76—599
Monty Kaser, Wichita, KS	74–82–72–74–75–74–74–74—599
George G. Smith, Asheville, NC	74–77–76–71–76–75–77–74—600
Alex Antonio, Jr., Hubbard, OH	74–79–73–74–76–79–76–70—601
Donald M. Headings, Springfield, MA	74–75–74–77–81–74–74–72—601
Roane H. Puett, Austin, TX	77–76–74–76–76–75–71–76—601
John A. Molenda, Warren, MI	75–74–74–78–79–78–70–74—602
Leon F. DeCaire, Canada	75–78–75–77–75–77–74–72—603
Rives McBee, Midland, TX	74–81–77–75–75–72–69–80—603
DeWitt T. Weaver, Cairo, GA	76–81–73–71–77–75–74–76—603

Harry Toscano's four-shot margin as medalist carried the banner for five other 1965 also-rans who returned to Palm Beach Gardens and gained eligibility. In the first brother act the Q School witnessed, Harold and Allen Henning both earned cards, although Harold was exempted from the tournament proper based on his recent victory in the Texas Open, to which he had gained entry via open qualifying. Martin D. Eichelberger is, of course, Dave Eichelberger, who was coming off a fine collegiate career at Oklahoma State and would go on to win four times on the PGA Tour.

1967
PGA National Golf Club
Palm Beach Gardens, FL

Bobby Cole, South Africa	69–68–71–75–66–74–73–76—572
Gibby Gilbert, Hollywood, FL	68–71–70–71–75–70–74–74—573
Ronald Cerrudo, San Rafael, CA	67–70–74–72–71–70–73–77—574
Deane Beman, Bethesda, MD	70–72–71–69–72–71–74–75—574
George Boutell, Phoenix, AZ	69–75–74–74–71–67–72–75—577
Bob Murphy, Nichols, FL	70–70–71–70–73–75–73–75—577
James Grant, Wethersfield, CT	69–72–74–72–73–73–73–72—578
Robert Smith, Sacramento, CA	69–70–74–69–78–72–74–74—580
Mike Higgins, Tomball, TX	71–73–73–71–74–77–71–70—580
Alvie Thompson, Willowdale, Canada	73–75–73–71–72–72–73–72—581
Richard Rhoads, Mamaroneck, NY	70–72–73–72–72–76–76–73—584
Tony Jacklin, England	74–76–76–70–74–68–74–72—584
Steve Eichstaedt, Miami Lakes, FL	69–75–75–71–74–71–77–73—585
Peter Townsend, England	72–74–73–74–75–75–66–76—586
Lee Elder, Washington, D.C.	76–73–74–73–74–70–73–73—586
Orville Moody, Lawton, OK	74–75–76–76–71–72–71–71—586
Barry Meerdink, Muscatine, IA	69–74–77–72–74–73–72–77—588
Marty Fleckman, Port Arthur, TX	70–78–76–71–76–72–72–73—588
Terry Winter, West Lafayette, IN	76–74–74–72–72–74–75–72—589
William Robinson, Tequesta, FL	73–73–77–76–73–69–71–78—590
Bunky Henry, Valdosta, GA	76–78–74–74–77–73–70–68—590

James Langley, Salinas, CA	70–69–72–76–78–74–75–78—592
Mya Aye, Burma	73–73–74–76–73–70–75–78—592
Jim Hiskey, Arlington, VA	71–78–77–71–74–70–76–76—593
Rodney Horn, Prairie Village, KS	74–70–73–73–76–76–75–76—593
Mike Hadlock, Marshall, TX	73–71–76–74–76–75–73–75—593
Richard Carmody, Long Beach, CA	71–75–76–74–74–76–76–76—594
Terry Comstock, Sioux Falls, SD	73–72–73–73–76–72–77–79—595
John Stevens, Wichita, KS	75–80–73–74–73–69–72–79—595

James Grant, with his tie for eighth place, completes the second half of an unlikely double as he becomes the second player from the Hartford, Connecticut, suburb of Wethersfield to succeed at tour school in only three years of competition. William R. Emmons had come out of Wethersfield to earn a card at the 1966 school. Alvie Thompson, a colorful pro from Ontario, is no relation to the patriarch of Canadian course designers, Stanley Thompson. Terry Comstock, who tied for 30th, is presumed to be the brother of Byron J. Comstock, also of Sioux Falls, South Dakota—as well as his family's proverbial fortunate son. Terry made it in "on the number" in what records indicate to be his first Q School attempt, while Byron was a distant 46th in 1965 but only two shots past the cut in 1966.

1968 Spring (PGA School)
PGA National Golf Club
Palm Beach Gardens, FL

Bob Dickson, Tulsa, OK	68–69–76–74–72–69–70–71—569
George Thorpe, Cleveland, OH	69–75–67–72–69–72–75–75—574
Jack Ewing, Bakersfield, CA	71–67–72–72–69–76–75–77—579
Hale Irwin, Boulder, CO	71–72–73–75–70–68–76–75—580

Larry Hinson, Douglas, GA	71–71–75–70–71–68–77–78—581
Joseph Porter III, Scottsdale, AZ	70–70–75–74–71–74–74–75—583
Clive Clark, Scarborough, York, England	76–71–75–70–76–70–71–74—583
Michael Hill, Tecumseh, MI	69–73–72–74–69–78–74–76—585
Hideyo Sugimoto, Japan	76–72–73–71–73–75–74–72—586
Benson McLendon, Jr., Birmingham, AL	75–74–72–69–76–73–74–73—586
John Shackleford, Shamrock, TX	68–74–71–71–73–75–75–81—588
John Jacobs, Oklahoma City, OK	74–71–74–75–69–74–74–78—589
Jim King, Chicago, IL	73–72–72–71–73–76–76–77—590
Kenneth W. Fulton, Canada	74–71–76–73–74–74–75–73—590
Dennis J. Rouse, Miami, FL	73–72–74–75–72–72–75–79—592

After having staged annual Q Schools in the fall for three consecutive years, the PGA split its program into spring and fall qualifiers. Of the 15 players who made it through this first bi-annual qualifier, Hale Irwin and Mike Hill are the most notable. Among the players failing to get a card at this school were Curtis Sifford and Butch Harmon, who would both opt to enroll in the breakaway APG qualifier later in the year. One other notable near-miss player in the spring of 1968 was Liang-huan Lu, the Taiwanese pro who would later experience a brush with immortality in the 1971 British Open at Royal Birkdale, where he was runner-up to Lee Trevino by a single shot.

1968 Fall (PGA School)
PGA National Golf Club
Palm Beach Gardens, FL

Grier Jones, Wichita, KS	67–78–67–73–72–70–72–72—571
Jimmy Day, Laurel, MS	70–75–72–74–73–67–75–70—576

Malcolm Gregson, Surrey, England 71–72–75–69–75–75–75–75—587

Donald Iverson, La Crosse, WI 77–68–72–75–75–71–73–77—588

Nathaniel Starks, Atlanta, GA 75–72–74–74–71–74–72–78—590

Gene Ferrell, Verona, PA 74–71–74–75–73–73–75–75—590

Greg Johnson, Columbus, GA 72–76–71–77–76–71–76–73—590

Jerry Heard, Visalia, CA 71–71–71–76–77–74–73–80—593

William Tindall, Seattle, WA 77–74–73–78–73–73–69–76—593

Jim Jamieson, Moline, IL 73–72–74–78–80–74–69–73—593

Jim Awtrey, Bronxville, NY 72–70–73–75–78–74–74–78—594

John Levinson, Kennebunk Beach, ME 74–74–75–73–71–79–73–78—597

Lawrence O'Hearn, Nova Scotia, Canada 75–70–77–71–74–74–75–81—597

Vern Novak, Timonium, MD 74–77–73–76–69–73–73–83—598

Jim Bullard, Wichita, KS 73–77–74–75–80–67–74–78—598

Robert Payne, Mt. Vernon, IL 75–74–74–76–74–72–73–80—598

Jeff Voss, Dallas, TX 77–77–77–74–72–73–74–74—598

Jim Hardy, Truro, MA 71–71–75–74–69–77–82–81—600

Roland Lamontagne, Carmichael, CA 74–74–81–73–74–72–74–78—600

Tom Bailey, Great Falls, SC 73–76–74–78–75–72–75–77—600

Dennis Lyons, Stamford, CT 72–77–80–76–71–72–73–79—600

Ras Allen, Garland, TX 73–77–76–70–75–76–76–77—600

Kenneth Ellsworth, Harbor City, CA 75–79–75–73–70–76–69–84—601

Edgar Sneed, Columbus, OH 75–75–80–75–75–72–71–78—601

David Bolman, Sheldon, IA 74–73–76–75–76–70–75–83—602

George Hixon, Tulsa, OK 70–76–77–78–77–73–74–77—602

Clayton Cole, Monroe, LA 75–75–77–74–73–77–74–77—602

Joseph McDermott, Franklin Park, IL 73–75–80–77–72–73–72–81—603

James Walker, Los Angeles, CA   72–76–77–75–74–79–72–78—603

Guy Bill, Oakland, CA   73–78–77–72–73–78–76–76—603

Of these 30 qualifiers, Ed Sneed's name may be the most recognizable, owing to Sneed's heartbreak in the final holes of the 1979 Masters. This eight-round school ended in barely playable weather conditions, which, along with exhaustion, boosted final-round scores to some of the highest for any qualifying group ever.

1968 Fall—APG School
Doral Resort and Country Club
Miami, FL

Martinus H. Roesink, Deventer,   75–78–73–65–74–74–71–75—585
  Holland
Robert Shaw, Bala Cynwyd, PA   77–74–69–72–74–73–73–76—588
Bob Panasiuk, Windsor, Canada   80–74–76–72–68–73–73–74—590
Ross Randall, Mamaroneck, NY   77–72–72–73–75–79–73–71—592
Jerry Don Barrier, Arkansas Pass,   74–77–76–72–72–73–77–75—596
  TX
Wayne Vollmer, Vancouver,   77–74–75–72–71–77–74–76—596
  Canada
Curtis H. Sifford, Los Angeles, CA   76–71–74–77–79–67–75–79—598
Randy Wolff, Beaumont, TX   71–77–79–81–71–71–76–72—598
Cesar R. Sanudo, El Cajon, CA   77–73–76–77–76–69–75–76—599
Bobby Lockett, Mt. Pleasant, TX   73–78–74–76–74–72–75–77—599
Roger Buhrt, Minneapolis, MN   84–77–72–74–69–71–77–76—600
Lawrence Sears, Waycross, GA   78–76–75–72–75–77–76–72—601
Leslie G. Peterson, Riverside, CA   83–79–71–75–75–71–76–74—604
Harry Taylor, Hayward, CA   82–75–70–72–76–77–78–75—605
Frank W. Mize, Jr., St. Louis, MO   77–73–75–80–78–72–76–75—606

Lee Davis, Jr., Los Angeles, CA	80–75–79–72–75–72–76–79—608
William A. Wakeham, Victoria, Canada	76–76–76–74–78–76–78–77—611
Howard Brown, Detroit, MI	79–75–76–78–80–74–72–77—611
Claude Harmon, Jr., New Rochelle, NY	73–76–75–75–80–79–79–78—615
Robert J. Pratt, Las Vegas, NV	79–77–80–76–78–76–75–74—650
Robert J. Cox, Richmond, Canada	77–76–77–82–77–73–75–78—550

This upstart, semiofficial qualifier would be the only Q School held at Doral until 31 years later, when the 1999 Q School goes to the Miami resort. The player from Hayward, California, who finished 14th, Harry Taylor, is not the same Harry Taylor who competed in the Q School on such a regular basis in the 1980s and 1990s.

1969 Spring
PGA National Golf Club
Palm Beach Gardens, FL

Robert Eastwood, Lodi, CA	74–71–73–73—291
Gerry Preuss, Woodland Hills, CA,	72–73–69–80—294
Gary Groh, Freeport, Grand Bahamas	73–77–73–72—295
Bobby Greenwood, Cookeville, TN	74–73–76–72—295
Donald Parson, Stratford, CT	75–71–74–75—295
Hal Underwood, Humble, TX	72–75–74–74—295
Charles Montalbano, Van Nuys, CA	73–72–78–74—297
John Schroeder, La Jolla, CA	79–72–74–72—297
Jon Cutshall, Houston, TX	69–76–75–77—297
Hugh Inggs, Vereeniging, South Africa	82–76–71–70—299
Rodney Curl, Redding, CA	76–76–75–72—299
John Miller, San Francisco, CA	74–78–73–74—299

Michael Nugent	76–72–82–70—300
Michael Reasor, Seattle, WA	75–73–77–75—300
Mahlon Moe, Albuquerque, NM	78–71–75–76—300

Following the tumultuous PGA-pro tour breakup year—in which three qualifiers were held and a flood of new players granted eligibility—the door was only held slightly ajar for aspiring tour players in 1969. This would be Johnny Miller's only tour school appearance.

1969 Fall
PGA National Golf Club
Palm Beach Gardens, FL

Doug Olson, Medford, OR	71–75–68–72—286
Michael Morley, Minot, ND	73–72–71–72—288
William J. Brask, Jr., San Diego, CA	75–72–71–71—289
Michael Mitchell, Houston, TX	76–72–70–73—291
Jack Lewis, Jr., Florence, SC	80–71–69–72—292
John Baldwin, Port Washington, NY	76–75–73–69—293
Brian Barnes, Sussex, England	68–76–79–70—293
Ben Kern, Mississauga, Ontario	72–78–73–71—294
Ronald Acree, Louisville, KY	73–73–74–74—294
James Barker, San Antonio, TX	74–71–77–73—29
Dennis Murphy, Long Beach, CA	71–73–75–77—296
Gary Bowerman, Toronto, Ontario	68–75–77–77—297

The early Q School rosters all tend to feature names of professionals who have gone on to the Senior PGA Tour. In this list, the senior we most recognize is Brian Barnes, famous for having defeated Jack Nicklaus in Ryder Cup singles matches twice in one day.

1970

Tucson Country Club

Tucson, AZ

November 1–7

Robert Barbarossa	279
Robert Clark	283
Dwight Nevil	283
Robert Bourne	283
Hubert Green	284
Victor Loustalot	284
Rik Massengale	285
John Lister	285
Richard Karl	285
James Dent	286
Charles Owens	286
Robert Lewis	286
Ken Fulton	287
Larry White	287
Ralph Johnston	287
Brian Allin	287
Roberto Bernardini	287
Steve Bogan	288

PGA Tour archives contain only final tallies for this qualifier, not round-by-round scores. Of the 18 players granted tour cards, two are African-Americans, Jim Dent and Charles Owens.

1971

PGA National Golf Club

Palm Beach Gardens, FL

Bob Zender	70–71–72–72–71–69—425
Lanny Wadkins	70–69–71–72–75–71—428
Sam Adams	69–74–76–70–70–69—428
Steve Melnyk	73–73–70–71–72–71—430
Tom Watson	71–71–73–72–71–75—433
Allen Miller	72–75–72–73–67–76—435
John Mahaffey	73–71–73–72–73–74—436
Bruce Fleisher	72–77–70–70–79–70—438
Jim Barber	74–73–71–75–73–73—439
David Graham	77–71–74–70–70–78—440
Forrest Fezler	76–72–68–75–75–75—441
Gary Groh	73–70–70–73–78–77—441
David Glenz	75–74–80–72–72–69—442
Leonard Thompson	76–73–76–73–71–73—442
Mike Spang	75–69–72–74–77–76—443
Bill Ziobro	76–72–75–74–72–74—443
Greg Powers	73–76–74–73–77–71—444
Wayne Peddy	69–76–74–78–76–71—444
Chuck Thorpe	68–76–74–73–79–74—444
Dave Haberle	74–73–74–75–73–75—444
Ray Arinno	73–75–75–73–74–74—444
John Gentile	73–72–73–75–75–76—444
Rogelio Gonzalez	76–74–72–73–71–78—444

This qualifier launched the stellar careers of Wadkins and Watson, neither of whom ever went back through the Q School grinder. "Graduates of the school are on probation for one year," declared the tour's 1971 player book, an odd comment given the prosper-or-perish nature of tour school.

1972
Silverado Country Club
Napa, CA
October 27–November 4

Larry Stubblefield	74–74–65–72–75–74—434
John Adams	78–72–70–75–69–70—434
Paul Purtzer	73–74–76–71–72–70—436
Jim Simons	76–76–70–70–73–71—436
Pat Fitzsimons	75–71–72–71–74–73—436
Lon Hinkle	79–72–69–71–72–74—437
Victor Regalado	70–72–72–71–76–78—439
Mike McCullough	76–75–78–71–71–70—441
Bruce Ashworth	75–77–70–77–69–73—441
Greg Edwards	77–75–70–73–77–70—442
Bob Allard	79–80–71–68–73–71—442
Tom Kite	77–73–75–72–74–71—442
Andy North	72–76–74–74–72–74—442
John Morgan	79–72–74–72–76–70—443
Tom McGinnis	75–74–74–76–74–70—443
Jim Ahern	81–73–72–70–74–73—443
Jeff Hewes	82–74–72–73–74–70—445
Lloyd Hughes	76–76–67–69–74–73—445
Gary Sanders	75–75–70–75–76–74—445
Don Padgett	78–75–74–72–73–74—446
Tom Jenkins	74–76–77–69–77–74—447
Artie McNickle	75–79–73–74–74–72—447
Tom Evans	77–68–75–75–78–74—447
Mike Kallam	79–77–74–75–70–72—447
Tim Collins	75–78–71–77–71–75—447

Neither Kite nor North would ever return to Q School after this year—each went on to become U.S. Open champion, while Kite would become one of the most successful players in modern PGA Tour history. Paul Purtzer, older brother of tour veteran Tom, would play the tour briefly before seriously injuring a shoulder and turning to the club-pro ranks. Gary Sanders of Anaheim, California, birdied the first hole in the final round of this qualifier, then stumbled, playing the next five holes in six strokes over par. Sanders reacted to his five-hole blowup by removing his wedding ring from a zipper pouch and putting it on. He had never worn his wedding band while competing before. Sanders played the next 12 holes in 3-under and earned his tour card with a final-round 74.

1973
Perdido Bay Country Club, Pensacola, FL
Dunes Golf Beach Club, Myrtle Beach, SC

Ben Crenshaw	69–72–67–73–67–72–70–68—558
Gil Morgan	74–66–70–68–75–74–70–73—570
Gary McCord	70–67–72–72–71–78–72–72—574
Richard Mast	72–68–66–70–77–73–75–73—574
Wally Armstrong	72–72–71–71–76–69–72–74—577
Joe Inman	78–70–72–69–73–73–73–72—580
Mark Hayes	76–69–73–71–75–70–72–74—580
Randy Erskine	68–69–72–71–74–74–76–76—580
Bobby Heins	70–70–76–70–72–76–74–73—581
Bob Unger	71–69–75–77–72–72–73–72—581
Spike Kelley	72–73–73–69–74–73–73–74—581
Nate Starks	71–74–73–70–75–72–72–74—581
Terry Diehl	76–72–67–69–71–77–71–78—581
Jim Masserio	74–76–70–74–72–75–70–72—583
Eddie Pearce	74–72–75–70–74–70–76–72—583

Ron Hoyt	74–72–71–67–74–77–71–77—583
Lyn Lott	73–73–72–74–73–75–72–72—584
Bobby Walzel	68–71–71–70–79–79–77–70—585
B. Thompson	69–72–69–74–78–79–71–75—587
Sam Farlow	71–73–74–72–74–72–72–79—587
W. Chancellor	79–71–74–70–77–72–73–72—588
Jim Blanks	75–73–72–78–74–67–76–73—588
Larry Nelson	70–74–71–72–78–72–75–76—588

This was the first of two consecutive experiments in split-sitting of Q School. Contestants played four rounds in Pensacola and traveled several hundred miles to Myrtle Beach. Crenshaw's margin of victory was a record 12 strokes over Morgan. Eddie Pearce, coming off a storied amateur career, emerged from this qualifier with a "can't miss" label he never lived up to.

1974
Silverado Country Club, Napa, CA
Canyon Country Club, Palm Springs, CA

Fuzzy Zoeller, New Albany, IN	70–71–73–74–72–72–71–69—572
Bob Risch, La Puente, CA	71–74–71–74–68–70–76–69—573
George Cadle, Half Moon Bay, CA	73–70–72–76–71–72–69–71—574
Peter Oosterhuis, London, England	71–83–71–68–75–70–73–73—575
Alan Tapie, Newport Beach, CA	72–72–68–75–70–74–75–70—576
Dave Newquist, Anaheim, CA	70–74–67–75–74–73–73–71—577
Rex Caldwell, Lompoc, CA	75–71–69–73–71–75–67–77—578
Bill Rogers, Texarkana, TX	71–75–70–78–73–72–70–69—578
Bobby Wadkins, Richmond, VA	71–71–74–71–72–71–76–74—580
John Abendroth, San Francisco, CA	74–74–72–76–74–71–67–73—581
Frank Conner, San Antonio, TX	70–71–76–73–74–73–71–73—581

Greg Trompas, San Diego, CA	68–76–70–79–78–72–71–70—584
Jack Spradlin, San Diego, CA	74–72–73–75–77–72–67–75—585
Roger Maltbie, San Jose, CA	77–72–69–74–75–72–74–73—586
Ray Carrasco, Huntington Beach, CA	71–74–72–73–75–74–71–76—586
Danny Edwards, Edmond, OK	74–71–75–70–75–74–75–72—586
Florentino Molina, Buenos Aires, Argentina	76–73–70–75–72–75–72–74—587
Dan Halldorson, Manitoba, Canada	72–74–72–73–72–75–74–77—589
Jimmy Wittenberg, Memphis, TN	76–71–74–75–72–72–77–72—589

Fuzzy Zoeller went on to become the first Q School medalist to win the Masters and the second Q School medalist to win a major championship (fall 1975 medalist Jerry Pate was first, with his victory in the 1976 U.S. Open). Jack Spradlin, who finished four strokes within the magic number at this qualifier would reappear as the tour school medalist in the spring 1980 finals at Pinehurst.

1975 Spring
Bay Tree Plantation
North Myrtle Beach, SC
June 9–14

Joey Dills	73–73–73–69–71–71—430
Howard Twitty	66–75–72–75–75–68—431
Tom Purtzer	72–74–73–70–73–69—431
Pat McDonald	71–75–76–73–71–68—434
Barry Jaeckel	72–71–72–72–75–72—434
Dan Elliott	74–75–72–70–72–72—435
David Lind	74–74–71–69–72–75—435
Calvin Peete	68–74–78–69–74–73—436

Dan O'Neill	72–76–75–75–72–67—437
Bruce Lietzke	72–74–74–73–71–73—437
Sammy Rachels	71–74–74–75–72–71—437
Randy Feather	71–76–75–74–72–71—439
Antonio Cerda	73–71–71–72–77–75—439

This qualifier is distinguished for having the smallest graduating class among the 44 played from 1965 to 1998. Decades later, Sammy Rachels can distinctly recall his introduction to Calvin Peete, the African-American odd-lot trader with the permanently crooked left arm who took up golf at age 23 and became perhaps the straightest hitter in PGA Tour history. "Calvin showed up on the tee wearing cowboy boots and flashing a big diamond in his front tooth," recalled Rachels. "I was sure somebody was trying to pull one over on old Sammy. Then I watched him play. Calvin was the only one of us who didn't need a golf course—he could play up and down sidewalks."

1975 Fall
Walt Disney World
Lake Buena Vista, FL
November 3–8

Jerry Pate	70–69–69–70–72–73—423
George Burns	68–77–69–70–71–70—425
Earl Humphries	72–71–70–72–72–70—427
Gary Koch	72–69–71–73–71–71—427
Bobby Stroble	67–75–74–70–70–72—428
Steve Veriato	71–73–73–69–71–71—428
Andy Bean	67–76–70–74–73–70—430
Stan Lee	73–71–73–73–71–70—431
Bob Gilder	71–72–72–69–73–74—431

Don Pooley	72–73–72–70–69–76—432
Dale Hayes	69–76–76–72–69–71—433
John Harris	71–72–71–73–75–71—433
Tommy McGinnis	69–75–73–73–69–74—433
Ray Leach	74–73–72–70–72–73—434
David Smith	76–72–76–71–67–73—435
Bill Mallon	69–76–74–74–70–73—436
Jim Thorpe	74–72–70–73–73–74—436
John Melnick	72–73–73–72–73–73—436
Ted Goin	74–73–70–75–71–73—436
Sandy Galbraith	68–71–73–74–73–77—436
Mark Pfiel	70–73–79–75–69–71—437
Gar Hamilton	72–74–74–74–72–71—437
Stan Altgelt	72–72–71–79–71–72—437
Guy Cullins	77–71–71–74–72–72—437
David Canipe	70–75–78–68–72–74—437

Pate's injury-shortened career began happily with this medalist performance. Andy Bean also emerged in fall of 1975 on his way to stardom. Bean would win over $3 million in the next 15 years before suffering injuries that led to a dramatic falloff in performance. Bean, after going back through Q School several times in the later '90s, was asked if he was priming himself for the Senior PGA Tour in 2003. "Forget the senior tour, that's four years away," answered Bean. "We got to eat now." Q School numerologists will appreciate the 436 turned in by John Melnick, of St. Simon's Island, Georgia. Melnick's performance ranks as one of the most consistent ever in a six-round tour qualifier.

1976 Spring
Bay Tree Golf Plantation
North Myrtle Beach, SC
June 8–13

Woody Blackburn	73–71–68–70–72–72—426
Robert Shearer	70–71–68–70–72–75—426
Bill Calfee	75–74–70–70–71–71—431
Al Brooks	73–76–73–72–70–68—432
Sam Farlow	71–72–72–67–77–73—432
Bill Kratzert	68–74–73–69–74–74—432
Jeff Hewes	71–75–73–73–70–72—434
Morris Hatalsky	75–72–72–75–69–73—436
Bob Impaglia	70–68–75–74–74–75—436
David Lind	72–70–73–75–73–73—436
Bill Brask	70–74–71–73–73–76—437
Mike Craven	74–72–74–73–74–71—438
Jim Knoll	71–72–72–74–75–74—438
Elroy Marti	72–76–73–71–74–72—438
Craig Stadler	72–70–72–75–72–77—438

Perhaps the most nondescript list of qualifiers in any tour school. The low name on the qualifying roster, Craig Stadler, turned out to be this school's only big winner on tour.

1976 Fall
Rancho Viejo Country Club
Brownsville, TX
December 9–17

Keith Fergus	70–69–69–74–68–68—418
Mike Sullivan	70–69–72–72–71–74—428
Mark Lye	72–73–68–70–74–76—433

Graham Marsh	68–69–75–70–74–77—433
Jimmy Wittenberg	68–68–76–79–73–70—434
Vicente Fernandez	69–72–76–73–73–72—435
Jay Haas	73–67–79–72–72–72—435
George Kunes	72–74–71–70–75–73—435
Jeff Mitchell	72–65–74–76–75–73—435
Greg Pitzer	70–74–67–77–76–71—435
Dick Mast	78–71–73–70–70–74—436
Alberto Rivadeneira Aguilar	73–74–72–77–69–71—436
John Abendroth	73–75–75–74–70–70—437
Jim Barker	73–76–71–74–75–68—437
Mark Pfeil	71–72–73–74–73–74—437
Bobby Stroble	71–76–70–73–74–73—437
David Canipe	73–69–75–73–73–75—438
Bruce Ford	68–71–75–75–77–72—438
Richard Friedman	72–71–74–72–73–76—438
Jack Newton	74–72–70–74–76–72—438
Doug Schryer	72–72–74–74–71–75—438
Ray Sovik	73–70–73–76–72–74—438
Larry Webb	68–73–73–76–76–72—438
Ray Arinno	72–73–77–71–75–71—439
Jim Booros	73–72–72–72–78–72—439
Peter Jacobsen	73–73–74–69–77–73—439
Don Pooley	67–72–73–78–75–74—439
Mike Reid	72–75–73–71–72–76—439
Ron Streck	72–68–77–73–73–76—439

1977 Spring
Pinehurst Resort and Country Club (Courses No. 2, 3, 5)
Pinehurst, NC
June 2–9

Phil Hancock	66–70–70–71–71–69—417
Lance Suzuki	63–71–69–76–73–66—418
Wayne Levi	71–71–65–71–71–69—418
Curtis Strange	67–68–70–71–72–71—419
Bill Pelham	67–66–73–70–71–73—420
Tom Tatum	69–71–70–74–67–71—422
Brady Miller	66–68–72–72–70–75—423
Tim Simpson	68–71–73–73–65–73—423
Ron Milanovich	72–71–70–69–76–67—425
Pat McDonald	66–71–69–74–71–74—425
Dave Sheff	69–73–64–74–73–72—425
Skip Dunaway	69–73–71–68–74–71—426
Jack Renner	75–70–71–73–71–67—427
Wren Lum	70–71–66–77–74–69—427
Alan Pate	75–70–66–74–72–70—427
Terry Catlett	68–69–71–76–72–71—427
David Brownlee	76–71–70–70–64–74—427
D. A. Weibring	69–69–76–69–72–73—428
Kim Young	75–66–74–70–70–71—428
Tom Valentine	69–69–72–73–76–70—429
Jack Spradlin	69–74–71–71–73–71—429
David Thore	73–73–67–72–72–72—429
Jim Chancey	72–72–67–75–75–69—430
Wayne Peddy	71–73–68–76–71–71—430
Terry Mauney	70–70–73–71–73–73—430

This massive gathering of 408 players would go down as the biggest final field ever in a Q School. The following year—even keeping its twice-yearly schedule of qualifying—the tour would bring back regional prequalifiers, thus cutting the size of the finals to 144. In *Golf World's* news story on the spring 1977 Q School,

Curtis Strange was tapped as the "most likely to succeed" among the 26 who earned their cards, a prediction that would prove rock-solid. Among the players who finished at 431 and missed getting their cards by a single stroke were the two Bymans, Bob and Ed.

1977 Fall
Pinehurst Resort No. 4
Pinehurst, NC
November 9–12

Ed Fiori	73–66–73–72—284
Lee Mickles	69–70–73–76—288
Buddy Gardner	69–74–74–72—289
Skeeter Heath	70–71–74–74—289
Gary Jacobson	69–72–73–76—290
Mike Shea	71–74–78–68—291
Bruce Robertson	72–70–75–74—291
Rick Beck	68–76–72–75—291
Dana Quigley	70–71–76–75—292
Parker Moore	72–69–74–77—292
Jeff Hewes	69–72–74–78—293
Perry Arthur	73–74–75–72—294
Dave Nevatt	75–73–75–71—294
Mitch Adcock	76–70–75–73—294
Gary Vanier	72–73–75–74—294
Jim Nelford	74–72–76–73—295
Don Brigham	76–72–74–73—295
Lon Nielsen	73–73–76–73—295
Mike Booker	76–71–74–74—295
Jaime Gonzalez	69–76–75–75—295

Bob Howerter	73–72–76–75—296
Pat McGowan	75–73–73–75—296
Bob Clark	71–73–75–77—296
Rob Ashby	73–74–73–76—296
Bobby Stroble	69–71–77–79—296
Mac Hunter	71–75–77–74—297
Jim White	74–72–75–76—297
Dave Shipley	73–72–79–73—297
Jim Ulozas	71–76–73–77—297
Gary Ostrega	75–72–78–72—297
Bobby Baker	72–71–76–78—297
Skip Guss	76–70–73–78—297
Dave Barr	70–74–75–78—297
Travis Hudson	71–74–72–80—297

The medalist in fall of 1977, Ed Fiori, turned out to also be the winningest tour member among the 30 who received cards that year. This Q School was a reunion of sorts for Jacobson, Guss, Mickles, and Nevatt, who all played at Arizona State University.

1978 Spring
University of New Mexico Golf Club
Albuquerque, NM
June 7–13

Wren Lum	68–68–70–73—279
Mark McCumber	70–69–73–69—281
Jim Mason	65–70–73–76—284
Brad Bryant	72–69–73–71—285
Adam Adams	69–71–73–72—285

Bob Byman	73–71–75–68—287
Mike Zack	71–70–73–73—287
Rocky Thompson	70–69–74–75—288
Bob Impaglia	72–68–72–76—288
Peter Chapin	71–74–69–74—288
John Adams	74–68–69–77—288
Ed Byman	71–72–71–75—289
Ron Mobley	72–69–71–77—289
Dan Pohl	74–70–74–72—290
Jim Knoll	70–73–73–74—290
Charley Gibson	72–71–74–73—290
Bill Murchison	75–70–75–70—290
Kip Byrne	68–74–72–76—290
Rocky Rockett	76–72–72–70—290
Don Baker	72–70–76–73—291
Elroy Marti, Jr.	72–71–76–72—291
Larry Degenhart	70–75–75–71—291
Joe Hager	69–74–74–74—291
Fred Voelkel	74–73–73–71—291
Wally Kuchar	72–71–73–75—291
Bill Sander	73–73–69–76—291
Mike Bodney	74–66–72–79—291

This qualifier was not McCumber's first try for a tour card, but it would be his last—McCumber's recurring nightmares notwithstanding (see chapter 7). Of the 28 who qualified in this edition of tour school, 15 of them scored either 290 or 291, making it one of the most tightly bunched classes ever. The roster of card-earners offers proof that before there was a Curt and Tom Byrum or a Brad and Bart Bryant on the PGA Tour, there was a Bob and Ed Byman.

1978 Fall
Waterwood National Country Club
Huntsville, TX
October 25–28

John Fought	72–68–70–75—285
Jim Thorpe	71–69–70–75—285
Robert Donald	68–76–73–71—288
Roger Calvin	73–72–71–72—288
Scott Simpson	72–73–71–73—289
David Edwards	73–68–73–75—289
Chip Beck	67–71–76–75—289
Tommy Valentine	78–68–69–75—290
Mark Mike	71–75–71–73—290
Dan Halldorson	73–72–71–74—290
Tommy McGinnis	69–74–73–73—290
Lindy Miller	73–71–73–74—291
Dick Mast	70–75–75–71—291
Jack Ferenz	71–74–72–74—291
Don Shirley, Jr.	73–74–70–75—292
Dana Quigley	74–73–74–71—292
Mike Brannan	75–77–69–71—292
Tommy Thomas	71–74–73–75—293
David Lundstrom	73–69–79–73—294
Tom Chain	71–72–78–73—294
Jack Sommers	76–72–78–69—295
Dennis Sullivan	74–75–73–73—295
Tony Hollifield	70–75–75–75—295
Buddy Gardner	74–74–74–74—296
Larry Webb	75–74–74–73—296
Sam Trahan	78–73–72–73—296
Bobby Baker	74–72–75–75—296

Buddy Gardner's score—four consecutive 74s—represents the only time in Q School finals history that a player tallied the same 18-hole score throughout the tournament. Robert Donald, who finished tied for third, is no relation to 1990 U.S. Open runner-up Mike Donald.

1979 Spring
Pinehurst Resort No. 6
Pinehurst, NC
June 6–9

Terry Mauney	70–69–71–74—284
Bob Proben	71–69–71–74—285
Dan Pohl	72–73–73–71—289
Mike Nicollette	72–73–71–73—289
David Eger	68–76–72–74—290
Mick Soli	72–77–70–72—291
Mike Schroeder	74–70–70–77—291
Chris Clark	73–73–74–72—292
Lee Carter	69–75–76–72—292
David Thore	75–72–74–72—293
John Mazza	78–73–70–72—293
Ray Arinno	76–70–72–75—293
Jim Von Lossow	77–72–75–70—294
Scott Steger	72–73–71–78—294
Beau Baugh	70–75–78–71—294
Larry Degenhart	75–74–72–74—295
Rodney Morrow	71–72–77–75—295
Wren Lum	75–72–75–73—295
Jeff Thomsen	74–75–71–75—295
Mike Colandro	71–77–71–76—295
David Canipe	75–75–73–73—296

Skip Dunaway   71–70–74–81—296
Pat Lindsey   75–78–75–68—296
Barry Fleming   72–73–79–72—296
Ed Byman   74–73–73–76—296

Closing scores of 68 and 81 by the narrowly escaping Skip Dunaway and Pat Lindsey represent a study in contrasts unusual for
the four-round Q Schools of this period. Wren Lum, who took
first place in one of the 1978 qualifiers, was back quickly for someone who had taken a tour-school medal. David Eger, who finished fourth, would eventually give up his professional
tournament-playing career and become a staff member of the
PGA Tour, in charge of Q School.

1979 Fall
Waterwood National Country Club
Huntsville, TX
October 31–November 3

Tom Jones   70–76–70–72—288
Chip Beck   75–73–70–71—289
Mike Peck   71–76–74–70—291
Bruce Douglass   70–76–75–71—292
Scott Hoch   72–71–73–76—292
Harry Taylor   71–76–73–74—294
Jon Chaffee   72–73–74–76—295
John Cook   74–76–72–75—297
Mike Donald   75–69–78–75—297
John Adams   72–77–73–76—298
Skeeter Heath   71–72–76–79—298
Tony Hollifield   79–71–74–74—298
Mike White   78–77–73–70—298

Stan Altgelt	74–74–76–75—299
Alan Fadel	78–72–72–77—299
Ron Milanovich	75–75–76–73—299
Mike Zach	73–76–76–74—299
Robert Donald	75–74–77–77—300
Ted Goin	78–72–77–73—300
Lance Ten Broeck	75–73–77–75—300
Jaime Gonzalez	72–74–76–78—300
Doug Black	76–76–72–77—301
Bill Murchison	77–78–72–74—301
Peter Teravainen	78–71–78–74—301
Jim Fellner	75–72–74–81—302
Mitch Mooney	72–78–75–77—302
Scott Watkins	77–77–69–79—302

For years, the PGA Tour media guide has mistakenly listed fall 1978 as Chip Beck's only qualifying performance at tour school. In fact, Beck had too low a finish on the 1979 money list and had to go back through qualifying, which he did with great success in this school. Given Beck's travails in the late 1990s, it is possible that despite his lifetime tour winnings in excess of $6 million, he will be forced to requalify.

1980 Spring
Pinehurst Resort No. 6
Pinehurst, NC
June 4–7

Jack Spradlin	75–69–71–73—288
Mike Gove	74–74–70–71—289
Vance Heafner	70–73–77–70—290
Robert Seligman	71–75–74–72—292

Jimmy Powell	68–72–77–75—292
Wren Lum	76–72–70–74—292
Bob Pancratz	73–73–76–71—293
Jim Barber	72–78–71–72—293
Sale Omohundro	74–74–73–73—294
David Brownlee	71–77–73–73—294
David Thore	78–72–69–75—294
Bill Loeffler	72–74–74–75—295
Mike Smith	71–72–76–76—295
Dennis Trixler	72–79–76–69—296
Dave Fowler	81–70–72–73—296
Mark Rohde	73–76–74–73—296
R. W. Eaks	77–72–75–73—297
Mike Holland	77–73–73–74—297
Bill Lytle	78–75–70–74—297
Gary Hardin	74–75–73–75—297
Jeff Hawkes	76–78–71–73—298
Mike Klein	77–74–75–72—298
Mike Harmon	79–71–76–72—298
Barry Harwell	73–73–81–71—298
Clint Doyle	77–74–71–76—298
Charlie Gibson	74–69–77–78—298
Bill Britton	71–73–76–78—298

Recent PGA Tour media guides have listed the much-traveled R. W. Eaks as having qualified in the fall 1980 school at Fresno. As shown above, Eaks in fact got his card at the spring school that year. Eaks had very little success as a PGA Tour player during the '80s, then emerged as a Hogan/Nike Tour regular who played the "developmental tour" for its first eight seasons, before finally earning PGA Tour eligibility when he won $117,000 to rank ninth on the Nike in 1997. Literally a graybeard, he is referred to as

"Gramps" by those who have played on the Nike Tour with him during that lengthy "developmental" period. Eaks didn't finish high enough on the PGA Tour money list to stay fully exempt, so he entered the 1998 tour qualifier but was forced to limp off the course during the fifth round with leg and back pain.

1980 Fall
Fort Washington Golf and Country Club
Fresno, CA
October 23–26

Bruce Douglass	65–69–67–70—271
Doug Black	69–71–69–69—278
Jack Ferenz	70–68–71–71—280
Jeff Hewes	67–70–71–72—280
Jim Booros	74–73–71–65—283
Keith Lyford	70–70–74–69—283
Gary Trivisonno	71–73–69–70—283
Allan Strange	68–70–74–71—283
Ted Goin	72–71–70–70—283
Curtis Worley	73–68–70–72—283
Mark O'Meara	72–75–67–71—285
Tim Norris	71–72–69–73—285
Dan Frickey	70–73–72–71—286
Rod Nuckolls	69–71–71–75—286
John Mazza	69–72–74–72—287
Perry Arthur	72–73–75–67—287
Loren Roberts	75–68–72–72—287
Darrell Kestner	73–71–71–72—287
Don Levin	72–73–69–73—287
John Jacobs	69–70–70–78—287
Scott Stegner	71–73–73–71—288
Brent Murray	73–72–72–71—288

Richie Adham	71–71–73–73—288
Bob Beauchemin	76–67–72–73—288
Fred Couples	67–76–71–74—288
Thomas Gray	72–70–70–76—288
Jimmy Paschal	69–73–72–76—288

Par at Fort Washington was 71, which makes Douglass's medal score of 271 slightly less torrid than it looks. Out of 27 card-earners at Fresno, two would become superstars, O'Meara and Couples. Among the other card-earners in this school was a player named Curtis and a player named Strange, but not the man you're thinking of. Allan Strange, Curtis's identical twin brother, got his shot at pro golf in the fall of 1980 but ended up in a Wall Street brokerage.

1981 Spring
Walt Disney World Resort (Palm Course)
Lake Buena Vista, FL
June 10–13

Billy Glisson	72–69–69–65—275
Charles Krenkel	68–73–67–68—276
Gavin Levenson	70–67–69–70—276
Denis Watson	67–72–70–70—279
Clarence Rose	68–70–71–70—279
Tom Woodard	67–66–73–73—279
Barry Harwell	71–72–65–72—280
Charlie Gibson	72–71–69–69—281
Jeff Thomsen	74–70–66–71—281
Skeeter Heath	70–69–72–70—281
Tom Chain	70–70–73–69—282
Payne Stewart	74–69–70–69—282

Bob Proben	72–73–67–70—282
Terry Anton	68–76–67–71—282
Jet Ozaki	68–68–73–73—282
Bill Loeffler	72–69–68–73—282
Mark Calcavecchia	74–69–72–68—283
Donald Reese	75–70–69–69—283
Rick Borg	75–69–70–69—283
Jim Bertoncino	73–68–72–70—283
Tom Inskeep	76–69–67–71—283
Larry Rinker	71–71–67–74—283
Gene George	72–71–71–70—284
Jeff Sanders	72–71–70–71—284
David Sann	74–70–68–72—284

Two of these 25 qualifiers, Stewart and Calcavecchia, went on to have superb careers, although Calcavecchia's would sputter at first and require him to requalify in 1982 and again in 1983. Two other members of this group, Denis Watson and Jet Ozaki, have achieved consistent success in their own right. Clarence Rose, who was 24 when he earned his card at this Disney World qualifier, would proceed through 14 up-and-down years before earning his privileges anew via the 1995 Q School, then win his first tournament (the 1996 Sprint International) a year later, only to find himself back in the qualifying trenches yet again in 1998. Billy Glisson, who took first-place money of $3,000 after sizzling through a final round of 65, would scarcely be heard from after the qualifier ended. Finishing first at tour qualifying has never been much of a harbinger for later success, but even at that Glisson goes down as one of the most disappointing Q School medalists ever. A check of tour records shows him recording his first payday of the 1982 season in July, at the Western Open, and basically disappearing after that.

1981 Fall
Waterwood National Country Club
Huntsville, TX
October 28–31

Robert Thompson	75–68–69–72—284
Tim Graham	71–69–75–69—284
Jay Cudd	74–73–69–70—286
Perry Arthur	80–63–72–71—286
Steven Liebler	74–68–73–72—287
Ronnie Black	71–70–72–74—287
Steven Jones	75–71–73–69—288
Ron Commans	74–70–74–72—290
Rick Pearson	72–75–71–72—290
Al Morton	72–70–71–77—290
Doug Black	77–72–72–70—291
Bill Buttner	74–74–75–68—291
Kenny Knox	73–69–78–71—291
Johnny Elam	75–71–76–70—292
Ray Barr, Jr.	71–74–73–74—292
Mike Nicolette	74–75–69–75—293
Michael Burke, Jr.	78–70–76–70—294
Hal Sutton	76–70–73–75—294
Paul Azinger	74–72–76–73—295
Scott Steger	77–73–70–75—295
Larry Mize	77–71–72–75—296
Scott Watkins	77–72–72–74—296
Blaine McCallister	70–78–71–76—296
Ken Green	74–68–74–79—296
Bob Burton	76–74–71–75—296
Clyde Rego	71–75–76–74—296
Rocky Thompson	72–73–77–74—296

Lance Ten Broeck	77–73–72–74—296
Tommy Armour III	72–72–77–75—296
Richard Zokol	76–74–73–73—296
Mike Booker	71–71–78–76—296
Buzz Fly	72–77–77–70—296
Steve Hart	75–69–75–77—296
Skip Dunaway	72–72–75–77—296

Three of the biggest winners on tour from this Q School, Sutton, Azinger, and Mize, can be found bunched at 294 and 295. Steve Jones, who had just turned pro and would return twice to Q School before becoming a seven-time tour winner and 1996 U.S. Open champ, is listed in the original PGA Tour records as Steven Jones, so this listing repeats the full-name entry. The obscure but memorable Buzz Fly inserts his name into posterity with his 296 at Huntsville.

1982
TPC at Sawgrass and Sawgrass Country Club
Ponte Vedra, FL
November 16–21

Donnie Hammond	66–68–71–65–74–75—419
David Peoples	72–72–70–74–73–72—433
Nick Price	77–70–69–69–74–74—435
Mac O'Grady	79–76–71–66–71–73—436
Tze-Chung Chen	69–76–69–75–73–74—436
Buddy Gardner	67–72–71–74–78–74—436
Bob Boyd	78–72–69–70–72–75—436
Richard Zokol	70–73–73–70–75–75—436
Dan Forsman	75–73–73–71–76–69—437
Gary McCord	73–74–72–70–74–74—437

John Mccomish	72–70–75–71–75–74—437
Mike Peck	74–71–75–72–76–70—438
Tom Jones	73–71–74–73–73–74—438
Joey Rassett	73–74–73–75–72–72—439
Ken Green	71–76–68–72–79–73—439
Jeff Sanders	71–73–71–77–71–76—439
Bill Sander	72–73–70–74–74–76—439
Rod Nuckolls	73–71–70–76–76–74—440
Lindy Miller	75–72–72–70–76–75—440
Steve Hart	78–73–72–71–70–76—440
Michael Brannan	76–71–70–72–72–79—440
Mick Soli	73–78–73–71–74–72—440
Lynn Lott	74–71–71–78–74–73—441
Doug Black	73–75–74–74–71–74—441
Curt Byrum	76–69–73–73–74–76—441
Larry Rinker	76–68–72–79–69–77—441
David Ogrin	81–70–69–73–75–74—442
Ivan Smith	76–69–74–74–74–75—442
Russ Cochran	68–71–73–74–75–79—442
Jimmy Roy	77–75–71–71–75–74—443
Bill Murchison	74–75–69–74–77–74—443
Loren Roberts	76–69–70–75–78–75—443
Tony Sills	74–77–70–74–72–76—443
Darrell Kestner	76–74–69–74–73–77—443
Wally Armstrong	69–73–72–77–74–78—443
Mike Gove	75–71–73–74–80–71—444
Ray Stewart	72–75–71–73–81–72—444
Mark Coward	72–72–75–82–70–73—444
Ronnie Black	74–78–69–79–69–75—444
Lonnie Nielsen	76–72–69–74–77–76—444
Blaine McCallister	76–69–74–73–75–77—444
Tom Lehman	71–71–71–75–78–77—444

Rafael Alarcon	77–74–67–71–76–79—444
Lars Meyerson	73–73–73–80–75–71—445
Jon Chaffee	74–72–75–74–79–72—446
Rick Pearson	72–80–69–75–76–74—446
Rick Dalpos	75–72–73–75–75–76—446
Sammy Rachels	73–81–71–74–70–77—446
Ken Kellley	75–76–69–72–75–79—446
Jeff Sluman	67–73–73–76–78–79—446

The tour school's format for final-round play has been 108 holes since 1982, when the return to once-a-year qualifying was enacted. The most noteworthy policy change covering graduates of this school is discontinuance of Monday, or "rabbit," qualifying for players earning their cards at tour school. The players from this 1982 school went forward secure in the knowledge that they could make up a schedule in advance and not have to reroute their travel according to whether they had made cuts or not. Donnie Hammond's best-ever Q School margin of 14 strokes is probably one of the most secure records in all of professional golf. Last-day scoring at this qualifier is among the highest ever. Boyd, Rachels, and Kestner would each later win a national PGA Club Professional Championship (in 1988, 1994, and 1996, respectively).

1983
TPC at Sawgrass
Ponte Vedra, FL
November 16–22

Willie Wood	71–70–70–71–72–72—426
Brett Upper	72–75–74–65–74–68—428
Bill Britton	77–70–75–74–68–68—432

Joey Sindelar	77–69–72–75–68–71—432
Griff Moody	70–73–69–75–72–73—432
Jay Cudd	69–72–73–67–77–75—433
Corey Pavin	78–72–76–68–74–66—434
Mark Brooks	77–69–72–69–76–71—434
Jodie Mudd	73–74–73–70–72–72—434
Bill Sander	73–73–70–71–72–75—434
Tom Lehman	76–72–75–67–76–70—436
Steve Leibler	77–74–73–70–71–72—437
Brad Faxon	73–70–76–73–75–71—438
Michael Putnam	75–70–74–71–74–74—438
David Peoples	76–71–77–69–70–75—438
Scott Watkins	75–79–68–75–70–72—439
Kenny Knox	76–78–70–71–72–72—439
Jim Kane	72–73–71–75–75–73—439
Loren Roberts	77–73–71–71–72–75—439
Adam Adams	77–74–73–73–72–71—440
Ken Brown	75–70–78–71–71–75—440
Clyde Rego	71–75–70–75–74–75—440
Gary Krueger	77–75–66–72–73–77—440
Curt Byrum	76–79–75–71–71–69—441
Randy Watkins	72–79–72–72–76–70—441
Ken Kelley	75–73–72–70–78–73—441
Mike Smith	77–72–70–69–80–73—441
Gary Marlowe	79–73–72–74–74–70—442
Jim Gallagher	77–72–73–74–73–73—442
Tom Lamore	79–72–73–74–70–74—442
K. C. Liao	77–77–72–70–72–74—442
Mark Wiebe	76–75–73–71–73–74—442
Tommy Valentine	72–74–71–73–75–77—442
John Hamarik	76–79–71–73–71–73—443
Lyn Lott	77–71–77–72–72–74—443

Bill Glasson	79–69–77–70–74–74—443
Rick Dalpos	75–75–73–72–74–74—443
Paul Azinger	74–70–77–71–77–74—443
Gene Sauers	75–78–76–72–74–69—444
Mark Calcavecchia	76–75–75–74–73–71—444
Larry Rinker	76–79–74–70–74–71—444
Bobby Stroble	74–77–70–77–73–73—444
Mike Cunning	80–74–72–71–74–73—444
Jack Spradlin	73–76–71–77–74–73—444
Jack Ferenz	72–81–71–71–76–73—444
Mick Soli	80–69–74–72–76–73—444
James Blair	77–73–73–75–71–75—444
Greg Farrow	77–74–73–71–74–75—444
Frank Fuhrer	76–70–75–72–74–77—444
Gary Pinns	73–76–78–75–71–72—444
Grier Jones	79–74–74–71–75–72—445
Gavin Levinson	77–74–73–69–80–72—445
Mike Gove	77–76–73–73–73–73—445
Kurt Cox	77–73–73–75–74–73—445
David O'Kelley	76–71–81–73–70–74—445
Mike Peck	74–81–73–68–75–74—445
Lee Rinker	75–74–75–72–75–74—445

When the PGA Tour announced plans to build its own golf course and clubhouse on land that would also contain a headquarters building, some players criticized it as a grandiose act that unfairly diverted tour income from the prize purses. In response, tour officials maintained that the facility would solve an annual problem of where to hold qualifying school. In 1982 and 1983, the TPC at Sawgrass was indeed used as a Q School site, but has not been used since. Future stars in this class of qualifiers include Calcavecchia, Pavin, and Faxon, who have not returned to the Q School mill since 1983, and Lehman, who would be back at school for a final time in 1984.

1984
Mission Hills County Club
Rancho Mirage, CA
La Quinta Hotel Golf Club
La Quinta, CA
December 12–18

Paul Azinger	69–71–69–70–67–72—418
Tom Sieckmann	72–70–69–69–67–72—419
Phil Blackmar	69–72–70–66–70–72—419
Mark Wiebe	70–73–73–66–72–71—425
Skeeter Heath	72–71–70–72–70–71—426
Wayne Grady	73–69–72–71–69–73—427
Steve Pate	67–69–68–74–75–75—428
Dennis Trixler	70–71–71–78–70–69—429
Bill Bergin	70–75–70–70–72–72—429
Mick Soli	70–72–71–72–70–74—429
Brad Fabel	67–69–72–76–71–74—429
Robert Wrenn	71–72–70–69–71–76—429
Mike Bright	71–72–75–73–67–72—430
Ken Green	73–72–73–70–70–72—430
Chris Perry	73–70–67–73–71–76—430
David Frost	73–74–74–69–73–68—431
Greg Twiggs	70–77–70–70–73–71—431
Andrew Magee	76–72–71–73–66–73—431
Jeff Hart	73–70–67–74–74–73—431
Tom Lehman	72–71–72–70–72–74—431
Mike Hulbert	69–73–72–70–72–75—431
Ernie Gonzalez	74–76–68–67–78–69—432

Jeff Sluman	74–74–69–70–74–72—433
Bob Tway	69–73–70–76–75–71—434
Ron Commans	69–75–70–73–75–72—434
Jeff Sanders	70–71–74–75–71–73—434
Jay Delsing	67–72–72–74–75–74—434
Steven Jones	72–69–72–71–74–78—434
Gordon Johnson	71–74–71–71–70–77—434
Kenny Knox	73–71–72–70–70–78—434
Tom Woodard	74–69–72–74–74–72—435
Woody Blackburn	71–73–71–74–73–73—435
Ivan Smith	70–74–69–75–74–73—435
Terry Snodgrass	71–70–72–73–76–73—435
Steven Bowman	68–69–73–70–82–73—435
Mike Barnblatt	74–71–73–74–69–74—435
Jeff Coston	72–71–75–72–70–75—435
David Thore	71–74–71–71–73–75—435
Bill Britton	71–70–71–73–72–78—435
Lennie Clements	73–72–74–74–70–73—436
Gary Pinns	74–73–71–72–72–74—436
Stuart Smith	70–74–69–71–78–74—436
Bill Buttner	71–70–72–71–78–74—436
Steven Liebler	74–71–71–70–72–78—436
Bob Lohr	71–70–72–70–75–78—436
John DeForest	70–72–70–71–75–78—436
Mike Gove	74–73–74–74–71–71—437
Dave Davis	77–72–71–69–75–73—437
Bill Glasson	72–72–70–72–77–74—437
David Lundstrom	75–71–75–71–69–76—437

This tour school final marked the entry of the La Quinta, California, courses into the regular rota of final-stage sites. The most notable scoring oddity in this field is the six-stroke gap between

Sieckman and Blackmar at 419 and Wiebe at 425. Of the eight PGA Championships held from 1986 to 1993, four of them were won by players who got tour cards at this Q School: Bob Tway (1986), Jeff Sluman (1988), Wayne Grady (1990), and Paul Azinger (1993).

1985
South and West Courses
Grenelefe Golf and Tennis Resort
Haines City, FL
November 20–25

Tom Seickmann	71–69–66–69–70–71—416
Tom Pernice, Jr.	70–69–73–67–66–72—417
Tom Byrum	67–72–69–69–70–72—419
Dick Mast	69–71–69–70–71–70—420
Peter Senior	70–71–69–68–72–71—421
Brian Mogg	69–67–73–71–72–70—422
Blaine McCallister	71–70–72–72–67–71—423
Davis Love III	66–74–71–73–68–71—423
Stu Ingraham	73–73–71–69–67–71—424
Jeff Grygiel	74–71–68–73–67–71—424
Robert Wrenn	67–73–70–71–72–71—424
Eduardo Romero	72–69–74–69–69–73—426
Mike Hulbert	69–72–72–70–69–74—426
Bill Israelson	70–73–72–69–71–72—427
Billy Pierot	67–75–70–71–71–73—427
Gregory Ladehoff	71–72–72–71–66–75—427
Dave Rummells	72–72–71–72–72–69—428
David Peoples	71–72–71–69–74–71—428
Mike West	70–69–71–72–72–74—428

Rick Fehr	72–72–78–66–74–67—429
Andy Dillard	71–73–78–69–66–72—429
Mike McCullough	74–75–70–68–70–72—429
Charles Bolling	73–68–72–67–75–74—429
Kris Moe	71–71–70–71–71–75—429
Antonio Cerda	72–73–72–72–73–68—430
Doug Johnson	75–71–73–69–73–69—430
Rocco Mediate	71–70–69–73–76–71—430
Mark Brooks	74–70–73–72–69–72—430
John McComish	69–72–74–70–69–76—430
Jim Dent	67–75–74–68–69–77—430
Mike Miles	69–76–72–69–75–70—431
Rod Curl	75–71–69–73–72–71—431
Jeff Lewis	71–76–70–73–69–72—431
Rick Cramer	71–72–71–74–68–75—431
Denny Hepler	74–72–73–71–71–71—432
Danny Briggs	72–74–69–73–71–73—432
Tom Gleeton	71–73–70–72–70–76—432
John Adams	67–71–77–70–71–76—432
Rick Dalpos	70–70–78–76–71–68—433
Mike Nicolette	74–72–75–72–72–68—433
Dennis Trixler	72–69–75–73–74–70—433
David Lundstrom	71–73–71–74–72–72—433
Bob Pancratz	70–72–75–71–73–72—433
Harry Taylor	74–75–66–70–72–76—433
Trevor Dodds	73–72–71–71–69–77—433
Mike Sullivan	77–72–74–70–71–70—434
Brian Claar	74–74–70–70–76–70—434
Adrian Stills	71–75–74–73–69–72—434
Mike Gove	72–74–77–69–70–72—434
Ernie Gonzalez	72–76–73–72–68–73—434

Seickmann earned a respectable $15,000 for first place, as Q School purse money was ratcheted up. That paycheck was equal to half his entire earnings from the regular 1985 season. The six-foot-five Nebraskan would be back for another pass at qualifying in 1987 before going on a successful six-year that included one tour victory, the 1988 Anheuser-Busch Classic.

1986
PGA West (Stadium Course)
La Quinta Resort (Dunes Course)
La Quinta, CA
December 3–8

Steve Jones	67–65–69–67–72–75—415
Steve Elkington	72–67–70–67–71–72—419
Philip Parkin	70–70–72–69–70–70—421
Rocco Mediate	69–69–73–71–67–72—421
Tom Garner	70–73–68–72–69–71—423
Bill Britton	68–69–70–69–75–73—424
Doug Johnson	76–68–66–65–75–74—424
Duffy Waldorf	73–69–73–72–68–70—425
Don Shirey, Jr.	69–73–73–70–69–71—425
Loren Roberts	72–68–72–71–70–72—425
Mark Brooks	74–73–68–70–70–71—426
Sam Randolph	69–72–70–72–72–71—426
David Peoples	71–74–71–70–73–68—427
Jim Carter	70–71–70–72–75–69—427
Ted Schulz	70–71–73–71–72–70—427
Keith Clearwater	71–73–70–71–71–71—427
Ray Barr, Jr.	72–69–73–70–72–71—427
Philip Jonas	67–71–71–71–73–74—427
John Inman	72–75–70–72–66–73—428

Ray Stewart	68–69–73–73–72–73—428
Brad Fabel	67–73–70–73–71–74—428
Jim Wilson	74–66–69–73–71–75—428
Perry Arthur	70–76–75–69–67–72—429
David Canipe	73–74–69–71–68–74—429
Trevor Dodds	72–69–70–72–72–74—429
John Horne	71–67–73–71–72–75—429
Jeff Lewis	74–74–71–71–72–68—430
Ted K. Lehmann	68–71–71–72–77–71—430
Rick Dalpos	70–77–69–73–69–72—430
Dave Eichelberger	72–69–68–72–74–75—430
Mike Bender	68–74–72–65–75–76—430
Jay Don Blake	74–68–75–69–78–67—431
Tim Norris	69–70–70–76–75–71—431
Bill Sander	74–70–65–71–79–72—431
Harry Taylor	72–73–75–76–69–73—431
Bruce Soulsby	75–69–71–70–73–73—431
Mike Smith	72–72–71–70–72–74—431
Vance Heafner	69–68–72–70–75–77—431
Brad Greer	71–70–75–70–75–71—432
Kenny Perry	69–70–79–71–71–72—432
John Riegger	74–70–73–70–72–73—432
Gary Krueger	72–72–71–69–75–73—432
Robert Wrenn	71–75–74–67–71–74—432
Robert Thompson	69–69–73–72–75–75—432
Aki Ohmachi	75–72–67–72–69–75—432
Denny Hepler	76–73–66–69–73–75—432
John McComish	70–72–74–70–68–78—432
David Hobby	70–74–74–73–76–66—433
Ed Dougherty	71–78–66–73–74–72—434
Tony Grimes	72–76–68–72–73–73—434
Richard Zokol	71–73–70–69–75–76—434

Mike McGee   71–70–75–70–71–77—434

Dewey Arnette   69–72–76–65–74–78—434

Purse money on the PGA Tour, after having risen at the rate of about $600,000 a year during the 1970s, was exploding in the 1980s at average annual increments of $2.8 million. Unfortunately for some of the names we begin to see repeating at Q School in this era—Dalpos, Peoples, McComish, et. al.—not everyone who got his hands on the sword could wrestle it out of the stone. Rocco Mediate's fifth-round 67 at PGA West in this tour school was more than just a necessary boost to his qualifying bid—Mediate described it years later as "the best round of my life."

1987
Matanzas Woods Golf Club
Pine Lakes Golf Club
Palm Coast, FL
December 2–7

John Huston   74–68–72–68–66–73—421

Jim Hallet   68–69–66–73–73–73—422

Jim Booros   71–71–73–68–66–74—423

Bill Buttner   73–67–75–75–71–67—428

Bruce Zabriski   76–67–77–71–69–68—428

Scott Verplank   71–70–75–74–68–71—429

Jim Nelford   73–72–72–68–72–72—429

David Canipe   72–70–71–75–69–73—430

Billy Andrade   74–70–70–73–70–73—430

Tommy Armour III   69–71–71–73–72–74—430

Clark Burroughs   70–72–71–70–72–75—430

Steve Lowery   68–76–79–71–68–69—431

Robert Thompson   72–74–71–74–71–69—431

Bob Proben   70–70–75–76–70–70—431

David Peoples	70–72–74–73–72–70—431
Brian Tennyson	71–76–73–69–73–70—432
Leonard Thompson	72–71–73–75–70–71—432
Greg Ladehoff	76–74–70–68–72–72—432
Joey Rassett	75–66–73–72–72–74—432
Paul Trittler	73–69–76–72–67–75—432
Tom Sieckmann	72–70–72–70–73–75—432
Jeff Coston	74–72–74–71–74–68—433
Jim Carter	73–69–75–69–73–74—433
Harry Taylor	72–71–76–76–68–71—434
Barry Cheesman	72–75–71–72–73–71—434
Tom Pernice	73–69–76–69–74–73—434
Mike Blackburn	70–74–72–76–68–74—434
Kim Young	72–68–73–72–73–76—434
Brandel Chamblee	68–66–74–76–74–76—434
Mark Brooks	72–72–75–76–73–67—435
Mike Bender	70–73–74–72–74–72—435
Billy Ray Brown	72–71–72–74–72–74—435
Steve Thomas	72–70–73–72–73–75—435
Richard Cromwell	71–72–75–77–71–70—436
Brian Mogg	73–73–71–72–76–71—436
Mark Maness	73–72–73–75–71–72—436
Tim Norris	72–70–75–74–73–72—436
Rick Pearson	73–70–73–74–73–73—436
Antonio Cerda	71–71–73–72–76–73—436
John Snyder	74–71–71–69–73–78—436
Bill Britton	76–69–75–70–77–70—437
Danny Briggs	73–73–72–76–72–71—437
Loren Roberts	72–70–76–73–75–71—437
Duffy Waldorf	73–75–71–71–72–75—437
Greg Farrow	69–74–75–72–72–75—437
Dillard Pruitt	68–75–73–72–72–77—437

Dave Eichelberger	68–71–81–73–70–75—438
Jeffrey Lankford	69–68–73–73–75–80—438
Brett Upper	69–75–73–75–72–74—438
Jay Delsing	74–69–74–75–67–79—438
Lance Ten Broeck	74–73–74–74–69–74—438
Roy Biancalana	71–73–74–76–69–75—438
Mike Hammond	75–73–71–73–73–73—438
Brad Bryant	75–67–72–72–74–78—438

Huston earned $15,000 for finishing first. The entire qualifying class managed relatively few scores in the 60s, which makes it interesting to note how many players at the very bottom of the final list opened with sub-70 scores, only to stumble forward from there and barely make their cards.

1988
La Quinta Resort (Dunes Course)
PGA West Jack Nicklaus Resort Course
La Quinta, CA
November 30–December 5

Robin Freeman	72–69–70–69–70–69—419
Brad Bryant	73–67–68–71–70–71—420
Don Reese	74–71–68–61–74–73—421
John Adams	70–66–73–72–69–72—422
Billy Andrade	73–68–67–71–71–72—422
Robert Thompson	65–68–67–71–77–74—422
David Tentis	72–70–71–71–70–69—423
Webb Heintzelman	71–70–73–68–70–71—423
Tony Sills	73–73–72–69–69–68—424
Ray Barr, Jr.	72–74–69–69–71–69—424
Nolan Henke	72–69–70–69–73–71—424

Billy Pierot	73–72–70–68–68–73—424
Jack Kay, Jr.	66–70–73–70–71–74—424
Miguel Martin	77–70–70–65–70–73—425
Ed Humenik	70–72–68–70–72–73—425
Karl Kimball	68–71–74–76–71–66—426
Ronnie McCann	73–67–75–71–70–71—427
Mark Hayes	72–71–67–73–71–73—427
P. H. Horgan III	69–73–70–70–71–74—427
Larry Silveira	71–68–70–73–70–75—427
Billy Mayfair	73–69–75–73–66–72—428
Rex Caldwell	71–75–68–72–70–72—428
Mike Miles	74–69–72–69–72–72—428
Bill Buttner	73–69–70–73–68–75—428
Ted Schulz	72–69–67–74–71–75—428
Don Shirey, Jr.	70–67–72–71–69–79—428
Roy Biancalana	72–73–70–69–73–72—429
Bob Wolcott	74–73–68–72–69–73—429
Trevor Dodds	70–72–70–74–69–74—429
Duffy Waldorf	72–72–71–70–66–78—429
David Jackson	73–74–71–69–71–72—430
J. L. Lewis	72–67–77–69–73–72—430
Bob Estes	74–73–70–68–71–74—430
Gregory Ladehoff	72–70–73–69–72–74—430
Tony Grimes	72–69–73–70–69–77—430
Lance Ten Broeck	73–71–72–69–78–68—431
John McComish	70–70–71–76–74–70—431
Kent Kluba	71–72–73–70–72–73—431
Jeff Hart	70–71–69–76–72–73—431
Rick Pearson	69–72–72–70–75–73—431
Jim Booros	75–73–70–67–72–74—431
Fred Funk	75–72–71–67–72–74—431
Jay Delsing	69–75–68–72–73–74—431

Steve Hart	72–72–69–70–72–76—431
Clark Burroughs	72–71–67–70–70–81—431
Joel Edwards	72–75–71–69–73–72—432
Doug Weaver	72–69–72–70–73–76—432
Charlie Bowles	70–72–69–78–70–73—432
Ray Stewart	73–71–69–72–70–77—432
Billy Tuten	76–69–72–67–72–76—432
Rick Dalpos	75–68–69–75–71–74—432
Greg Twiggs	71–70–70–72–74–75—432

Robin Freeman was "the kid from the pro shop" when he surprised himself and everyone else by winning the $15,000 first prize in this qualifier. A PGA West assistant pro when he entered, Freeman had the advantage of home cooking and home-course knowledge when he reached final stage. Being an inexperienced traveler, Freeman had all he could do to get from place to place during the 1989 season. His spotty play that year would earn him further opportunities to go through Q School, leading to his unique distinction of being the only two-time Qualifying Tournament medalist ever (Freeman was comedalist with Ty Armstrong and Dave Stockton, Jr., in 1993). This Q School's most compelling footnote, however, is the fourth-round 61 shot by Don Reese. In the annals of PGA Tour Qualifying, Reese's 11-under score is not only a record, it is a full two shots better than any other score on par-72 course by a qualifying player. The other one-round score that tends to jump off this page in the record books is the whopping 81 shot by Clark Burroughs in the final round. Coming off 67–70–70, Burroughs made the needle jump with his closing score.

1989
TPC at the Woodlands
The Woodlands Inn and Country Club (North Course)
The Woodlands, TX
November 29–December 4

David Peoples	73–67–69–72–67–72—420
Tommy Moore	70–71–68–69–71–72—421
Jerry Haas	69–71–69–68–73–72—422
David Canipe	71–72–67–69–71–73—423
Bob Eastwood	73–69–71–67–73–71—424
Emlyn Aubrey	72–70–71–70–68–73—424
Ray Barr, Jr.	71–67–74–71–75–68—426
Jim Woodward	73–70–69–70–76–69—427
Fred Funk	74–72–66–72–71–72—427
Dennis Harrington	76–71–69–75–70–67—428
Greg Bruckner	76–69–70–74–71–68—428
Michael Allen	74–69–68–71–76–70—428
Jay Delsing	75–67–68–74–73–71—428
Peter Persons	73–73–69–69–72–72—428
Greg Hickman	71–72–64–76–73–72—428
Lee Janzen	71–71–68–69–77–72—428
Patrick Burke	70–71–68–71–73–75—428
Neal Lancaster	74–69–72–72–73–69—429
Ed Dougherty	74–71–73–73–68–70—429
Tom Eubank	75–71–73–69–74–68—430
Steve Lamontagne	75–71–70–72–72–70—430
Jeff Wilson	70–73–72–71–73–71—430
Sonny Skinner	69–73–76–69–71–72—430
Bob Wolcott	76–70–70–70–72–72—430
Grant Waite	73–71–70–69–75–72—430
Rick Todd	71–69–74–69–74–73—430

Tony Sills	73–71–70–71–70–75—430
Brian Kamm	72–70–69–74–70–75—430
Bill Buttner	73–72–66–71–72–76—430
Steve Hart	71–74–72–72–70–72—431
Kirk Triplett	76–71–68–69–75–72—431
Mick Schuchart	72–73–69–68–76–73—431
Mark Hayes	75–73–69–71–75–69—432
Carl Cooper	78–69–70–70–76–69—432
Rick Fehr	73–71–72–72–71–73—432
Pat Fitzsimons	70–73–70–71–73–75—432
Larry Silveira	76–74–71–71–73–68—433
Tom Silva	74–72–71–70–78–68—433
Dillard Pruitt	71–73–75–73–71–70—433
Joel Edwards	73–72–72–71–75–70—433
Harry Taylor	72–73–74–69–73–72—433
Robert Gamez	75–73–69–73–70–73—433
Jerry Anderson	72–72–70–73–73–73—433
Sean Murphy	71–70–73–70–76–73—433
Nolan Henke	71–72–72–73–71–74—433
Dewey Arnette	72–74–67–69–75–76—433
Mike Smith	72–72–68–67–77–77—433
Mitch Adcock	72–77–69–73–71–72—434
Lennie Clements	74–69–68–73–72–79—434
Ted Tryba	72–75–71–74–67–76—435
Paul Trittler	72–74–70–72–75–72—435
Jeff Hart	75–72–69–75–70–74—435
Jack Ferenz	74–68–72–74–73–74—435
Brian Claar	79–70–70–71–78–67—435
Clark Dennis	72–74–72–71–75–71—435
John Dowdall	77–73–66–71–74–74—435
Richard Zlokol	73–74–71–72–73–72—435

P. H. Horgan III   74–69–70–72–72–78—435
Brad Fabel   76–72–68–71–74–74—435

For tour-school perennial David Peoples, medalist honors at the 1989 qualifier had to be particularly satisfying. Ten years later, Peoples' career is on the blink, while fellow qualifiers of the same vintage, such as Fred Funk and Lee Janzen, are among the tour elite. Consider the vagaries of tour qualifying: If Pat Horgan had managed to shave one stroke off his gaudy final-round 78, he would have become the 50th qualifier and knocked out all 10 of the "and ties" players who, along with Horgan, shot 435. At a total of 59, this was the largest single-school group of qualifiers ever. With the coming of the Hogan/Nike Tour a year later, Q School was on its way to a contracted graduating class. Since 1989, the number of card-earners at Q School has been pared from low 50 and ties to the current level of low 35 and ties.

1990
La Quinta Resort (Dunes Course)
PGA West Jack Nicklaus Resort Course
La Quinta, CA
November 28–December 3

Duffy Waldorf   68–67–72–67–70–69—413
John Inman   67–71–69–69–72–67—415
Scott Gump   73–73–65–68–67–70—416
Bryan Norton   76–70–69–67–71–66—419
Carl Cooper   70–71–72–66–68–72—419
Brandt Jobe   70–66–73–69–69–72—419
Brandel Chamblee   76–72–70–68–66–68—420
Bill Buttner   70–68–72–69–65–76—420

Ronnie Black	70–69–72–65–73–71—420
Dillard Pruitt	71–70–71–72–72–65—421
Greg Whisman	71–66–73–70–69–72—421
Bart Bryant	74–66–68–75–68–71—422
Greg Bruckner	72–69–71–69–75–66—422
John Daly	71–68–70–71–69–73—422
Karl Kimball	67–72–70–69–71–73—422
Mike Standly	72–66–75–71–69–70—423
Ken Schall	71–72–69–73–66–72—423
Trevor Dodds	74–68–66–74–68–73—423
Sean Murphy	69–70–71–72–71–70—423
Jerry Haas	67–72–70–68–73–73—423
Larry Silveira	74–67–71–72–71–69—424
Brad Bell	75–69–72–69–69–70—424
Marco Dawson	71–71–70–71–69–72—424
Perry Arthur	75–73–68–65–69–74—424
Dudley Hart	73–66–71–69–71–74—424
Jim Benepe	71–74–68–71–71–70—425
Robert Thompson	69–73–73–70–72–68—425
George Burns	73–72–68–69–69–74—425
Clark Dennis	69–71–73–69–71–72—425
J. C. Anderson	68–67–74–74–70–72—425
John Wilson	69–66–70–73–70–77—425
Michael Allen	71–71–74–68–70–72—426
Brad Lardon	69–73–72–72–70–70—426
Craig Rudolph	71–69–69–72–72–73—426
Brian Kamm	72–69–72–67–73–73—426
Kim Young	74–71–68–71–74–69—427
David Sutherland	70–72–68–75–71–71—427
Joel Edwards	73–71–69–70–71–73—427
Sam Randolph	70–71–72–69–71–74—427
Dan Halldorson	68–72–69–72–73–73—427

Bobby Clampett	68–67–70–75–74–73—427
Barry Cheesman	73–70–71–73–73–67—427
Brian Watts	67–68–72–71–75–74—427
Mark Hayes	71–73–73–71–67–72—427
Dave Rummells	73–72–68–71–74–70—428
Greg Ladehoff	72–68–70–73–71–74—428
Dicky Thompson	75–71–73–68–72–69—428
Neal Lancaster	68–70–70–79–70–71—428
Charlie Bowles	75–69–70–73–69–72—428

Purse inflation throughout the '80s and '90s has resulted in a slew of repeat Q-Schoolers, but Carl Cooper's unusual three-year run from 1989 to 1991 still draws the eye. The University of Houston grad not only entered all three of those years, but got a card each time and even moved up in the final standings each time. He was 31st in 1989, tied for fourth in '90, and destined to finish by himself in second place in 1991. Tied for 36 in this batch of qualifiers are Bobby Clampett (coming through Q School again, 10 years after first earning a card) and Sam Randolph, two classic blue-chippers who had disappointing careers, although Clampett did get off to a flashy start.

1991
West and South Courses
Grenelefe Golf and Tennis Resort
Haines City, FL
December 4–9

Mike Standly	67–71–67–70–69–68—412
Carl Cooper	67–64–68–73–73–70—415
Tom Byrum	68–69–70–71–73–66—417
Kelly Gibson	72–68–68–71–69–69—417

Sonny Skinner	71–66–67–69–73–71—417
Paul McIntire	69–74–70–67–67–71—418
Jon Chaffee	72–74–68–65–70–69—418
Steve Hart	71–69–71–68–71–71—421
Fran Quinn	67–69–73–69–75–68—421
Patrick Burke	74–69–66–73–71–68—421
Donnie Hammond	71–71–69–68–73–69—421
Emlyn Aubrey	70–77–73–66–67–69—422
Mike Cunning	76–73–69–69–68–68—423
Greg Lesher	73–68–73–67–71–71—423
John Ross	71–68–71–68–71–74—423
Greg Whisman	74–71–67–72–67–72—423
J. P. Hayes	73–72–70–71–69–69—424
E. L. Pfister	73–69–66–71–76–70—425
Mark Carnevale	74–72–68–69–71–71—425
Robert Friend	72–72–69–72–72–71—425
Jim Woodward	72–73–65–73–70–72—425
Doug Martin	72–69–70–71–69–74—425
John Inman	72–74–69–69–73–69—426
Mitch Adcock	71–74–64–70–75–72—426
Bruce Zabriski	76–69–72–65–72–72—426
David Toms	72–73–70–69–70–72—426
David Ogrin	66–72–72–70–73–73—426
Richard Zokol	71–70–69–61–72–73—426
Chris Tucker	73–73–70–69–68–73—426
Tray Tyner	72–70–64–73–78–70—427
Michael Allen	73–70–69–73–73–69—427
Dicky Thompson	74–70–66–74–73–70—427
Brandel Chamblee	71–72–74–69–73–68—427
John Riegger	74–71–72–68–70–72—427
Jim McGovern	73–66–70–67–75–76—427
John Elliott	73–70–70–70–74–71—428

Kim Young	74–71–70–69–73–71—428
Marco Dawson	70–79–69–68–73–69—428
Robin Freeman	72–74–71–67–72–72—428
David Peege	72–75–70–70–74–67—428
Greg Hickman	75–68–69–69–72–75—428
Dave Schreyer	73–73–69–70–72–72—429
Mike Sullivan	74–74–70–69–70–72—429
Lon Hinkle	74–71–71–71–72–70—429
Dick Mast	70–74–71–71–70–73—429
Brad Bell	76–68–71–70–75–69—429
Greg Kraft	73–73–68–71–70–74—429
Steve Lamontagne	72–70–71–73–68–75—429

The 1991 school at Grenelefe—so far, anyway—has not been a big career-launcher for any of the graduates. Bob Friend's tie for 18th at this qualifier stands out in retrospect, given the historic final-round score of 63 Friend shot six years later at Grenelefe to get himself back on the big tour.

1992
TPC at The Woodlands
The Woodlands Inn and Country Club (North Course)
The Woodlands, TX
November 28–December 3

Massy Kuramoto	70–71–72–69–71–70—423
Skip Kendall	79–67–69–70–67–71—423
Brett Ogle	70–70–71–72–69–71—423
Perry Moss	71–74–66–70–71–71—423
Neale Smith	67–72–71–70–71–72—423
Jimmy Johnston	70–71–69–70–73–71—423
Harry Taylor	72–67–69–69–76–71—424

Dave Rummells	72–69–72–67–72–72—424
Gene Jones	66–72–75–71–71–70—425
Willie Wood	70–70–69–70–74–72—425
Tad Rhyan	67–70–70–73–72–73—425
Mike Schuchart	74–69–71–72–71–69—425
Robin Lee Freeman	70–71–69–73–73–70—426
Carl Cooper	72–68–72–68–75–71—426
David Ogrin	66–69–72–74–74–72—427
Lennie Clements	72–74–71–72–70–69—428
Joe Durant	72–72–71–69–75–69—428
Paul Goydos	72–69–72–71–73–71—428
Bill Murchison	73–72–70–70–71–72—428
Grant Waite	70–71–74–71–71–72—429
Dave Peege	73–75–67–72–69–73—429
JC Anderson	69–71–71–72–71–75—429
Barry Cheesman	69–74–73–72–73–69—430
Dennis Trixler	68–75–72–73–72–70—430
Brandel Chamblee	72–74–72–68–73–71—430
John Elliott	72–73–69–72–72–72—430
Greg Twiggs	71–74–68–71–74–72—430
Kim Young	70–77–66–73–70–74—430
Tom Byrum	71–69–71–74–70–75—430
Trevor Dodds	71–69–73–70–77–71—431
Marty Schiene	72–72–72–70–73–72—431
Jeff Cook	68–73–72–71–73–74—431
Greg Cesario	77–70–70–70–68–76—431
Michael Bradley	69–71–71–71–72–77—431
Jay Overton	73–73–68–73–74–71—432
John Dowdall	69–75–71–74–74–69—432
Michael Allen	68–73–69–70–73–79—432
Eddie Pearce	70–71–76–67–77–71—432
Greg Kraft	70–76–73–70–75–68—432

Tim Conley	68–71–72–71–77–73—432
Lee Porter	74–71–73–72–69–73—432
Len Mattiace	71–72–72–72–72–73—432
Dave DeLong	75–70–70–70–74–73—432

By far the biggest gangsome of comedalists at any Q School, the group at 423 has not prospered much since sharing top honors in the 1992 qualifier. Ogle, an Australian, won tournaments in 1993 and 1994, but he later lost his exemption. The others haven't contended much at all, although Kendall appears to be finding himself in the late '90s. Jay Overton's success in this qualifier is noteworthy, given that Overton was a fully employed director of golf at a Florida resort at the time. He made scant use of his eligibility during the 1993 season. To understand how diverse are the roads to qualifying, compare Len Mattiace's steady march toward 432 with Michael Allen's roller-coaster ride to the same on-the-number finish. And if you're keeping tabs on Kim Young, this is the Texan's fourth successful pass through tour school.

1993
La Quinta Resort (Dunes Course)
PGA West Jack Nicklaus Resort Course
La Quinta, CA
December 1–6

Ty Armstrong	71–70–68–71–67–68—415
Dave Stockton, Jr.	68–72–66–68–70–71—415
Robin Freeman	70–68–68–68–70–71—415
Jesper Parnevik	65–66–79–67–67–72—416
Jeff Woodland	68–69–71–69–68–71—416
Pete Jordan	71–65–69–72–68–71—416
Joey Rassett	74–71–66–66–72–68—417

Clark Dennis	69–72–70–68–69–71—419
Morris Hatalsky	69–71–70–71–68–70—419
Dennis Paulson	70–70–71–69–69–71—420
Glen Day	69–71–71–73–68–69—421
David Feherty	76–70–69–66–68–72—421
Yoshi Mizumaki	73–74–67–67–71–69—421
Todd Barranger	67–73–71–68–73–69—421
Steve Rintoul	68–71–68–72–73–69—421
Bob Burns	70–69–67–70–67–78—421
Steve Gotsche	74–68–74–68–67–70—421
Tim Simpson	71–71–71–68–67–74—422
Guy Boros	72–70–68–70–71–71—422
Paul Goydos	71–71–72–65–72–71—422
John Wilson	70–70–70–73–68–71—422
Thomas Levet	67–71–66–76–72–70—422
Steve Stricker	71–73–73–69–65–71—422
Mark Wurtz	74–69–69–68–72–71—423
Dicky Pride	70–71–65–72–68–77—423
Esteban Toledo	70–68–73–70–70–73—424
Paul Stankowski	66–71–74–70–71–72—424
Steve Brodie	70–73–71–72–73–65—424
Rocky Walcher	72–69–73–68–70–72—424
D. A. Russell	73–71–67–72–67–74—424
Mike Heiner	68–70–75–67–76–68—424
Don Reese	71–67–76–72–69–70—425
Ed Kirby	75–66–72–69–71–72—425
Steve Lamontagne	73–71–72–70–70–69—425
Bill Britton	73–75–66–68–74–69—425
Bill Kratzert	70–71–73–70–72–69—425
Charles Raulerson	70–72–71–70–69–74—426
Rob Boldt	70–72–73–71–72–68—426
Shaun Micheel	73–68–69–76–73–67—426

Mike Brisky	69–69–72–72–69–75—426
Chris Kite	68–75–71–71–69–72—426
Brad Lardon	73–69–72–70–73–69—426
Phil Tataurangi	68–72–69–75–71–71—426
Jim Furyk	70–71–74–71–69–71—426
Brad King	68–74–70–67–73–74—426
Tom Garner	71–70–71–68–74–72—426

Though Stockton, Jr. was a comedalist in 1993, this was not to be his finest hour at a tour school. Coming back from the sabbatical he took to during the 1998 tour season to be with his wife and gravely ill infant daughter, Stockton would return to the qualifying wars at La Quinta that fall and feel no golf pressure whatsoever, qualifying in a tie for fourth place at 20-under 412. Qualifier's Hiccup Award for this school goes to Bob Burns and Jesper Parnevik, who each broke form for just one day—Burns closing with a 78 when his previous high round was 70, and Parnevik elevating to a 79 in round three, surrounded by four scores in the 60s. Late-rally prize goes to Steve Brodie, who cooked up a 65 in round six after failing to break 70 in any previous round.

1994
West and South Courses
Grenelefe Golf and Tennis Resort
Haines City, FL
November 30–December 5

Woody Austin	70–68–72–68–69–67—414
Eduardo Romero	71–69–68–71–69–70—418
Tray Tyner	70–70–67–74–72–66—419
Bruce Fleisher	69–70–68–70–73–69—419

Harry Taylor	73–67–68–72–70–70—420
Dudley Hart	69–72–70–69–74–67—421
Pat Burke	72–70–67–72–71–69—421
Bill Porter	66–71–69–73–71–72—422
Ronnie Black	67–70–70–71–72–72—422
Doug Martin	72–71–66–71–75–68—423
Mike Brisky	72–72–69–71–71–68—423
Charlie Rymer	71–73–67–68–74–70—423
Omar Uresti	73–74–68–64–72–72—423
Don Reese	70–71–74–68–69–71—423
Jeff Leonard	71–75–67–69–74–68—424
Joey Rassett	68–74–71–70–73–68—424
Bart Bryant	65–67–71–74–77–70—424
Mark Wurtz	69–68–72–73–71–71—424
Lee Rinker	71–76–69–69–68–71—424
Marco Dawson	71–78–69–69–65–72—424
J. L. Lewis	72–69–68–68–75–72—424
Steve Gotsche	70–70–74–71–71–69—425
Phil Blackmar	65–74–66–73–77–70—425
Kelly Gibson	71–72–69–68–74–71—425
Tommy Tolles	71–71–72–71–69–71—425
Dicky Thompson	69–74–67–71–73–71—425
J. P. Hayes	69–70–67–69–78–72—425
Joe Acosta, Jr.	76–71–68–68–70–72—425
Scott McCarron	73–74–74–67–69–69—426
Jonathan Kaye	60–76–74–69–69–69—426
Scott Ford	69–70–70–72–75–70—426
Keith Fergus	74–71–67–74–70–70—426
Ray Stewart	74–70–71–71–72–68—426
Kawika Cotner	70–73–65–75–75–68—426
Tony Sills	69–66–71–70–77–73—426

Tim Loustalot	72–74–73–67–67–73—426
Jay Williamson	70–73–73–70–71–70—427
Tom Hearn	75–70–69–69–74–70—427
Clark Burroughs	73–73–70–70–71–70—427
Bill Britton	68–72–68–72–77–70—427
Michael Allen	72–75–71–66–73–70—427
Mike Smith	72–73–69–70–73–70—427
Ryan Howison	72–73–75–68–69–70—427
Carl Paulson	72–71–71–70–72–71—427
John Adams	74–72–71–70–72–71—427
Steve Hart	69–71–73–72–68–74—427

The most serious game face on the 1997 Nike Tour belonged to Woody Austin, whose career has been one of the most dramatic up-and-down stories in the recent annals of pro golf. With an eighth-place finish on the 1997 Nike Tour money list, Austin was able to play his way back onto the PGA Tour. A crippling knee injury he had suffered during the 1987 Q School in Palm Coast knocked Austin out of golf for two years, during which time he worked as a teller in a credit union. He took his momentum from this 1994 tour school and went on a rampage, earning Rookie of the Year honors on the PGA Tour at age 31. Austin won the 1995 Buick Open and finished in the top 30 on the big-tour money list in both 1995 and 1996, then fizzled in 1996. He earned a Nike Tour card at the 1997 Q School, then used it to earn some redemption. Finishing in the middle of the 1994 pack was Tommy Tolles, who had won two Nike Tour events and was ready to make the leap. Tolles just barely kept his full PGA Tour exemption in 1995, but over the next two years he would have 15 top-10 finishes and amass nearly $1.7 million in earnings.

1995
Bear Lakes Country Club
West Palm Beach, FL
November 29–December 4

Carl Paulson	70–65–69–65–69–71—409
Omar Uresti	70–67–71–67–68–67—410
Steve Hart	67–70–68–69–68–68—410
Shane Bertsch	71–68–68–69–69–66—411
Joey Gullion	71–68–72–64–69–67—411
Olin Browne	70–68–65–68–70–70—411
Tom Byrum	71–68–68–71–64–69—411
Kevin Sutherland	70–67–66–68–68–72—411
Tim Herron	71–69–65–68–69–70—412
Russ Cochran	69–70–69–67–66–71—412
Steve Jurgenson	68–70–68–70–67–70—413
Clarence Rose	67–67–68–72–69–71—414
David Peoples	69–68–68–67–70–72—414
Scott Medlin	69–69–69–71–64–72—414
Robert Wrenn	67–68–70–71–74–65—415
Lucas Parsons	67–68–69–68–73–70—415
Paul Stankowski	66–67–69–77–66–70—415
Hisayuki Sasaki	74–64–70–69–68–70—415
Brian Tennyson	69–71–68–65–70–72—415
Billy Ray Brown	75–68–68–67–71–67—416
Frank Lickliter, Jr.	73–75–65–67–67–69—416
Len Mattiace	71–68–72–69–67–69—416
Jeff Gallagher	66–74–66–72–69–69—416
Ronnie Black	71–68–70–64–72–71—416
Steve Rintoul	72–65–69–70–69–71—416
Scott Dunlap	70–73–68–71–68–67—417

Joe Daley	67–71–73–69–68–69—417
Bart Bryant	70–68–69–70–69–71—417
Jarmo Sandelin	74–72–67–68–70–67—418
John Maginnes	71–71–69–68–72–67—418
Taylor Smith	69–69–71–73–69–67—418
Greg Kraft	71–73–67–67–71–69—418
Jeff Julian	73–67–74–67–68–69—418
Jay Williamson	70–68–68–72–70–70—418
Joel Edwards	67–70–66–70–72–73—418
Mike Swartz	70–65–70–69–71–73—418
Jeff Hart	67–73–69–74–67–69—419
Andy Bean	74–67–70–68–71–69—419
Gary Rusnak	73–72–66–72–68–68—419
John Elliott	70–69–72–69–70–69—419
Ron Whittaker	74–68–69–70–71–67—419
Bryan Gorman	72–68–67–70–71–71—419

This is the great take-it-low Q School of the 1990s. The 69 shot by Carl Paulson in the fifth round of this qualifier is one of three scores altered in this archive from what was originally found in PGA Tour records. The tour's player guide showed Paulson shooting 59 in that fifth round, which would have resulted in a final total of 399. That mistake notwithstanding, Paulson's performance was tops in an unusually low-scoring Q School final. (The other two intentionally altered numbers from tour records are the closing 68s by Steve Hart, who tied for second place—the player guide has them mistakenly as 58s.) Two semisleepers from this pro golf "draft" were Stankowski and Lickliter, each of whom has gone on impressive hot streaks several times in his PGA Tour career.

1996
La Purisma Golf Club Lompoc, CA
Sandpiper Golf Club, Goleta, CA
December 4–9

Allen Doyle	72–70–70–72–68—352
Jimmy Johnston	71–72–68–71–70—352
Doug Barron	70–72–71–71–69—353
Chip Sullivan	74–70–71–67–71—353
Jimmy Green	71–77–70–67–69—354
Tom Pernice, Jr.	70–69–74–71–70—354
Brent Geiberger	67–73–70–73–72—355
Phil Tataurangi	67–74–71–71–72—355
Gabriel Hjertstedt	72–71–75–71–67—356
Larry Silveira	70–74–73–72–67—356
Tommy Armour III	74–74–72–68–68—356
Shaun Micheel	70–73–72–71–70—356
J. P. Hayes	69–71–74–70–72—356
Mike Standly	69–69–75–70–73—356
Shane Bertsch	69–71–75–67–74—356
Donnie Hammond	74–71–72–72–68—357
David Sutherland	73–71–70–73–70—357
Robert Damron	71–72–68–74–72—357
Hideki Kase	72–71–71–71–72—357
John Dowdall	72–72–71–70–72—357
Jack O'Keefe	72–77–71–72–66—358
Kevin Burton	74–69–74–72–69—358
Sonny Skinner	72–74–71–71–70—358
Jeff Hart	71–74–74–69–70—358
Craig Kanada	70–75–72–70–71—358
Adam Mednick	72–72–71–72–71—358
Larry Rinker	69–75–72–70–72—358

Rafael Alarcon	74–68–74–70–72—358
Tom Byrum	69–78–70–68–73—358
Todd Demsey	72–70–70–73–73—358
Billy Ray Brown	70–71–71–73–73—358
Tray Tyner	72–75–69–68–74—358
Kevin Sutherland	71–74–76–67–71—359
Jim McGovern	70–72–70–75–72—359
Tony Mollica	71–71–74–70–73—359
Frank Lickliter	70–73–72–71–73—359
Tim Simpson	74–73–71–72–70—360
Dave Barr	73–73–73–71–70—360
Bob Wolcott	71–75–74–70–70—360
Jay Delsing	69–74–72–74–71—360
Bradley Hughes	72–75–71–71–71—360
Stuart Appleby	69–77–73–70–71—360
Spike McRoy	70–75–76–68–71—360
Paul Tesori	77–71–72–69–71—360
Craig Bowden	71–76–70–70–73—360
Brad Sutterfield	75–71–72–69–73—360
Anthony Rodriguez	67–74–73–71–75—360
Brian Henninger	74–71–69–71–75—360
Paul Claxton	68–73–68–72–79—360

A misbegotten final stage, and the only five-round tour school on record. The 1996 final was held at two fine golf courses located 45 minutes apart and subject to vastly different weather conditions. Cold winds and driving rain plagued the finals throughout, shortening the competition by 18 holes and breaking the hearts of players who began their final rounds well enough to bring their aggregate score (versus par) back within the cut line. Several contestants were in this position on the course, only to be called back in when rains intensified and informed that their play in the final round would not count.

This was the year Rex Caldwell, a popular tour journeyman who enjoyed one stellar year among his 20-plus seasons, shot a final-round 60 in second-stage qualifying, but fell just short of the score necessary to reach final stage. Allen Doyle, a comedalist, would achieve only one top-10 finish in 1997 and end up 189th on the money list. At age 47, however, the career amateur who had only turned pro in 1995 had the easier pickings of the Senior PGA Tour to gear up for. Doyle, born in June of 1948, showed up on the senior circuit right on schedule, Monday-qualifying his way into six events and winning nearly $165,000. Doyle followed that up by winning medalist honors at the Senior PGA Tour national Q School, making him the first player ever to achieve that redoubtable double. He has already won a senior-circuit tournament in his short time out there.

1997
West and South Courses
Grenelefe Golf and Tennis Resort
Haines City, FL
December 3–8

Scott Verplank	66–64–67–70–69–71—407
Blaine McCallister	67–70–68–72–66–70—413
Stephen Ames	70–68–69–69–70–70—413
Lee Porter	70–71–67–69–71–68—416
Franklin Langham	72–71–68–68–66–72—417
Spike McRoy	69–71–69–71–68–69—417
Sonny Skinner	71–70–66–73–69–69—418
Jim McGovern	75–66–68–69–72–68—418
Kent Jones	72–70–67–64–71–75—419

John Riegger	70–69–70–72–68–70—419
Bob Gilder	67–72–69–74–68–69—419
Richard Coughlan	73–66–70–70–71–69—419
Hugh Royer	67–71–69–70–71–71—419
Guy Hill	69–67–69–73–69–72—419
Vance Veazey	73–68–66–71–71–70—419
Bruce Fleisher	69–72–69–69–71–69—419
Niclas Fasth	73–67–74–72–63–71—420
Kevin Wentworth	72–69–68–73–68–70—420
J. P. Hayes	71–69–67–74–66–73—420
Esteban Toledo	71–72–70–70–66–72—421
Tim Conley	70–73–73–71–69–65—421
Jim Estes	71–72–71–71–70–66—421
Steve Jurgensen	74–67–67–73–69–71—421
Keith Nolan	71–70–68–70–70–72—421
Tom Pernice, Jr.	71–69–67–70–70–74—421
John Morse	74–70–70–72–66–70—422
Mike Weir	71–68–69–72–71–71—422
Clark Dennis	71–72–69–74–66–70—422
Jeff Gallagher	71–67–69–73–69–73—422
Craig Barlow	76–67–70–71–71–67—422
Bradley Hughes	70–73–67–74–68–70—422
Dickey Pride	72–68–69–72–69–72—423
Tim Loustalot	71–71–69–68–69–75—423
Mark Wurtz	75–69–66–76–67–70—423
Lan Gooch	69–68–70–71–73–72—423
Iain Steel	68–75–72–72–67–69—423
Bobby Gage	69–77–66–69–70–72—423
Bob Friend	76–69–76–69–70–63—423

Winning by the largest margin since Donnie Hammond's record-setting medal year in 1982, Scott Verplank treated the tour school as his personal Lourdes. The injury-plagued Verplank never looked back from his first-place showing at Grenelefe, sweeping up $1.2 million in official money for 1997. For runner-up Mc-Callister, who just barely kept his full eligibility by finishing 125th on the 1997 money list, Grenelefe in 1997 was very nearly a prelude for La Quinta in 1998. Bruce Fleisher may have done the best job of all in springboarding off this qualifier—within 14 months, Fleisher would have scored back-to-back victories as a rookie on the Senior PGA Tour.

1998
La Quinta Hotel (Dunes Course)
PGA West (Jack Nicklaus Resort Course)
La Quinta, CA
November 18–23

Mike Weir	75–65–66–68–70–64—408
Jonathan Kaye	65–71–64–69–72–70—411
Deane Pappas	73–67–68–68–66–69—411
Dave Stockton, Jr.	67–69–70–70–69–67—412
Pete Jordan	66–72–68–67–70–69—412
Greg Chalmers	66–69–67–69–71–70—412
Geoffrey Sisk	67–74–69–67–65–70—412
Mike Brisky	67–71–70–68–70–67—412
Rich Beem	69–68–70–71–69–66—413
Cameron Beckman	71–74–66–66–68–68—413
Brent Schwarzrock	66–69–68–68–73–70—414
P. H. Horgan III	68–70–72–71–67–67—415
Briny Baird	71–66–68–68–70–72—415
John Elliott	73–68–67–69–70–69—416
Ted Purdy	65–67–73–72–68–71—416
Rick Fehr	62–71–70–67–72–74—416

Alan Bratton	69–70–72–70–69–67—417
Charles Warren III	68–71–69–70–70–69—417
Robert Allenby	71–70–69–68–69–70—417
Chris Couch	69–70–67–68–71–72—417
Bo Van Pelt	73–70–67–70–65–72—417
Craig Barlow	67–70–69–70–68–73—417
Katsumasa Miyamoto	67–73–71–69–71–67—418
Jeff Brehaut	73–70–68–67–71–69—418
Ty Armstrong	71–67–73–67–68–72—418
Steve Jurgenson	69–69–72–72–68–70—420
Jay Delsing	68–69–69–69–73–72—420
Jay Williamson	72–73–66–71–66–72—420
Chris Smith	66–71–69–67–72–75—420
Chris Riley	74–70–71–71–66–68—420
Danny Briggs	71–71–69–71–70–69—421
Dicky Pride	72–66–70–73–69–71—421
David Seawell	67–72–71–69–74–68—421
Brian Gay	64–70–73–71–68–75—421
Carlos Franco	68–75–71–69–66–73—422
Tim Loustalot	69–66–68–70–76–73—422
Scott Dunlap	65–73–68–71–72–73—422
Clarence Rose	68–68–70–73–69–74—422
Perry Moss	67–71–68–69–71–76—422
Rory Sabbatini	69–71–76–69–70–67—422
Kent Jones	70–71–71–75–64–71—422

The medalist, Mike Weir, was forced to go back through qualifying after receiving a card in 1997 but totaling insufficient purse money. The unprecedented $50,000 he earned out of the newly beefed-up Q School purse must have eased the sting of returning. Kent Jones pulled one of the finer late-stage miracles of this Q School final, shooting 64 after a series of 70-plus rounds to pull him back into contention. Jones said his wife had told him, on the eve of the fifth round, "They give you a lot of chances to shoot a low score in this tournament"—a rare example of someone turning the six rounds of final stage into a positive. The unflappable Jay Delsing moved into a select company of repeat qualifiers by playing his way to a tour card via Q School for the fifth time. Rick Fehr's 62 deserves recognition for being one of the two or three lowest competitive rounds in the history of Q School final-stage competition.

AFTERWORD

Q School is considered the season's final examination for would-be tour players, which makes the halfway point on the tour schedule a sort of midterm exam for the pros whom Q School (and the Nike Tour as well) has sent into battle. This book's final chapter was originally going to be titled "Epilogue," but epilogues and the PGA Tour Qualifying Tournament don't quite go together because the tournament draws contestants through its portals again and again. The Q School offers no true end point—at least not in reference to an individual player's career. And thus it offers no clear vantage point from which to write a true epilogue.

That being the case, it is a simple matter to study the midyear money list and calculate the progress of our most recent PGA Tour qualifiers, be they Q School graduates or players who earned eligibility via a top-15 finish on the Nike Tour. For anyone who has dwelled at length upon the doings and difficulties of aspiring tour players, it is natural to pick up the list and hope to find many members of the current Q School crop sitting pretty at midyear, with earnings high above the top-125 safety line. Unfortunately, at the middle of the 1999 season that is hardly the case.

With 22 events having been played, only nine of the pros who earned their PGA Tour cards at La Quinta in November of 1998 are among the top 125 money winners for 1999. Nor has the Nike Tour graduating class of 1998 fared much better: A mere seven of them have come through the British Open checkpoint with winnings of $185,052 or better—the total needed for top-125 status. And it's not even a matter of these qualifiers knocking at the top-125 door. Over one-third of the pros who were able to grind out a score of 422 or better at La Quinta are ganged up in the 175th to 210th place segment of the money list as of late July. There is even a batch of Q Schoolers—Bo Van Pelt, Deane Pappas, Charles Warren, Clarence Rose, and Steve Jurgensen—who have competed in 10 or more tournaments without playing their way beyond the $30,000 level. The term "behind the 8-ball" is common among midyear pros mired deep down the money list. For Van Pelt, Pappas, et. al., that 8-ball must look like the boulder that chased Indiana Jones down the mountainside.

On the bright side, 1998 medalist Mike Weir sits at 46th place with nearly $600,000 in prize money. Rich Beem—not just a Q Schooler but a raw rookie on the PGA Tour—earned a two-year exemption from the dreaded tour-school wringer, thanks to his victory at the 1999 Kemper Open. But Beem will probably not be your rookie-of-the-year on tour in 1999. Carlos Franco, the Paraguayan longshot who learned to play golf barefoot, took first place at the 1999 Greater Milwaukee Open. As impressive as the victory is, Franco's rookie season money total of $1.4 million, based on 15 starts, is even grander. Franco, Weir, and Beem have cycled out of the Q School orbit, perhaps never to return. Chris

Riley, Scott Dunlap, and Dicky Pride have also fared well in the first half of 1999, although each needs to keep the high finishes coming in order to retain his card.

Watching the Q School process become increasingly competitive, I have been tempted to believe that the annual qualifier has the power to enflame the tempers of its graduates in a way that ensures many, if not most, of them success on the PGA Tour. But obviously the tour itself tempers its players with an even hotter flame. When the Q School was inaugurated in 1965, the PGA understood that each generation of graduates was needed to replenish the herd. There were competitors too old or too weak to keep up, and the new arrivals who replaced them would make the entire population stronger. These days, the top 125 on the PGA Tour money list contains far fewer players who are natural candidates for thinning out. Maybe Mac O'Grady was right when he said you could send the top 125 money winners back through Q School and—assuming 125 cards were made available—find that 110 or more would requalify.

For a Q School graduate, that means you have to come out of the qualifying process a different man than the one who went in. Or, as Bill Ziobro put it, you need to emerge from tour school as that man you always knew you could be.

1999 PGA TOUR MONEY LIST THROUGH BRITISH OPEN CHAMPIONSHIP AS OF JULY 18, 1999

Rank	Player	Events	Earnings
1	David Duval	15	3,019,406
2	Tiger Woods	15	2,624,105
3	Payne Stewart	16	1,879,442
4	Vijay Singh	21	1,824,490

Rank	Player	Events	Earnings
5	Jeff Maggert	16	1,694,700
6	Davis Love III	16	1,577,068
7	Justin Leonard	19	1,402,084
8	Carlos Franco†	15	1,380,204
9	Steve Pate	19	1,379,255
10	Hal Sutton	17	1,270,111
11	Jeff Sluman	21	1,262,080
12	Tim Herron	19	1,198,677
13	John Huston	17	1,176,887
14	Chris Perry	20	1,050,973
15	Loren Roberts	16	1,016,177
16	Phil Mickelson	16	999,256
17	Tom Lehman	15	997,336
18	Stuart Appleby	20	958,167
19	Ernie Els	11	906,306
20	Jim Furyk	17	876,505
21	Jose Maria Olazaba	8	854,247
22	Nick Price	13	841,424
23	Jesper Parnevik	14	838,038
24	Scott Hoch	19	8326,024
25	Glen Day	18	835,925
26	Bob Estes	18	825,917
27	Steve Elkington	14	813,476
28	Scott Gump	19	809,811
29	Ted Tryba	20	802,364
30	Bill Glasson	14	793,422
31	Rocco Mediate	17	783,125
32	Gabriel Hjertstedt	20	781,630
33	Dennis Paulson‡	19	777,944
34	Frank Lickliter	19	733,089
35	Andrew Magee	17	727,964

Rank	Player	Events	Earnings
36	Olin Browne	16	700,801
37	Greg Kraft	18	699,779
38	Duffy Waldorf	16	680,685
39	Fred Funk	21	673,859
40	Mark O'Meara	13	663,854
41	Tommy Armour III	18	622,220
42	Stewart Cink	17	609,858
43	David Toms	20	601,790
44	Lee Janzen	17	601,790
45	Steve Stricker	17	600,050
46	Mike Weir†	19	598,748
47	Fred Couples	13	594,692
48	Craig Parry	16	582,076
49	Paul Goydos	19	568,482
50	Skip Kendall	20	561,443
51	Brian Watts	15	549,032
52	Paul Lawrie*	1	546,805
53	Kirk Triplett	16	541,219
54	Brent Geiberger	18	530,071
55	Dudley Hart	17	527,542
56	Billy Mayfair	19	524,939
57	Rich Beem†	16	508,005
58	Greg Norman	9	470,612
59	John Cook	19	443,752
60	Tommy Tolles	15	439,990
61	Kevin Sutherland	18	439,041
62	Bradley Hughes	20	433,162
63	Craig Stadler	13	432,813
64	Corey Pavin	18	424,118
65	Jerry Kelly	23	423,149
66	Steve Flesch	19	415,548

Rank	Player	Events	Earnings
67	Harrison Frazar	20	414,185
68	Mark Calcavecchia	20	380,069
69	Jim Carter	19	380,010
70	Paul Azinger	16	371,966
71	Chris DiMarco	20	360,135
72	Mike Reid	14	358,395
73	J. P. Hayes	18	350,047
74	Scott Verplank	18	343,490
75	Len Mattiace	21	333,985
76	Joey Sindelar	17	332,652
77	Lee Westwood*	7	324,577
78	Mark Brooks	21	322,308
79	Brandel Chamblee	16	321,524
80	Franklin Langham	18	319,298
81	Chris Riley**	17	317,108
82	Jay Haas	17	306,876
83	Bob Tway	18	306,011
84	Scott Dunlap**	14	303,158
85	Billy Ray Brown	15	301,472
86	Mark Wiebe	17	301,386
87	Dicky Pride†	18	298,473
88	Kenny Perry	17	292,342
89	Omar Uresti	21	292,008
90	Dan Forsman	18	291,686
91	Billy Andrade	19	291,530
92	Larry Mize	14	291,026
93	David Frost	16	289,546
94	Jean Van De Velde*	1	289,026
95	Eric Booker‡	20	288,064
96	John Maginnes‡	18	283,008
97	Jonathan Kaye†	19	276,953

Rank	Player	Events	Earnings
98	Neal Lancaster	21	268,554
99	Brad Fabel	18	267,531
100	Nolan Henke	16	266,672
101	Doug Dunakey‡	19	266,237
102	Barry Cheesman	22	264,534
103	Esteban Toledo	22	262,755
104	Kevin Wentworth	16	260,651
105	Colin Montgomerie*	9	257,651
106	Robert Allenby†	18	248,848
107	Naomichi Joe Ozaki	11	246,184
108	Paul Stankowski	18	245,389
109	Michael Bradley	18	237,454
110	Doug Barron	20	233,779
111	Emlyn Aubrey‡	15	229,275
112	Scott McCarron	16	228,857
113	Robert Damron	19	225,075
114	Steve Lowery	20	224,877
115	Greg Chalmers†	20	216,173
116	P. H. Horgan III†	17	214,824
117	Phil Blackmar	17	214,601
118	Brad Faxon	12	212,182
119	Jay Don Blake	18	211,657
120	Sergio Garcia	4	202,650
121	Tom Scherrer‡	17	201,447
122	Rory Sabbatini†	16	192,973
123	Grant Waite	18	186,042
124	Trevor Dodds	18	185,258
125	Mike Sposa‡	17	185,052
126	Scott Simpson	14	179,006
127	Steve Jones	11	177,777
128	Craig Barlow†	16	176,856

Rank	Player	Events	Earnings
129	Peter Jacobsen	14	175,095
130	David Sutherland	18	170,190
131	Clark Dennis	20	168,486
132	Jay Williamson**	18	167,397
133	John Daly	17	165,565
134	Blaine McCallister	18	164,887
135	Ronnie Black	10	160,885
136	Mike Hulbert	20	158,273
137	Brian Henninger	19	156,893
138	Angel Cabrera*	1	156,230
139	Bernhard Langer*	7	155,282
140	Rick Fehr†	14	152,148
141	Danny Briggs**	15	149,554
142	Frank Nobilo	19	147,439
143	Brett Quigley	12	146,015
144	Joe Ogilvie‡	17	144,576
145	Ben Bates	21	143,099
146	Tom Watson	12	141,410
147	Tom Byrum	17	135,632
148	Sean Murphy‡	15	134,185
149	Jimmy Green‡	16	125,784
150	Jeff Gallagher	21	122,916
151	Mike Brisky†	16	122,504
152	Woody Austin‡	17	122,082
153	Miguel Angel Jimenez	7	122,021
154	D. A. Weibring	11	120,993
155	J. L. Lewis	20	118,378
156	Bob Friend	23	116,900
157	Curtis Strange	13	113,263
158	Jim Gallagher, Jr.	18	112,563
159	Chris Couch**	17	112,392

Rank	Player	Events	Earnings
160	Joe Durant	16	111,414
161	Kaname Yokoo*	7	111,395
162	Patrik Sjoland*	7	108,527
163	Darren Clarke*	6	106,618
164	Chris Smith†	16	106,319
165	Ian Woosnam*	6	104,478
166	Tom Pernice, Jr.	20	104,358
167	Charles Raulerson‡	18	103,704
168	David Ogrin	11	93,143
169	Willie Wood	17	92,702
170	Russ Cochran	17	92,424
171	Bob Burns‡	18	91,815
172	Shigeki Maruyama*	7	79,137
173	Eric Rustand*	2	77,229
174	Lee Rinker	19	76,678
175	Guy Hill*	3	74,616
176	Doug Martin	20	73,911
177	Katsumasa Miyamoto†	12	73,904
178	Notah Begay III‡	17	73,779
179	Pete Jordan†	17	73,341
180	Robert Karlsson*	2	72,800
181	Alan Bratton†	18	71,708
182	Dave Stockton, Jr.†	18	71,396
183	Per-Ulrik Johansson	7	70,073
184	Geoffrey Sisk**	19	70,003
185	Brandt Jobe*	4	70,000
186	Lee Porter	20	69,782
187	John Elliott**	15	69,253
188	Donnie Hammond	6	68,952
189	Briny Baird†	15	65,057
190	Sandy Lyle	9	64,265

Rank	Player	Events	Earnings
191	Jay Delsing†	14	60,316
192	Bruce Lietzke	8	59,487
193	Doug Tewell	8	58,821
194	Robert Gamez	12	58,355
195	Ty Armstrong**	16	55,097
196	Retief Goosen*	2	54,368
197	Kent Jones†	15	52,412
198	R. W. Eaks	8	51,296
199	Perry Moss**	11	51,137
200	Spike McRoy	5	49,701
201	Tim Loustalot†	15	48,995
202	Fulton Allem	17	44,618
203	Cameron Beckman†	16	44,505
204	David Berganio, Jr.	4	43,431
205	Jeff Brehaut†	15	42,139
206	Tsuyoshi Yoneyama*	1	40,620
207	Phil Tataurangi	16	38,530
208	Brian Gay†	14	37,280
209	Fuzzy Zoeller	14	37,071
210	Nick Faldo	9	36,707
211	Ted Purdy†	16	36,089
212	Robin Freeman‡	17	34,128
213	Larry Rinker	18	33,765
214	Kelly Gibson	9	33,458
215	Brian Claar	4	32,927
216	Sven Struver*	2	32,135
T217	Andrew Coltart*	1	32,027
T217	Costantino Rocca*	1	32,027
219	Kyoung-Ju Choi*	2	31,457
220	Tom Kite	15	31,030
221	Bo Van Pelt†	16	30,564

Rank	Player	Events	Earnings
222	Andy Bean	9	29,000
223	Mike Springer	20	27,002
224	Steve Allan*	2	26,343
225	Deane Pappas**	17	24,484
226	Gary Hallberg	9	24,110
T227	Miguel Angel Martin	1	23,903
T227	Peter O'Malley*	1	23,903
229	Thomas Bjorn*	7	23,516
230	Charles Warren†	15	22,717
231	Clarence Rose†	10	22,575
232	Ray Floyd	2	22,480
233	Wayne Grady	11	21,737
234	Mark Carnevale	4	21,179
235	Padraig Harrington*	1	21,091
236	Dave Stockton	2	20,920
237	Brad Bryant	13	20,533
238	Jason Gore*	2	20,385
239	Phillip Price*	2	19,815
240	Bobby Wadkins	3	19,113
241	Don Pooley	5	19,063
242	Steve Jurgensen†	13	18,694
243	Pierre Fulke*	1	18,056
244	Stephen Ames	5	17,900
245	Wayne Levi	9	17,653
246	Mike Standly	8	17,491
247	Chip Beck	16	17,089
T248	Paul Affleck*	1	14,842
T248	Peter Baker*	2	14,842
T248	Mark McNulty*	1	14,842
251	Mark James*	1	13,592
T252	Mike Sullivan†	3	12,765

Rank	Player	Events	Earnings
T252	Mark Wilson*	1	12,765
254	David Howell*	2	12,675
255	David Lebeck*	1	12,060
256	Michael Walton*	1	11,921
257	Tom Purtzer	12	11,605
T258	Thomas Levet*	1	11,275
T258	Peter Lonard*	1	11,275
T258	Neil Price*	1	11,275
T258	Dean Robertson*	1	11,275
T258	Katsuyoshi Tomori*	1	11,275
263	Lanny Wadkins	12	10,890
264	Dan Pohl	2	10,868
265	Keiichiro Fukabori*	1	10,400
266	Chris Tidland*	1	10,305
T267	Santiago Luna*	1	10,253
T267	Jeremy Robinson*	1	10,253
269	Johan Rystrom*	1	9,921
270	Jarmo Sandelin*	1	9,764
271	Lee Thompson*	1	9,608
272	Jason Tyska*	1	9,562
273	Brian Davis*	1	9,491
T274	Derrick Cooper*	1	9,374
T274	Shingo Katayama*	1	9,374
T274	Martyn Thompson*	1	9,374
277	David Peoples	1	8,970
278	Jim McGovern	6	7,940
279	Mike Nicolette	1	7,225
280	Keith Fergus	4	6,818
281	David Ishii*	1	6,614
282	Jeff Freeman*	4	6,270
283	Ted Schulz	2	5,980

Rank	Player	Events	Earnings
284	Mathias Gronberg*	3	5,961
285	Greg Meyer*	1	5,850
286	David Edwards	5	5,840
287	Oscar Serna*	1	5,730
288	Ed Fiori	6	5,610
289	Jarrod Moseley*	2	5,534
T290	Mike Malizia*	1	5,434
T290	Mark McCumber	2	5,434
292	Dave Barr	1	5,375
293	Gary Koch	1	5,250
294	Chip Sullivan*	3	5,225
295	Michael Burke, Jr.*	3	5,198
296	Bob Gilder	7	5,152
T297	Jack Nicklaus	2	5,075
T297	Hidemichi Tanaka*	3	5,075
299	Brian Hull*	1	5,033
300	Rod Butcher*	1	5,000
T301	Chris Patton*	1	4,950
T301	Craig A. Spence*	4	4,950
303	David Seawell**	13	4,900
304	Cliff Kresge*	2	4,876
305	Joel Kribel*	3	4,692
306	Mike Donald	2	4,416
T307	Mark Hayes	3	3,841
T307	Andy North	2	3,841

† 1998 Q School qualifier

** Q-School Grad/Nike Tour member

‡ 1998 Nike Top-15 finisher

* Non-Tour member